WHO IS A PERFECT MAN?
WHO IS A PERFECT WOMAN?

WHO IS A PERFECT MAN? WHO IS A PERFECT WOMAN?

A BIBLE STUDY SERIES

Bamidele A. Kings

[30% of the proceeds of this book go to the Church Complex Building Fund, Food & Shelter for the Poor!]

Copyright © 2024 by *Bamidele A. Kings*

All rights reserved. No part of this publication may be reproduced, distributed, or transmitted in any form or by any means, including photocopying, recording, or other electronic or mechanical methods, without prior written permission of the copyright owner and the publisher, except in the case of brief quotations embodied in critical reviews and certain other noncommercial uses permitted by copyright law. For permission requests, write to the publisher, addressed "Attention: Permissions Coordinator," at the address below.

ARPress
45 Dan Road Suite 36
Canton MA 02021
Hotline: 1(888) 821-0229
Fax: 1(508) 545-7580

Ordering Information:
Quantity Sales. Special discounts are available on quantity purchases by corporations, associations, and others. For details, contact the publisher at the address above.

Printed in the United States of America.

ISBN-13	Paperback	979-8-89330-352-0
	eBook	979-8-89330-353-7
	Hardback	979-8-89330-354-4

Library of Congress Control Number: 2024900549

THE STUDY OF PSALMS 15

PREFACE

"Every WORD of GOD is pure, He is a shield unto them that put their trust in Him; therefore, I receive the WORD of GOD, not as the word of men, but as it is in truth the WORD of GOD, which effectually worketh also in me that believe. And so I am holding forth the WORD of Life, that I may rejoice in the Day of Christ, that I have not run in vain neither laboured in vain." Amen!

Psalms 15
A PSALM OF DAVID

<u>*Psalm 15*</u> *is one of the Psalms of David, you ask "why I said it's one of the Psalms of David, didn't David write the entire Book of Psalms?" Well, as we must know, David didn't write all of the Book of Psalms:*

Some have referred to the Psalms as Israel's hymnbook, which is partially true but overall is insufficient to account for all that is in the Book of Psalms.
More than one-third of the collection is made up of prayers to God. Therefore, it contains both hymns and prayers that were used in the context of Israel's worship!

Many of the Psalms have names prefixed to them, some of which we will see as "The Psalms of David." Since the Book is a collection of many different psalms written over a long period of time, there is not just one author.

By far the most common designation in the titles is "A Psalm of David," which probably means that David is the author of those Psalms.
David's role as a musician in Saul's court [I Samuel 16:14-23] as well as his many experiences as a shepherd, a soldier and king make him a likely candidate for writing many of these Psalms.

Other authors include Solomon, Asaph, the sons of Korah, Ethan, Heman son of Korah, and Moses; in the case of Asaph, although he was one of David's chief musicians [I Chronicles 6:39], the name itself became associated with a group of musicians bearing the same name, [Ezra2:40-41]: Ezra is perhaps the collector and compiler of Psalms in its present form.

The Psalm can be divided into classes. There are hymns [145-150] and songs of thanksgiving [30-32]. Psalms of lament [38-39] are prayers or cries to God on the occasion of distressful situations.

Royal Psalms [2; 110] are concerned with the earthly king of Israel. Enthronement Psalms [96; 98] celebrate the kingship of the Lord. Penitential Psalms [32; 38; 51] express condition and repentance, and wisdom or didactic Psalms [19; 119] tend to be proverbial.

Message And Purpose Of The Book Of Psalm!

There are myriad messages scattered through the 150 Book of psalms, but overall, this record of the responses of God's people in worship and prayer serves the purpose of teaching us how to relate to God in various circumstances of life.

The Psalms also demonstrate God's sovereignty and goodness for His people in order to instill confidence in those who trust in Him.

<u>Psalm 15</u> is called "The Second Psalm of The Righteous:" while <u>Psalm 1</u> is the "First Psalm of The Righteous:" this Psalm starts with two very important questions, the same now became the Title, which we will explore and study in this book!

In my Study Bible, the super inscriptions on this Psalm 15 says, "<u>A Psalm of David</u>" 'The Great Question of Man.' This Psalm to many is just one of the Psalms that they might think nothing to other than just to read like a literature book or like any other story book as they think of other Psalms, but I tell you, it is a very, very interesting chapter of the Book of Psalms so short in five verses as it is to study, as I believe you will enjoy every bit of the study!

And so to all our readers, who buy this book keep it in your library after studying completely, it is a treasure, if your focus and destination as a child of God is Heaven, to abide and dwell with The Father after your tenor here on earth; I welcome you to '<u>A Systematic, Expository Study of God's Word</u>;' here in this *wonderful Bible Study Book, we will study this chapter of the Book of Psalms, <u>Psalm 15</u> precept upon precept, line upon line.*

The Bible says in the Book of <u>Isaiah 28:13</u>, "But the Word of the LORD was unto them precept upon precept, precept upon precept; line upon line, line upon line; here a little, and there a little; that they might go, and fall backward, and be broken, and snared, and taken!"

Again! I welcome us all to a world of study in the Word of God; this chapter 15 of the Book of Psalms will take us from Genesis through the Bible to Revelation. And I pray that the LORD will open your heart to receive the teachings, the instructions, corrections and knowledge as you focus on Him!

May God Bless you richly as you read this great Bible Study Book with us!

Welcome to the World of Study!!!

DEDICATION

I dedicate this book to The Mighty God of Heaven:

THE ADONAI - The LORD My Great GOD:
The Master and Majestic LORD. GOD, our Total Authority!

EL - The STRONG ONE:
He is More Powerful than any false god. He overcomes all obstacles. The LORD on WHOM we depend!

EL ELOHE YISRAEL - GOD, The GOD of Israel:
He is distinct and separate from all false gods of the world!

EL ELYON - THE GOD MOST HIGH:
He is The SOVEREIGN GOD: In whom we can put our trust. El Elyon has supremacy over all false gods!

ELOHIM - THE ALL-POWERFUL ONE CREATOR:
GOD is the all-powerful Creator of the universe. Our GOD knows all, creates all, and is everywhere at all times. 'The Plural of "Eli"

EL OLAM - THE ETERNAL GOD, THE EVALASTING GOD:
He is the Beginning and the End. The ONE who works His purposes throughout the ages. He gives strength to the weary!

EL ROI - THE GOD WHO SEES ME:
There are no circumstances in our lives that escape His fatherly awareness and care. GOD knows us and our troubles!

EL SHADDAI - THE ALL SUFFICIENT ONE. THE GOD OF THE MOUNTAINS, GOD ALMIGHTY: GOD is the all-sufficient source of all our blessings. GOD is all-powerful. Our problems are not too big for GOD to handle!

IMMANUEL - GOD WITH US "I AM"
Jesus Is God in our midst. In Him all the fullness of Deity dwells in bodily form!

JEHOVAH [YHWH] - "I AM," THE ONE WHO IS THE -SELF-EXISTENT ONE:
GOD never changes. His promises never fail. When we are faithless, He is faithful. We need to obey HIM!

JEHOVAH JIREH - THE LORD WILL PROVIDE:
Just as GOD provided a ram as a substitute for Isaac, He provided His Son Jesus as the ultimate sacrifice. God will meet all our needs!

JEHOVA MEKADDISHKEM - THE LORD WHO SANCTIFIES:
God sets us apart as a chosen people, a royal priesthood, holy unto God, a people of his own; He cleanses our sin and helps us mature in Him!

JEHOVAH NISSI - THE LORD IS MY BANNER:
God gives us victory against the flesh, the world and the devil. Our battles are His battles of light against darkness and good against evil!

JEHOVAH RAPHA - THE LORD WHO HEALS:
God has provided the final cure for spiritual, physical, and emotional sickness in Jesus Christ. God can heal us of both spiritual and physical sickness of whatever kind!

JEHOVAH ROHI - THE LORD IS MY SHEPHERD:
The Lord protects, provides, directs, leads, and cares for His people; God tenderly takes care of us as a strong and patient shepherd!

JEHOVAH SABAOTH - THE LORD OF HOSTS, THE LORD OF ARMIES:
The Lord of the hosts of heaven will always fulfill His purposes, even when the hosts of His earthly people fail!

JEHOVAH SHALOM - THE LORD IS PEACE:
God defeats our enemies to bring us peace. Jesus is our Prince of Peace. God brings inner peace and harmony!

JEHOVA SHAMMAH - THE LORD IS THERE, THE LORD MY COMPANION:
God's Presence is not limited or contained in the Tabernacle or Temple, but is accessible to all who love and obey Him!

JEHOVAH TSIDKENU - THE LORD OUR RIGHTEOUSNESS:
Jesus is the King who would come from David's line, and He is the One who imparts His righteousness to us!

YAH, OR JAH - "I AM" THE ONE WHO IS THE SELF-EXISTENT ONE:
God never changes. His promises never fail. When we are faithless, He is faithful. God promises His continuing Presence!

YHWH - "I AM," THE ONE WHO IS THE SELF-EXISTENT ONE:
God never changes. His promises never fail. When we are faithless, He is faithful!

TO OUR LORD JESUS CHRIST: SON OF GOD THE FATHER

He is the Founder, the President, the Leader, the General Overseer and the Director General of Wells of Salvation Ministries & Dominion Center for All Nations!

He Is:
THE KINGS OF KINGS:
THE LORD OF LORDS:
THE ALFA AND THE OMEGA:
THE BEGINNING AND THE END:
THE ADVOCATE:
THE LAMB OF GOD:
THE RESURRECTION AND THE LIFE:
THE SHEPHERD AND BISHOP OF OUR SOULS:
THE JUDGE, THE RULER:
THE MAN OF SORROWS:
THE HEAD OF THE CHURCH:
THE MASTER:
THE FAITHFUL AND TRUE WITNESS:
THE ROCK:
THE HIGH PRIEST:
THE APOSTLE:
THE DOOR:
THE LIVING WATER:
THE BREAD OF LIFE:
THE ROSE OF SHARON:

THE TRUE VINE:
THE MESSIAH:
THE TEACHER:
THE HOLY ONE:
THE MEDIATOR:
THE BELOVED:
THE BRANCH:
THE CARPENTER:
THE GOOD SHEPHERD:
THE LIGHT OF THE WORLD:
THE IMAGE OF THE INVISIBLE GOD:
THE WORD OF GOD:
THE CHIEF CORNERSTONE:
THE SAVIOUR:
THE SERVANT:
THE AUTHOR AND FINISHER OF OUR FAITH:
THE ALMIGHTY:
THE EVERLASTING FATHER:
THE SHILOH:
THE LION OF THE TRIBE OF JUDAH:
THE I AM:
THE PRINCE OF PEACE:
THE BRIDEGROOM:
THE ONLY BEGOTTEN ONE:
THE WONDERFUL COUNSELOR:
THE IMMANUEL; EMMANUEL:
THE SON OF MAN:
THE DAYSPRING:
THE AMEN:
THE KING OF THE JEWS:
THE PROPHET:
THE REDEEMER:
THE ANCHOR:
THE BRIGHT MORNING STAR:
THE WAY:
THE TRUTH AND THE LIFE:
THE CHOSEN ONE:

Who Is A Perfect Man? Who Is A Perfect Woman?

THE MESSENGER OF THE COVENANT:
THE LAST ADAM:

<u>TO THE HOLY SPIRIT</u>:

The Exsecutor, The Co-Founder, The Teacher, The Leader and The Co-Director of Wells of Salvation Ministries & Dominion Center for All Nations!

THE EXECUTOR AND THE BEST TEACHER

ACKNOWLEDGEMENTS

My Gratitude And Love Goes First To my wonderful and beautiful dear wife and Partner in the ministry, Pastor [Mrs.] Veronica O. Kings [a prayer warrior] for believing in me and giving me her total support for writing this book, also for her wisdom and dedication to the work of God in our hands, for her encouragements, for upholding me in prayers continually; more importantly, for the giving of her total self and commitment to Wells of Salvation Ministries & Dominion Center For All nations. Her life of intercessory has been tremendously upholding and blessing. May the Lord continue to encourage, strengthen and bless you!

To my spiritual fathers and mentors, Pastor W.F. Kumuyi, [General Superintendent, Deeper Christian Life Bible Church] my Church of orientation; Pastor E. Adejare Adeboye, [General Overseer, The Redeemed Christian Ministries]; Apostle Dr. Gabriel & Rev. Roselyn Oduyemi [Founders Bethel Ministries]; Pastor Benny Hinn, The Divine Healing Ministry] under whom I attended Benny Hinn School of Ministry; Bishop Dr. David Olaniyi Oyedepo, [Director-General Winners Chapel]; Dr. David Jeremiah, [Shadow Mountain & Turning Point Worldwide Ministry USA]; Bishop Ransom Bello, Founder, [Calvary Life International Ministries]; Dr. Mike Murdock [Founder The Wisdom Center, Texas USA]: To My dear friend and Brother In Christ, Dr. Tony Evans, [The founder and Senior Pastor, Oak Cliff Bible Fellowship in Dallas. USA] all of whose ministry is blessing me and others all over the world! And to a Great Man of God whom I love to listen to and whom I also love so dearly, Pastor James MacDonald, the

Founder, [Walk In The Word Ministries USA!] Your lives so much inspired and impacted in me the strongest and greatest experience of the meaning and depth of the Gospel. I love you all!

Also, to a man I greatly admire, A Global Model, a philosopher, a Theologian, a man of love and peace, a man of integrity who is so burdened about the global peace always appealing and soliciting people to unite, a man of God in the person of 'Pope Francis' [Jorge Mario Bergolo!] May you forever be blessed; may the Lord keep you and help you fulfill your heart desire in your calling.

My special greetings to a Great Woman of God Nancy Leigh DeMoss of [Revive Our Hearts], a woman whom the Lord has raised and ordained for this end time to impact, to shape, to mentor, to teach and to minister to the women at large, your ministry is changing and modeling women for Christ, you are a woman whom the Lord is using to call the women to freedom, fullness and fruitfulness in Christ and as you have found your calling in reviving the hearts of women, may the Lord continually renew and revive you to continue to affect our generation!

Writing this book would not have been possible but for your inspired word of wisdom that has inspired me immeasurably and brought me this far; humbly, I receive you all as the prophets of the Most High God; with due respect to you all, and with all of your permissions, I access what you all carry and I possess the same in Jesus name Amen!

May the Lord Continue to strengthen you all and keep you till the end of time as you continue to make exploits for His Kingdom!

My gratitude also go to our associates pastors, Pastor Gani Babatunde Bisiriyu [a former Muslim], Pastor [Mrs.] Veronica Kings, Pastor Rod Mulford, who have constantly made themselves available come rain come shine in the service of the Lord, they and the Leaders who are always at the Bible Study beginning from Elder John O. Adeosun, Elder Sister Joyce Mulford, Deacon

Dennis Ateli all of whom have never missed to sit at the Feet of Christ learning; they have always been a source of encouragement and inspiration to me, to my wonderful wife, and to the entire congregation; they have both been faithful in everything, their attendance have been excellent and impeccable! May The Lord God reward you and fill you all with His knowledge and wisdom!

How can I forget to acknowledge the entire members of our great ministry Wells of Salvation Ministries & Dominion Center For all Nations, who I also owe a debt of gratitude for their quest, their desire to learn and receive the truth unadulterated teachings of the Word of God; and have been very wonderful in their attendance to our weekly Wednesdays Bible Study, also to all the regulars at the Bible Study for the duration of eight weeks of the study of this special book entitled "Who Is A Perfect Man: Who Is A Perfect Woman" May your desire to know more and have the knowledge of the God of Heaven adequately be rewarded in Jesus name!

INTRODUCTION

More and more, God is teaching me to trust in Him every day for every step I take and everything I do; for teaching me how to wholly and completely depend on Him. He constantly calls me to stretch beyond what's comfortable which made me to always learn something at the end.
To walk through new territory when I would rather stay with the familiar.
To face difficult, physical, mental, and emotional challenges. To do things I know I can't achieve by myself without His Power.
Each time something is required of me that I'm certain I am unable to accomplish in my own strength, I see a picture of just one or two steps being illuminated, while those before and after are engulfed in darkness and cannot be seen.
This describes my walk with God. I trust Him for each day of my life, for sustenance, for supply, my health and that of my wife and our wellbeing. I am so very grateful for every breath, while I determined to look for the blessing in the moment, no matter what the circumstances.
I follow His lead-- even when I can't see where I'm going, even when it scares me to do so--because deep within my spirit I know that these simple steps of faith are preparing me for eternity! He is my strength and inspiration!

HAPPY READING AND HAPPY STUDY!!!

[Please note that all Bible references used in this book are from King James Version]

Before we go into this wonderful study of the WORD of GOD let us Pray!!!

Our God in Heaven, we thank you very much for this Bible Study Book, the Study of Psalms 15; "Who Is A Perfect Man" "Who Is A Perfect Woman." We thank you for the help, the support, the provision and the strength You have given towards the production of this Bible Study Book to Your Glory. We Thank You for the great desire You've given us to be able to purchase this Book and study Your Word; we know You're preparing us for something great and wonderful now and in the future.

And Lord we pray, as You are taking all the pains to prepare us, we too will be yielding to You, and submitting to You to be well prepared for what You have for every one of us in Jesus' name.

We pray Lord that these Words in this Study Book will not only enrich our lives, it will make us to enrich the lives of other people around the world at large, and Lord as we study, we will be doers of the Word, and obedience to the Word which will bring blessings to our lives, blessings and security into the lives of people around us and around the world in Jesus' name.

Open our eyes of understanding and open our hearts to receive, that we may behold wondrous things even in Your Word as we study this Book. Bless us Lord and let Your name be glorified in all of our lives and the world at large. In Jesus' name we pray. Amen!

Psalm 15

Vs.1, "LORD, who shall abide in THY tabernacle? who shall dwell in THY HOLY Hill?
Vs.2, He that walketh uprightly, and worketh righteousness, and speaketh the truth in his heart.
Vs.3, He that backbiteth not with his tongue, nor doeth evil to his neighbour, nor taketh up a reproach against his neighbour.
Vs.4, In whose eyes a vile person is contemned; but he honoureth them that fear the LORD. He that sweareth to his own hurt, and changeth not.
Vs.5, He that putteth not out his money to usury, nor taketh reward against the innocent. He that doeth these things shall never be moved."

CHAPTER ONE

THE SOVEREIGN GOD

EL ELYON - THE GOD MOST HIGH:
He is The SOVEREIGN GOD: In whom we can put our trust. El Elyon has supremacy over all false gods!

Psalm 15:1

Vs.1, "LORD, who shall abide in THY tabernacle? Who shall dwell in THY HOLY Hill?"

This chapter of the Book of Psalms have five wonderful verses that speaks the mind of God to us as well as speaking to our hearts; the first verse of this great **Psalm** starts with the word **_"LORD,"_** anytime we see this Word 'LORD' in our Bible written in capital **'L' capital 'O' capital 'R' capital 'D'** this is referring to *God* The Father Himself, **The Elohim The Creator of All and the Owner of All**. His name is **JEHOVAH!** And for your information as a reader of this book, we're going to be dealing with this word *"LORD"* a great deal in this book so that we know who is saying what, whom we are talking about and who said what in a particular instance. **The LORD GOD of Heaven, GOD The FATHER Himself, The AMEN! Hallelujah!!**

So, this **_Psalm 15_** starts with two questions, the number one question is *"LORD, <u>who shall</u> abide in Thy Tabernacle?"* and the second question goes again like this: *"Who shall dwell in Thy Holy Hill?"*

Literally, the two questions are one, to *'abide'* and to *'dwell'* but they have conditions, I mean to be able to *'dwell'* and *'abide.'* Now these questions are what we're here in this book to study, to examine and to explore! The question is can we as human being, as we are, live righteously to be able to **'Dwell'** and **'Abide'** with **God the Father** after our tenor here on earth? It is an important factor if you've been a Christian all your years, going to church, paying your tithes, giving offerings, never engage yourself in anything frivolous; but you're missing it and struggling in just one area, and it could be an area that will bring all your services to amount to zero as we understood that with God, fail in one is fail in all! May we not labour in vain in Jesus' name? Amen!

The phrase **_'Thy Tabernacle'_** is parallel to **_'Thy Holy Hill'_** and refers to the Sanctuary of **Jehovah GOD, YAHWEH** is **HIS** name! This is the place of God's Presence and protection, your focus, my focus and the focus of all His children, Heaven the Habitation of the Almighty!

> *"I will abide in thy tabernacle forever: I will trust in the covert of thy wings. Selah."* **_Psalm 61:4_**

"THY TABERNACLE" is used here in a way similar to *"house"* or *"temple"* as a figurative reference to **Jehovah's Presence**. Being in Jehovah's Presence is the hope of all the faithful; **_[Ps.15:1]_**. The truth is, certain people are not allowed in God's Presence because of His Holiness;

> *"For thou art not a God that hath pleasure in wickedness; neither shall evil dwell with thee:" vs.5, "The foolish shall not stand in thy sight: thou hatest all workers of iniquity."* **_Psalm 5:4-5_**

The term here *'pleasure'* as underlined above is the same word translated as *"delight"* in **_Ps.1:2_**, but here, it is negated. Not only does **GOD** have no desire for **_wickedness_**, but it also cannot even exist in His Presence.

The arrogant, those who practice evil, liars, and the violent including the **_false prophets_** are all included in the explanation of those who

shall not stand in GOD's ***sight***. The word *'stand'* as in ***Ps.2:2 [read]***, describing those who *"set themselves"* against ***GOD***.

To set oneself is often used in military contexts to describe preparation for battle: The ***kings*** and ***rulers*** are not just specific groups, but they represent all governing authorities and dignitaries ***on the earth***:

How can we go into battle with Him? Can we ever win? Because here, it describes you and I in whichever category we might find ourselves how we are ***setting ourselves against the LORD!***

- When we are working against the ordinances of GOD, doing our own thing, when we claim to be in the service of the Lord but have a secret agenda, to extort, to deceive, to manipulate and to give false ***prophecies*** in other to line our pockets or extort: we are sinning and setting ourselves against God!
- When we are for many years still a babe in the Lord, always a ***convenient Christian***, in other words, we want to be pleased in any church we attend, instead of pleasing God; we want to tele-guide the preacher, the pastor of the ***church of Jesus Christ*** must listen to us, must preach what we want to hear especially if we give more in ***tithes and offerings***; we want to control the church, we want to control the pastor and the entire congregation:
- When we want to control everyone and control everything and whatever we say goes. When we want to be recognized above others, when we want the church to accept whatever we do right or wrong and it must not be talked about, when we have our own favorites and neglect others; and when all of what we want is not happening, we revolt, we rebel and leave the church: then we are inviolation of His commandments! With pride in our hearts.
- When we want to bring carnality into the church, pollution into the church, when we want to bring the ideas of worldly meetings into the church, worldly parties into the church when we're always asking questions that gender strifes, when we're dividing the people, inciting the people against the leadership;

we're never stayed humble, we are rebellious, and we refuse to grow:

- When we are always right in our own eyes the Bible says in **Proverbs 12:15** that we are fools...
- When we operate in anger in the church of Jesus Christ and in His Presence, **"pastor offended me, his sermon is directed at me, someone told him of what I did,"** and we can go on and on with that anger forever: when our focus and our motives are not pure, but our emphasis is on money and not in the **WORD**:

We are setting ourselves up against the Lord; we're also setting ourselves up for failure. The pastor or the minister is human not an angel everyone is bound to make mistakes, but we are holding on to errors to judge and rebel *instead of praying for the Man of God;* Job says, *"Who has rebelled against Him and prospered?"*

We are in battle against the Lord; especially when all we want is not happening, we forsake the assembly of the righteous; we leave the church to another church, and again we want to be an adversary in that new church we went, we're never satisfied wherever we are, we want to boss everyone; we want to be recognized. **Ps.2:2** describe us as standing against the Lord! What we have is called a domineering spirit and if we are not delivered from that evil spirit, we cannot **"dwell"** and **"abide"** with the Father!

When we are in a Bible believing church where the anointing is awesome, where the Spirit of God is and moves, a fasting and a praying church, a church of excellence where prayers are being answered, a place where we both can testify to all the miracles through God, that we constantly receive, yet you're filled with **resentment** against the church, and if we are restless and cannot *dwell* and *abide* in a local church how can we *dwell* and *abide* with Him in heaven?

"The kings of the earth set themselves, and the <u>rulers take counsel together</u>," we always group people together to fight the principles of the church because it's not done our way, we unite people together to destroy, to scatter, we asks question that generates strife, to sow seeds of discord amongst the brethren, we're always working against the rules loving only ourselves and standing against the guidelines of the church; we are against the anointing: ***Ps.2:1-5*** speaks of us!

When we are looking for a perfect church here on earth *[no, not here on earth]* and we're restless in our search, soon we become professional visitors, haven visited a number of churches yet we have no resting place, our search will soon be over *[because there is no perfect church here on earth]*; and believe it or not, if we are operating as described above, the spirit of *Nebuchadnezzar* is ruling in us, the Bible says, we are wicked and as such, we need deliverance! We cannot *"dwell"* and *"abide"* with Him!

There is no contest between these wicked people and GOD; they cannot get anywhere near the **LORD** to attack **HIM**. The desire of God's people is to be in **His Presence** forever; look at what ***Ps.65:4*** says!

Remember we are talking here about **THE SOVEREIGN GOD; EL ELYON - THE GOD MOST HIGH;**

> ***Psalm 65:4****, "Blessed is the man whom thou choosest, and causest to approach unto thee, that he may dwell in thy courts: we shall be satisfied with the goodness of thy house, even of thy Holy Temple."*

In Thy courts is equivalent to ***house*** or ***temple***, all of which represent being in **JEHOVAH's Presence**. The ***goodness*** as underlined refers to spiritual refreshments that a person experiences in **GOD's Presence**. This is often pictured as a feast *[**Ps.23:5**; **Ps.36:8**]*.

> ***Ps.23:5****, "Thou preparest a table before me in the presence of my enemies: thou anointest my head with oil; my cup runneth over."*

The image shifts from shepherd to friend. The identification of Jehovah with a shepherd emphasizes His care and protection for those who are His, the question is, are you one of His children? Am I one of His? Are you one of His disciples? Am I one of His disciples? Are we born again? Are we really His children?

The fact also is He is more than that to and for a person who is in close relationship with Him, who is in close fellowship with Him. While protection from enemies is still implied, it is intensified with the image of a banquet [table] that is served while the enemies look on.

In Jewish society ***oil*** was a symbol for rejoicing,

> ***"And wine that maketh glad the heart of man, and oil to make his face to shine, and bread which strengthen man's heart;" Ps.104:15***

To make a man's ***face*** to ***shine*** with oil figuratively describes the abundance of God's provision and the satisfaction of rich foods. ***Bread*** denotes any type of food. Oil was also used in the welcoming of important guests:

> ***"Thou lovest righteousness, and hatest wickedness: therefore God, thy God, hath anointest thee with the oil of gladness above thy fellows:"***

Did we see that, *"above your fellows;" [Ps.45:7]:* all these when we are in Him, and through Him *"Dwelling"* and *"Abiding"* with *"Him:"*

> ***"But my horn shalt thou exalt like the horn of a unicorn: I shall be anointed with fresh oil:" Ps.92:10***
> To exalt a horn is a figurative expression denoting restored vitality and power *[Ps.89:17], being **anointed*** with oil, means consecration for service *[Lev.8:10-12]* oil also refers to an act of hospitality that symbolizes favour *[Ps.23:5]*.

Who Is A Perfect Man? Who Is A Perfect Woman?

"My head with oil thou didst not anoint: but this woman hath anointed my feet with ointment:" Lk.7:46

Here from *vs.44-47*, Jesus drew a contrast between the Pharisee's lack of hospitality and the woman's profuse service. Jesus did not mean that the Pharisee had little sin to be forgiven, but that he did not think of himself as a sinner *[like many of us]*, while the woman was profoundly aware of her sinfulness, but we always like to hide our sins and pretend that all is well.

In order for us to be able to *'Dwell'* and *'Abide'* with the Father we must not sweep our sins under the rug and act as if we're clean and that, *'there is no sin in us, we deceive ourselves and there is no truth in us'* the Bibles says in *[I John 1:9]*. When there is a sin un-repented of, when there is an un-addressed iniquity, and we act as if we haven't done anything bad is self-deceit.

WE must be able to examine ourselves to the point of conviction as to where we want to spend eternity except where we are trying to believe the lie of the devil that there is no eternity, whether we believe in the existence of eternity or not, our unbeliever in hell or heaven does not erase the facts of existence.

What is our goal as children of God, heaven or the other side? But the certainty is, there is no middle to it and we cannot have it both ways: and so, the question we should be asking ourselves is:

"Am I really a Christian, am I a child of God the Father, can people around testify to the fact that I am a Christian, then why can't I abide by the heavenly rules?"

So, we're asking, "what are the heavenly rules?" well, we can go back to the 'Ten Commandments' that which was originally given to us written by the Finger of God and given through the hand of Moses in Two Tablets of Stones: so, we can line up our lives with the rules and examine ourselves!

***Psalm 84:3-4**, "Yea, the sparrow hath found an house, and the swallow a nest for herself, where she may lay her young, even thine altars, O Lord of Hosts, my King, and my God:"*
vs.4, "Blessed are they that dwell in thy house: they will be still praising thee. Selah."

The heart describes the minds of the godly, their thoughts focused on the ascent to Zion!

Man of God, Woman of God, Children of God, what is your desire, what is my desire, where is our focus as Christians, what else do we need, where else can we go at the end of this journey, to whom do we belong, what other God can satisfy us and meet us at our point of need, or de we want to labour in vain? Absolutely not!

Think about this great question of man!

"LORD, Who Shall Abide in Thy Tabernacle? Who Shall Dwell in Thy Holy Hill?"

You say, *"but I am born again,"* congratulations and welcome into the fold! But that is just the beginning of the journey, that is the first step, but it's not all that qualify us to *'Dwell and Abide"* with Him; and we cannot do it on our own, we have to do it with Him, He is the One who can perfect us, but we must follow Him closely.

Before we continue, let us realize that our God is a Holy God, He is a purposeful God and He is **THE SOVEREIGN GOD**; He is the God of all creation, do not forget that He knows us because He created us. He is always willing to help us *[if and when we allow Him]* but then we must be faithful unto Him and live Holy!

Listen to what Jeremiah 29:11 says,
"For I know the thoughts that I think toward you, saith the LORD, thoughts of peace, and not of evil, to give you and expected end!"

Friends, don't we want to know the depth of His 'thought toward us,' shouldn't we try to find out what kind of 'expected end' He wants to give us? If we are ready for the truth, and we really want to know the truth; here is the answer *[are we ready]?*

It lies in **Psalm 42:7** *"Deep Calleth Unto Deep!"* Just what am I trying to get into, what am I trying to tell us? *[see the illustration below and let the Spirit of God give us a revelation here!]* but I will try and give us some *clues into what I am trying to get across to us.*

ILLUSTRATION:

- Ground water is separated by 240 plus feet of clay. 1st aquifer is ground water (coli form bacteria),
- 2nd aquifer is arsenic traced – As-Pollution - As-pollution is a by-product of the reduction of sedimentary iron ox-hydroxides.
- 5x World Health Organizations allowed amount.
- Clean water – Ancient - sets at the 3rd aquifer that is as much as 350 ft. below the surface.

In order to get a safe well, you have to drill a hole through the first 2 aquifers and past the 240 plus feet of clay to the 3rd aquifer where the safe water sets. *[First entry into Christianity: Getting Born again!]*

There are plenty of **wells** *[churches]* everywhere, but no healthy **water** *[sound doctrine of the Word of God]*. Our pulpits are invaded with messages of grace and sayings of prosperity emphasis are laid more on money: but digging deep into the WORD of GOD is the only prosperity I know of and it's what brings prosperity to our spirit soul and body!

- The prosperity preachers don't go deep enough into the Word, and no seal was placed in the hole to stop cross-contamination between the 3 aquifers or levels of water.

  "[Every wind of doctrine that contaminates" **Eph.4:14]**.

- Government paid to have wells dug, but then the payoffs for government officials and contractors caused the wells to be only 200 ft. deep.

  "[By the sleight of men, and cunning craftiness," <u>Eph.4:14</u>].

- These inferior wells cause sickness and death to animals, as well as humans who depend on the wells for their water.

  "[By the sleight of men, and cunning craftiness, whereby they lie in wait to deceive," <u>Eph.4:14</u>].

When gifted people, anointed men and women of God, ordained preachers of the Gospel and the rest preachers of the truth of the Word of God equip the church, the community of faith will evidence stability in precept and practice.

- *<u>Jeremiah 5:31</u>, "The prophets prophesy falsely, and the priests bear rule by their means; and my people love to have it so: and what will ye do in the end thereof?"*

We always like it cheap, and the WORD of GOD is not cheap, the Bible says, "Every WORD of GOD is pure, He is a shield unto them that put their trust in Him; therefore, I receive the WORD of GOD not as the word of men, but as it is in truth the WORD of GOD, which effectually worketh also in me that believe! [Multi-references].

First is to believe it is the **WORD** of **GOD** and we receive it as such and believe the same, and put our trust in the **WORD** of **GOD**, and **NOT** receive it as the word of men, we will not take the WORD of GOD as cheap and that's from where our failure begins when we take lightly the things of GOD.

The Bible says in *<u>Psalms 138:2c</u>, "For Thou hast magnified Thy Word above all Thy name."*

If this is indeed true as I know it is, why do we take His Word lightly and take it as cheap when the Owner of His WORD magnified His WORD above <u>ALL HIS NAME</u>!

Many of children of God like to receive the WORD of GOD as the word of men that's why we go to churches where the emphasis is more on mundane things and not the WORD of GOD, **emphasis on something else like** *money, like fashion parade, like a place to flaunt wealth* and we end up after each service not understanding His purpose for that service but fulfilling all righteousness by going to the church as a customary thing; so we tend to scratch on the surface and not knowing how to dig deep!

So, when we are digging wells there, I tell the driller – "Dig Deeper"

- 350 feet = 105 meters" but no one wants to dig deeper because:
- As you dig deeper, you encounter obstacles: *[discouragements]*.
- Rocks, Hard Clay: *[distractions]*; listen people of God,
- Digging deep means more time.
- Digging deep means more work.
- Digging deep means more materials.
- Digging deep means more cost.
- Digging deep means more dedication; the question is, am I willing to give more time, am I willing to put more materials, am I willing to expend some resources and give more, lastly, am I willing to be more committed and rededicate myself to this great calling?

<u>II Timothy 2:15</u>, "Study to shew thyself approved unto God, a workman that needeth not to be ashamed, rightly dividing the word of truth!" Digging deep, digging deep, to engage in the art of studying the Word of God!

We like things on the surface.
- We like things easy.
- We like to remain in our comfort zone.
- We like things to not mess up our daily routine.

- We don't like to have to work to get something
- Quick and easy, that's how we usually want things.

  - *Mark 10:17-25 "And when he was gone forth into the way, there came one running, and kneeled to him, and asked him, Good Master, what shall I do that I may inherit eternal life?"*
  - *vs.18: "And Jesus said unto him, why callest thou me good? there is none good but one, that is, God."*
  - *vs.19: "Thou knowest the commandments, do not commit adultery, do not kill, do not steal, do not bear false witness, defraud not, honour thy father and mother."*
  - *vs.20: "And he answered and said unto him, Master, all these have I observed from my youth."*
  - *vs.21: "Then Jesus beholding him loved him, and said unto him, one thing thou lackest: go thy way, sell whatsoever thou hast, and give to the poor, and thou shalt have treasure in heaven: and come, take up the cross, and follow me."*
  - *vs.22: "And he was sad at that saying and went away grieved: for he had great possessions."*
  - *vs.23: "And Jesus looked round about, and saith unto his disciples, how hardly shall they that have riches enter into the kingdom of God!"*
  - *vs.24: "And the disciples were astonished at his words. But Jesus answereth again, and saith unto them, Children, how hard is it for them that trust in riches to enter into the kingdom of God!"*
  - *vs.25: "It is easier for a camel to go through the eye of a needle, than for a rich man to enter into the kingdom of God."*

Rich young ruler
- Wanted it quick: *"just get born again and all your problems will be over]*; is that how it works, problems that have been there for as long as we were born into planet earth, to be gone in a swift; is that how it works; are we not looking for magic instead of relationship that brings miracles?

- Just buy it now: *[because many of the so-called false prophets will put a tag price on every ailment or problem]* and you got to pay why? Because you want a quick, but temporary solution; ***Jeremiah 5:31*** puts it this way:

"The prophets prophesy falsely, and the priests bear rule by their means; and my people love to have it so: and what will ye do in the end thereof?"

- How much does it cost, a visit or more to the herbalists or prophets, or with the star gazers, or the sorcerers, or the necromancers or the magicians or the stargazers?
- Many never thought there might be more to this than a shallow list of do's and don'ts: many so called Christians are running away from good Bible believing churches because of their sinful lives and because of responsibility, also many don't want to be committed; ***"[say your prayers and I will say Amen, and they are out to continue their old lives; such is the life of many]"*** no string attached, they don't even have a home church, they are professional visitors visiting churches all year round and are still searching, no home church, no Word no resting place! If care is not taking, they will remain professional visitors until Jesus comes.
- Many thought they could just scratch the surface and find salvation.
- Some thought all you had to do was throw a few bucks on the plate.
- They didn't realize that it was going to take a whole lot more than shallow commitment.

I'm asking every child of God to **Dig Deeper**, to be more committed, to aspire to grow. A brother after he got converted to Christianity from another religion, he began attending some of these churches for years where all they do is to light candles all over the place, they have a particular kind of long white dress, rituals of all kinds including stream bath and breaking of eggs. Ministers will take both married and unmarried women for stream baths ***I've never seen that in my Bible]***. The brother yearned for growth, and he began to ask himself some questions, is this all there is to Christianity, isn't there anything like study to know and have more? He concluded and convinced himself that there must be something better than this; then he left the 'sect *[because unknowingly to him, he was in a cult-like-religion' as there are many gospels that are not the gospel of Jesus Christ even though the carry Bibles]*; he went to a Living church where the Word of God is being taught precept upon precept, line upon line, he became so zealous and he began to learn more and more about the God of the Bible. Soon he began to teach the Word of God and preach wonderful, vibrant sermon, blessed be the name of the Lord, now he is an associate pastor!

> *Why? 'Study to shew thyself approved unto God, a workman that needeth not to be ashamed, rightly dividing the word of truth:" II Timothy 2:15*
>
> *Eph.4:14, "That we henceforth be no more children, tossed to and fro, and carried about every wind of doctrine, by the sleight of men, and cunning craftiness, whereby they lie in wait to deceive!"*

Otherwise, without knowing the WORD of God, we are open to all kinds of teachings that will pollute our minds and we don't know what to believe any more.

- I believe it's time that we begin to look deeper into God's Word.
- I believe it's time that we begin to pray deeper than we have in the past.
- It's time that our commitments toward the things of God grow deeper.
- I believe it's time to give more of our time, talents and treasure to the service of God who is the giver of all things!

But remember, deeper means more work.
- It means more time.
- It means more materials.

- It means more cost and more dedication.
- It means more responsibility and commitment.

You can't have a deep walk with God and get it easy.
- You can't have a deep walk with God without working for it.
- Quick and easy are just not going to work if we want a relationship with God that affects those around us.

Scripture, *"Deep calleth unto deep."*

If you're struggling with depression, worry, financial difficulty, relationships, sin, feeling like you are not saved dig deeper.
- Pray More.
- Fast Often.
- Ask God to help you.
- He's waiting for you to turn your heart to Him.

If you want a closer walk with God dig deeper. Don't settle for a run-off walk with God.
- That's where all the crud is.
- The rainwater washes all the junk into one place and then [spiritual] bacterial sets in.
- *[spiritual malnutrition, cholera epidemics]* start from this level of shallow well, because we are microwave oven Christians, no Word, no commitment, no Bible Study, no church attendance, we are once a while church attendee kind of people, we are weak and not zealous, we choose when to present ourselves before the LORD.
- When a professed Christian don't have a home church, no permanent place of worship, when a Christian will not be in any church for weeks, months, even years and are comfortable parading ourselves as Christians; when we are good and comfortable at other places but churches.
- Whenever we are any church service, we are restless, we want to have a 30-minute service and in a hurry to leave, even to places that are not glorifying to God.

- Think about a relationship like I just described if its real, if we're really Christians, if our salvation is not questionable!
- Let the truth be told, are we not running away from commitments? Are we not running away and hiding from responsibility? We don't want to be committed to any church, so we don't have to participate in anything nor give!

Our well needs to go deeper.
- Go deeper by reading our Bible.
- Go deeper by praying.
- Go deeper by attending Bible Studies.
- Go deeper by making church a priority.
- Go deeper by making commitments to God.

"Deep calleth unto deep"

Jesus is not shallow.
- His commitment to us is not frivolous.
- It was not cheap.
- It cost Him something.
- It cost Him everything.

Punch through the ground water experience.
- Don't settle for the very next spiritual experience you find past the runoff.
- Water either.
- Dig deeper.
- Get down into the ancient water.
- Get down into the Promises of God.
- Go past the 240 feet of clay.
- It may not seem like there's anything down there but keep drilling! And I promise you will find HIM; he is there waiting!

I had an experience one time at my early stage in life as a staff when I witnessed at the Horticulture Center of the Ministry of Agriculture; water is needed for the crops, crops need a lot of water especially during the dry season, and a team of drillers came to drill, searching for pure quality water; soon the drilling began for days, for weeks and for months; during this process, we saw all kinds of color and layers of earths, and in amazement, species of stones that you could never imagine are down out there in different sizes and the depths kept going down and down and down, finally the breakthrough came and suddenly we saw the gush of this spring water, so crystal clean, so pure and ready to drink! I tell you; it was exciting!

And once you find this precious water in this precious fountain, don't forget to seal the well.
- Don't let cross contamination occur.

After all the drilling, they find out that water from the 2nd aquifer leaches down into the third aquifer by following the hole you drilled. They have to pour concrete or betonies (swells 18 times its size) down the hole to seal it.

Once you find the deep experience with God, seal some things off, seal away some sinful friends, cut away from wrong associations, seal your walk and position in Christ with His Blood.
- Don't let your past cross contaminate your future.
- Get into your Bible, Get into the WORD
- Learn how to study.
- Learn how to pray.
- Learn how to fast.
- Make going to church [a Bible believing church] a priority: Remember, it is God Himself who can perfect us to fit into His Kingdom and His Presence as we get closer to Him!

BACKWARD OR FORWARD?

Every New Year keeps looking forward; we treasure our memories and the experiences of the past. We want to recount former blessings, and we also want to retain the lessons we've learned along the way. But our dreams are bigger than our memories and we should always be excited about what God is planning for the future. With creative genius, God made His universe in spheres and circuits. Because the earth rotates on its axis, we have a new day every twenty-four hours. Because the world circles around the sun every 365 days, we have endless supply of new years and new starts.

God designed it that way to keep us looking forward and living life to its fullest; time only moves in one direction, and it's forward. there is no "reverse" on the clock or calendar.

> ***Isaiah 43:18-19**, "Remember not ye the former things, neither consider the things of old: Behold, I will do a new thing; now it shall spring forth; shall ye not know it? I will even make a way in the wilderness, and rivers in the desert!*

Why not let Him do a new thing in us, why not let Him perfect us, let Him break us, mold us to fit and make us ready for His Glory. The apostle Paul stuck this same note in his verse of testimony in **Philippians 3:12-14**,

> *"Not as though I had already attained, either were already perfect: but I follow after, if that I may apprehend that for which also, I am apprehended of Christ Jesus!"*

> *"[Not that I have already attained, or am already perfected; but I press on, that I may lay hold of that which Christ Jesus has also laid hold of me. One thing I do, forgetting those things which are behind and reaching forward of those things which are ahead, I press toward the goal for the prize of the upward call of God in Christ Jesus!]" NIV*

STRENGTH TO STRENGTH:

According to **Psalms 84**, God's people are those who have set their hearts on pilgrimage. Though they sometimes pass through valleys, they locate the springs, refresh themselves, and go ***"from strength to strength"*** until they appear before God in Zion.

Sometimes we feel like we're going from weakness to weakness. But God's way is from strength to strength; and we should adopt His attitude about that. Strength will rise as we wait upon the Lord.

Our prior experiences are the foundation stones of future service. Our past mistakes have taught us irreplaceable lessons, and our sins are under the Blood of Christ. Yesterday's victories have paved the way for tomorrow's progress. The Second Coming of Christ is nearer than it's ever been, and the word has never needed the hope of the Gospel more. There's never been a better time to live life to its fullest through Christ our Lord and Saviour. The Lord God of our Salvation!

"Understand this!"

SALVATION IN THE OLD TESTAMENT:

The concept of salvation in the Old Testament features a variety of applications, including deliverance, rescue, safety, and even welfare. In ***Exodus 14:30, "the LORD saved Israel"*** from the hand of the Egyptians. This usage of the term is typical of the times when salvation focuses on physical deliverance from a specific danger. Another nuance involves forensic or legal rescue, which is observed in passages like ***Deuteronomy 23:27*** where a woman who is the subject of sexual attack in a field has no one to rescue her.

But the most significant use of the concept and the one most commonly perceived is the stereological emphasis in which the fallen spiritual nature of humankind stands in need of salvation or redemption by God.
Implicit in all uses of *"salvation"* are the perceptions of need and even inability. As often as not, God is featured as the only One who can affect a rescue or bring salvation, which is especially true of the eternal salvation of the individual. Passages such as ***Isaiah 51:8*** contrast the ephemeral nature of physical realities with a salvation that is for all generations. In the famous passage magnifying the beauty of those who bring good news and proclaim salvation, the

rescue in view seems to be spiritual and eternal *[Isaiah 52:7]*. *Isaiah 59:17* employs language later invoked by New Testament authors such as Paul, who speaks of *"breastplate of righteousness"* and *"the helmet of salvation" [Eph.6:14,17].*

In Jonah's prayer from the belly of the great fish, he declares that *[Jonah 2:9]*. While it could be argued that the prophet's thought is only about his abysmal physical circumstance, most would see a more profound avowal, *[an open declaration]* anticipating god's sovereign redemption of the soul.

Salvation in the Old Testament is also linked with other concepts such as redemption, atonement, and righteousness. Such ideas express the means of salvation *[atonement], the goal of salvation [righteousness]*, or the nature of salvation *[redemption]*. For example, the Passover was designed not only to depict the exodus from Egypt but to also remind the Israelites of the more profound significance of the role of sacrifice in salvation. A lamb dies and its blood is sprinkled on the door posts so that the death angel will pass over, sparing the life of the firstborn *[Exodus 12:1-14]*. The rituals associated with the Day of Atonement also focused on a vicarious, substitutionary atonement for the sins of the people *[Leviticus 16:1-34]*.

Isaiah 53 conveys the message of a sacrificial act on the part of the Suffering Servant, who made His Life and offering for sin that would *"justify many."* By His stripes we are healed and the iniquity of us all was laid on Him as He was struck by God for the transgressions of us all.

God is the sole author of salvation. The human family, horribly marred by sin, cannot affect salvation 'even by the keeping of the law.' This raises the question of how salvation is appropriated in the Old Testament. Genesis 15:6 declares that Abram believed *"in the LORD; and He counted it to him for righteousness."* Paul makes this passage central to his whole argument in *Romans 1-8. "For what saith the Scripture? Abraham believed God, and it was counted unto him for righteousness" [Romans 4:3]*. While there seems to be general recognition among Christians that righteousness and holiness are required to stand before God, many erroneously believe that salvation was attained in the Old Testament by the keeping of the law. Both Genesis and Romans agree in declaring that salvation may be attained only through faith *[believing God]*. As the sacrificial system perpetually illustrates, atonement must be made. *Isaiah 53* presented the Suffering Servant as the One who would ultimately make that atonement. Paul demonstrates explicitly what is always implicit in the Old Testament, the law could save no one. Salvation is extended in any era on the basis of God's grace appropriated by faith of human beings.

Old and childless. Abraham believed in the LORD, that is, he affirmed that God is dependable. God counted it to him for righteousness that is He judged or accounted that Abram measured up to the standard, conformed to the norm. Abram's faith and God's gracious response to it served as a paradigm [a pattern] of the Christian experience in three New Testament Books [Romans 4:3; Galatians 3:6; James 2:23].

James continues with the theme of being *"hearers"* as well as *"doers"* of the Word of God *[read James 1:19-27]* by focusing on the relationship between faith and works!
The distinction between the *"hearer"* who *"forgetteth"* and the *"doer"* of the Word who *"continueth* is whether he allows *"the perfect law of liberty"* to shape his life's course. The person who puts faith into action and is *"blessed"*, his worship influences his life. In the same way, the person who refuses to hold his *"tongue"* is deceived about his faith. He hears and talks, but he does not act on what he has heard. James' definition of **pure** and **undefiled** religion is based on action, not heedless hearing and meaningless lip service.

We cannot be *"hearers"* of His Word and not be *"doers"* of the Word, but we can be regenerated if and when we give heed to His Word for this is the WILL of God for us as His children, remember, we cannot change ourselves neither can we help ourselves but He alone can change us, He alone can help us and He alone can perfect us, all we need to do is to love the Lord with all our hearts, obey His commandments, again to love our neighbours as we love ourselves, embrace the Lord, give our life completely and let Him lead us, let Him direct us, there can never be a better Leader for Him Alone is Worthy:

He is ....
THE *EL ELYON--THE GOD MOST HIGH:*
*He is The **SOVEREIGN GOD**: In whom we can put our trust He will be with us, lead and guide us to be able to 'Dwell and Abide with Him!" Amen!*

CHAPTER 2

EL ROI - THE GOD WHO SEES ME:
There are no circumstances in our lives that escape His fatherly awareness and care. GOD knows us and our troubles!

Psalm 15:2

Vs.2, He that walketh uprightly, and worketh righteousness, and speaketh the truth in his heart.

"HE THAT WALKETH UPRIGHTLY"

How do we walk uprightly? This is simply referring to a life of integrity, if we look at **Psalm18:23; Psalm 119:1**

In **Ps.18:23**, it says, *"I was also upright before Him, and I kept myself from mine iniquity:"*

Here is the psalmist's statement of innocence as a part of thanksgiving for answered prayer, indicating why God delivered him from his calamity.

He said in <u>verses 20 & 24</u>, how *"the LORD rewarded me according to my righteousness; according to the cleanness of my hands had He recompensed me." <u>vs.24</u>, Therefore hath the LORD recompensed me according to my righteousness, according to the cleanness of my hands in His eyesight!"*

When we walk before the Lord in righteousness and in uprightness He surely rewards; righteousness is further clarified as cleanness of .... hands, meaning integrity in his obedience to God's commands.

He says, *"He that hath clean hands, and a pure heart; who hath not lifted up his soul unto vanity, nor sworn deceitfully:"*

It's the use of rhetorical questions about those who are worthy to enter into **Jehovah's** Presence and ***"Dwell with Him,"*** as the question we are examining right now. *'Clean hands' and 'a pure heart'* represent innocence and integrity:

<u>**Ps.73:13**</u> says, *"Verily I have cleansed my heart in vain, and washed my hands in innocency:"* washing hands was part of an oath of innocency, *"[I will wash my hands in innocency: so will I compass thine altar, O LORD: That I may publish with the voice of thanksgiving, and tell of all thy wondrous works.]"*

<u>**Ps.26:6-7**</u>: Washing **hands** was part of an oath of purification symbolizing innocency: The psalmist was not absolutely perfect and free from sin, but he was upright in terms of his faithfulness to God, any unaddressed sin always brings a curse, in other words, it is an act of pride for us to act as if we have everything going well and have not sinned; any sin unaddressed in the church of Jesus Christ automatically becomes the sin of the church and it calls for repentance: *[see church discipline]*.

Any man or woman who wronged another or wrong the church actually knew what he or she did or was doing, but to pretend as like nothing happened when the victim is hurting is a sin in itself and when someone is hurting as a result of our action or wrong doing, God is also hurt and thereby, He is not happy with us until we agree that we have wronged someone and we go immediately to apologize, and put things right; how can we pretend like we did nothing.

The most terrible thing is, we're waiting for the person we wronged to come and bow before us, remember in <u>**vs.2c**</u>, *"he that speaketh the truth in his heart:"* the Bible says, *"[to do unto others as we*

want them do unto us]" without speaking the truth in our hearts, if we think in all of these we can **"Dwell and Abide"** with The Father we deceive ourselves. It is **_Pride that_** is not letting us accept our sin. The spirit of Nebuchadnezzar is in us; it is the sin of **_pride_**.

When we don't respect other people's views, anything we do or say goes, when we can tell anyone anything, but nobody tells us anything, we are always right in our own eyes, when we underrate others and belittle them as if they are nothing, we are not being truthful. It is pride, the sin of **_Nebuchadnezzar_**; to walk uprightly, and to speak ***truthfully***, is to continually audit our daily walk with Him and see where we have offended God before we go to bed, repent of our sins and get right with the Lord!

Please do not forget what He says in the Book of Jeremiah 1:5,

> ***"Before*** *I formed thee in the belly I knew thee;* ***before*** *thou camest forth out of the womb I sanctified thee, and I ordained thee a prophet unto the nations!"*

The sense in which God forms man in the womb is by being the Author of nature and the creator of the law of reproduction whereby all creatures and things in nature reproduce themselves.

Here in **_Jeremiah 1:5_**, The prophet was told that God chose *[knew]* him before He formed him in the womb. Similar concepts are used in the call of the Servant of God **_[Isaiah.49:5]_** and the apostle Paul **_[Galatians 1:15]_**. God had more than an intellectual knowledge of **_Jeremiah_**; He had a personal relationship with him. So, for us to think that God does not know or have more than intellectual knowledge of us, we are deceiving ourselves, He created each of us uniquely, one in a trillion people will have a matching **_DNA_** that's how uniquely created us, we are in His awesome wisdom, He knows us and deals with each person individually:

The Book of **_Psalms in Chapter 139_**: Celebrates the attributes of God; God's attributes of Omniscience are beyond human comprehension;

when he says, **in _verse 7_**, *"Wither shall I go from thy spirit: of wither shall I flee from thy Presence?"* The psalmist could not remove himself from the realm of God's transcendence, nor could he run from God's immanent and personal engagement with Him: *[Jeremiah 23:24; Amos 9:2-4; Hebrew 4:13]*. The concept is both frightening and comforting.

> *Jeremiah 23:23-24, "Am I a God at hand, saith the LORD, and not a God afar off? Can any hide himself in secret places that I shall not see him? saith the LORD."*

God is not a pagan local god confined to His shrine or temple. He is both immanent [at hand] and transcendent *[a far off]*.

> *Amos 9:2-4, "Though they dig into hell, thence shall mind hand take them; though they climb up to heaven, thence will I bring them down:"*
> *vs.3, "And though they hide themselves in the top of Carmel, I will search and take them out thence; and though they be hid from my sight in the bottom of the sea, thence will I command the serpent, and he shall bite them:"*
> *vs.4, "And though they go into captivity before their enemies, thence will I command the sword, and it shall slay them: and I will set mine eyes upon them for evil, and not for good!"*

This portion of the Book of Amos we just read though, none of the Israelites will be able to hide from God, *[vs.3]*, not even you and I, so the language here is hyperbole *[exaggeration for rhetorical effect]*. Obviously, no one can literally climb into heaven or hide at the bottom of the sea.

> *Hebrew 4:13, "Neither is there any creature that is not manifest in his sight: but all things are naked and open unto the eyes of him with whom we have to do!"*

The author of this chapter of **Hebrew chapter 4 verses 1-16**, now drew the reader into examining their own personal faith as the Word of God shines its penetrating light upon the inner man. Faithfulness begins with a proper internal disposition. The **quick** and **powerful** Word of God probes into the deepest part of a person like a surgeon's knife to discern his innermost **thoughts and intents**: which must be closely followed and obeyed if and when we are sure to enter into His rest to "Dwell and Abide!" God's Word reveals to him both his ingrained wickedness and the saving way of faith. At that critical point, when the divine judge reveals Himself through His Word, the hearer must **labour** to enter the divine rest by believing. If the result of unbelief and disobedience to God is exclusion from divine rest, then the result of true faith and faithfulness to God is entrance into everlasting divine rest.

> <u>**Hebrew 4:8**</u>, *"For if Jesus had given them rest, then would he not afterward have spoken of another way."*

<u>**Jesus**</u> in this <u>**verse 8**</u>, refers to Joshua, the son of Nun, Everlasting rest was not available through the ministry of Joshua in the Old Testament since it was reserved for the ministry of the New Testament **"Joshua."** The name **"Jesus"** is a Greek derivative of the Hebrew name Joshua, which means **"The Lord Is Salvation."** The ministry of Joshua did not bring people Sabbath rest. Only through the Superior Ministry of Jesus the Son of God may a person enter divine rest. Only through **The Great High Priest**, who has come from Heaven and identified with man in his weakness, may we boldly approach the **"Throne of Grace!"**

> <u>**Jeremiah 1:5**</u>, *"Before I formed thee in the belly I knew thee; <u>before</u> thou camest forth out of the womb I sanctified thee, and I ordained thee a prophet unto the nations!"*

The man Jeremiah was called <u>sanctified</u> or separated <u>***"to be holy"***</u> or ***"set apart"*** to the Lord of the entire world, and so, it is natural as the GOD of All, that His message would extend <u>unto the nations.</u>

'I knew,' meaning, **[I know everything about you, because I created you; I know your capabilities and I know your weakness and your shortfalls], yet, [I approved of you]**, chose you, set you apart and *'**Sanctified you,**'* meaning, you are an *'Ecclesiastes'* in other words, *'I Ordained you*, meaning that, **[I commissioned]** you before you were born; that is *'Grace!'*

There is nothing about you that is hidden from Jehovah God; ***There are no circumstances in our lives that escape His fatherly awareness and care. GOD knows us and our troubles!*** God is willing to receive us as we are, to sanctify us, ordain us and renew us, but we must live a life of separation from the world and eschew evil ***[to desist from sinning]***!

> *"O LORD, thou hast searched me, and known me: Thou knowest my down sitting and mine uprising, Thou understandest my thought afar off: Thou compassest my path and my lying down, and art acquainted with all my ways: for there is not a word in my tongue, but lo, O LORD, thou knowest it altogether:" [Ps.139:1-4]*

<u>**Psalm 139**</u> speaks of *'Praise to All Knowing God,'* this Psalm celebrates the attributes of God: The Hebrew verbs can be interpreted as timeless truth; *"You search, and You know me."* God's attributes are not restricted to time.

The words *'known,' 'understandest,' 'compassest,'* and be *'acquainted'* speak of God's Omniscience. The word 'compassest' comes from the Hebrew root *'zara,'* which means *"measure."* The Hebrew word for ways does not necessarily denote literal walking but daily behaviour.

God's Omnipresence guarantees protection; in <u>***vs.5***</u> of <u>***Ps.139***</u>, ***"God's hand upon me,"*** denotes absolute control over the psalmist, who was subject to the Lord's loving care and discipline.

Therefore, God demands for us to live Holy if we want to possess our possession and fulfill our calling; the question is, 'what are we doing with our commission, [as in *Jeremiah 1:5*]; what are we doing with our calling, how often do we win souls with our mandate? As leaders in the church of Jesus Christ, workers and members in our local assemblies, how uprightly is our walk with the Lord; are we really good examples that others can follow, do we gang-up against the authority, do we garner people around us to plot evil, to gender strive against the anointing instead of getting busy winning souls?

> *"The kings of the earth set themselves, and the rulers take counsel together, against the LORD, and against His anointed, saying: Let us break their bands asunder, and cast away their cords from us: He that sitteth in the heavens shall laugh!" [Ps.2:2-4]*

Kicking against the brick is a hard thing to do, God will not hold us guiltless, our disobedience, disloyalty, our non-zealousness, stone-headedness, strive, grumblings, lies, deceits, jealousy and pride in the house of God, are daring to God and cannot be excused. When we have assignments in the house of God, we take off without looking back, dis-countenancing the Head, even as leaders, we leave our assignments to others without realizing how disappointing it is to God, we're not walking uprightly, neither are we speaking truthfully. God will not hold us guiltless! How can we then *"Dwell and Abide'* with Him!

THE BIBLE AND WOMEN!

The Bible highly esteems women. It teaches that they are co-bearers of the image of God-that He crowned them with honour and glory and gave them charge to exercise dominion over the earth.
Women, along with men, have the enormous dignity, privilege, and responsibility to put the glory of God on display *[Isaiah 43:6-7]*.

The Bible highly esteems women, but unfortunately, women do not always highly esteem the Bible. Some disregard the Bible--they are apathetic and lackadaisical, unwilling to exert the effort to sharpen their Bible Study habits, and unconcerned about applying the Word of God to their lives.

Others disrespect the Bible--they think that they have the right to choose which parts are and are not applicable to women today. Others deride the Bible--claiming that since the writers were exclusively men, Scripture is flawed and insufficient for women. The tendency for women to disrespect and deride the Bible is particularly prevalent in our post-feminist society, even amongst those who claim to follow Christ.

Two women who had an enormous respect for the Bible were Eunice and Lois, Timothy's mother and grandmother. Paul credits them with Timothy's conversion:

> *"When I call to remembrance the unfeigned faith that is in thee, which dwelt first in thy grandmother Lois, and thy mother Eunice; and I am persuaded that in thee also:" [II Tim.1:5]*

> *Paul and Timothy both had a heritage of faith. When Paul said he prayed for Timothy continually night and day, he used a common expression for continual prayer. Timothy was on His mind and in his prayers throughout each day. [I Timothy 1:3-4]*

He also credits them with carefully teaching Timothy Scripture and doctrine. Timothy's father was not a believer, so he didn't contribute to Timothy's spiritual training;

> *"Then came he to Der-be and Lystra: and behold, a certain disciple was there, named Timotheus, the son of a certain woman, which was Jewess, and believed; but his father was a Greek: [Acts 16:1]*

It was Eunice and Lois that acquainted Timothy with **"the Holy Scriptures,"** taught him what they meant, instructed him in the ways of the Lord, and ensured that he received instruction for salvation through faith in Christ Jesus:

> ***"But continue thou in the things which thou hast learned and hast been assured of, knowing of whom thou hast learned them:***
> ***vs.15, And that from a child thou hast known the Holy Scriptures, which are able to make thee wise unto salvation through faith which is in Christ Jesus:" [II Tim.3:14-15]***
>
> ***"Train up a child in the way he should go: and when he is old, he will not depart from it:" [Proverbs 22:6]***

Paul reminds Timothy about his mother and grandmother's attitude toward Scripture and their skill in studying, understanding, and applying it. He wrote the well-known verses about all Scripture being inspired by God and **"profitable for doctrine, for reproof, for correction, for instruction in righteousness,"** to make us perfect, **"thoroughly furnished unto all good works"** in the context of the outstanding job that Eunice and Lois did equipping Timothy *[II Tim.3:14-17]*. These two women did not disregard, disrespect, or deride the Bible. They held it in highest esteem.

In order to influence for Christ those who are in our relational sphere, women need to have the same regard for Scripture that Eunice and Lois had. We need to be students of the Bible, and diligently study the Bible, so we can correctly teach the Word of truth:

> ***"Study to shew thyself approved unto God, a workman that needeth not to be ashamed, rightly dividing the word of truth:" [II Tim.2:15]. Study here means, 'Study, it means, to be 'Zealous; it also means, to Handle Scripture correctly!***
>
> ***"Rightly dividing" "correctly teaching, cutting straight, holding a straight course, doing right]"***

> *"For of this sort are they which creep into houses, and lead captive silly women laden with sins, led away with divers lusts:*
> *vs. 7, Ever learning, and never able to come to the knowledge of truth:"* [II Tim.3:6-7]

Because of their guilt from their past, these unstable women laden with sins were particularly susceptible to the asceticism and legalism of these false teachers: they themselves have no doctrine and what you do not have, you cannot give, hence they are un-able to give proper training and directions to their children; therefore the children grow up into the same old styles of living like their parents: in other words, what your children see you do is what they will do, if they see you not caring about the things of God, they will grow up not caring about the things of God, not even caring about anything: if they see you as nonchalant, not a prayerful person, not a lover of God, not a giver and always selfish not caring to share with anyone; guess what? They will be the same and do the same. We are the first teacher God gave to our children, first mentor to mentor them and train them in the way of the Lord so they will live longer and no in disobedience.

> *"Train up a child in the way he should go: and when he is old, he will not depart from it:"* [Proverbs 22:6]

Women who highly esteem the Bible, and have a good grasp of doctrine, will be able to be *"teacher of good things,"* and will have a tremendous impact in mentoring their children and friends in the ways of the Lord:

> *"The aged women likewise, that they be in behaviour as becometh holiness, not false accusers, not given to much wine, teachers of good thi9ngs:*
> *vs.4, That they may teach the young women to be sober, to love their husbands, to love their children!"* [Titus 2:3-4]

The teaching in these verses is practical and focuses on the domestic sphere. Paul emphasizes that older *women* can help model for *young women* what it means to be a wife and mother: Parents especially mothers, *[women]* are the first teachers God gave to their children but now the roles are switched, children controls their parents, parents are afraid to teach, train and correct their children the results are what we see on our streets daily; our streets are no more safe both for the lawful and the innocent children and are not safe either for the rebellious ones; same reason they are ***dying young!*** *"Honour your parent ....]"* the Bible says, *"so you can live long"* has a deep meaning, in other words, *'disobedience children tread the parts of death, they follow disobedience friends who then lure them to death!'* The warnings, the rules, the instructions and commandments in the Bible are there for us and for our children to respect and to obey, the Bible is the **GPS** given to us by the *Heavenly Father* to keep us from getting lost in the crowd of life, to keep us from evil as well as keeping us away from trouble, troubles that will shorten our lives!

<u>Exodus 20:12</u>, "Honour thy father and thy mother: that thy days may be long upon the land which the LORD thy GOD giveth thee:"

A stubborn and a rebellious son who refused other discipline could be taken before the elders for judgment, that is to the law for correction, now the correction could be in any form and in the case of a son who commits murder, the judgment could mean death penalty *[read all references: Deut.21:18-21; Lev.19:3]*; Eli's sons showed contempt for their father and for the Lord, which resulted in death, that's the verdict of disobeying parents and not focusing on God! *[I Sam.2:12-17, 22-25, 29-30]*. The respect and kindness that Jacob and Ruth showed to their respective parents provide positive examples.

Failure to honour parents was one of the sins that Ezekiel listed in a description of the people of Jerusalem before the city was destroyed *[<u>Ezek.22:7</u>; <u>Mic.7:6</u>]*. Long life for individuals is also a possible interpretation is also mentioned elsewhere as an outcome from the Lord for loyal obedience *[Exo.23:26]*.

Food For Thought:

Elementary school teaches the 3R's and habits of mind. Habits can be good or bad. Teachers try to teach or promote good habits and correct bad ones as they see them forming. Good habits can be in the realm of hygiene, moral judgment, group behavior, and study habits. Inappropriate behavior includes the inability to take turns, wait to vocalize and ask questions, to share, and to conform in group activities and schedules. A good preschool or daycare facility strives to ameliorate these problems. As we get older, change is often harder to accomplish, as we get 'set in our ways'.

It is necessary to correct children and have them accept the correction. Modern educational theory says children should be given the freedom to make many more choices than in generations past. Let's not assume children will know what the best choice or correction should be. They need an adult's wisdom to help point to a better way. The inability for students to accept corrections means that there is no hope of a better outcome. If you can't listen to an alternative, then there is NO HOPE.

Teachers try to teach discipline in school with academic studies and via the act of practice in sports and the arts. It is only with discipline that correction can be achieved. The unstructured home environment commonly found today undermines much of this effort. Students suffering a lack of self-control can't focus academically, play musical instruments or use art materials. They can spend their entire academic day talking out of turn and fidgeting. If you can't control yourself, nothing will work out for you. Discipline means being able to change from a bad situation to a better one. This ability is necessary for any correction to take place. I call this skill the ability to change gears in your life.

Who Is A Perfect Man? Who Is A Perfect Woman?

Why, however, listen to correction if there is no respect for the person who is giving the advice? If there is no concept of authority in the home, no effective authority in the school system, and no authority arising from a nonexistent church life, no one will likely pay attention. This is where the issue reaches biblical proportions, because the Word of the Lord is the ultimate authority, and without the fear of God and His Word, these various edicts seem arbitrary. The child centered educational philosophy of today is underlined by the traditional American disrespect for authority in general. Children are more and more confused as to which way to turn these days and it is unfair to expect children to have to make decisions that are not yet prepared for. We are at a point where children are running the show. Teachers are increasingly being accused of poor student performance, and students are being passed on to the next grade unqualified. At home, children often have their parents horse collared. This is a tragedy for the children and for society. As an adult, if you can't take correction from your boss, the police, your doctor, your pastor, or your God, you're lost and completely lost!

Andy Meacham!

It's amazing the way some parents treat their children without respect, many called them various negative names while insulting and raining curses on them. Some will say, *[because he [the father now] is nothing, never achieved anything, his child cannot be anything]* who said that? Because that is not in my Bible neither is it in yours? When we treat our children with dignity and care, they will be who we want them to be. Moses' mother saw the potential in Moses and went all the way to protect the future deliverer of his generation. May the Lord open the eyes of parents to see their tomorrow in their children and pay all the necessary price to secure, develop and protect this precious gift of their life.

Joseph's brother were parochial in their thinking and allow their emotion to overwhelmed them because of Joseph's dream and they could not see their future in that dream rather out of their selfish emotion they want to destroy their tomorrow thinking it is only Joseph that will be affected, they would have die of hunger because God promoted Joseph from the dungeon, from the prison to the place!

David's parents do not recognize the future of Israel in David and that is why they abandoned him on the field when other older ones are at home to take part in the sanctification process for anointing the next King. They kept him out of the scene, but God's destiny in every child shall be fulfill, hence Samuel said go and bring that neglected child we will not sit down until he comes.

Many parents are suffering today because of the neglect on their children who will give them the dividend of their investment. It is better to train a child than to correct an adult. When we don't curb and train our children, they tend to go into areas where angels fear to tread. They go into drug trafficking; they go into serious crimes. Crime is robbing many people of hope, including our children and their life is wasting away, they rot out there in jails as we have more teens and more people in prisons than higher institutions. Life is very precious, don't waste your time, don't allow crime to rob you of hope. Every life is precious to God!

Walking uprightly with the Lord includes the training of our children in the way of the lord, judging from the life of Eunice and Lois above; these two great women were the backbone of Timothy's walk with the Lord; how about us and our children, what training did we or are we giving them to make them to be more grounded in the Word of God? How will our children become good citizens or good leaders tomorrow if we neglect these basics, or are we not thinking of tomorrow? Are we raising vagabonds to be in power tomorrow? What will tomorrow be like with murderers in power? What will tomorrow look like with looters in power? What will tomorrow look like with rapists in power? What will tomorrow be like with convicts in congress? Don't we see our streets and what they do and is there nothing we can do about it for tomorrow's sake?

The LORD GOD said this about Abraham in **Genesis 18:19**, *"For I know him,"* does the Lord know you as a disciplinarian who will train his child in the way of the Lord? Because God wants children that will inherit and walk in the Abrahamic covenant thereof:

> *"For I know him, that he will command his children and his household after him, and they shall keep the way of the Lord, to do justice and judgment; that the LORD may bring upon Abraham that which he hath spoken of him!"*

We will explore that statement, *"that the LORD may bring upon Abraham that which He hath spoken of him!"* Here it is!

> In the Book of **Genesis 17:4-8**, God said in His Promises to Abraham: *"As for me, behold my covenant is with thee, and thou shalt be a father of many nations:*
> *vs. 5, Neither shall thy name any more be called Abram, but thy name shall be Abraham; for a father of many nations have I made thee:*
> *vs. 6, And I will make thee exceeding fruitful, and I will make nations of thee, and kings shall come out of thee. vs. 7, And I will establish my covenant between me and thee and thy seed after thee in their generations for an everlasting covenant, to be a Gods unto thee, and to thy seed after thee:*
> *vs. 8, And I will give unto thee, and to thy seed after thee, the land wherein thou art a stranger, all the land of Canaan, for an everlasting possession; and will be their God."*

These verses contain the fullest presentation of God's *covenant* with Abram. Eight different aspects of the covenant are presented in these verses. Most of these promises are not new, but nowhere else are they put together in one place. The new aspect is where God changed the patriarch's name, thus indicating His authority over him: instead of *Abram ["Exalted Father"]*, his new name would be ***Abraham ["Father of a Multitude"]*** in other words, ***"Father of nations."***

God now placed one final covenant-related demand on Abraham and his seed: circumcision. This surgical removal of the foreskin on new born *[Jos.5:2-3]* was performed when the boy was ***eight days old***: no form of female circumcision was authorized. This surrender of the first portion of the bodily instrument used to fulfill God's first command to humanity ***["Be fruitful and multiply," He says, [Gen.1:28]*** symbolized the individual's willingness to submit all of himself to God and to all His covenant commands.

The fact that every ***man child among*** them was to be circumcised had a leveling effect within the Israelites community; whether wealthy or poor, master or slave, all shared a common experience and a common mark. All were equal before God. So vital was the acceptance of the sign on the body that anyone who lacked it was to be ***'cut off from His people' [means death in most cases]*** because he has ***broken*** the ***covenant***. God did this and the purpose is to protect His name and to protect His covenant with Abraham and his seed and his children.

What father will leave an inheritance worth of trillions and trillions and more to a gangster or a vagabond to squander? So if we are walking uprightly enough we should be able to train our children in the way of the Lord so that there can be peace in the family, peace in the community, peace in our nation and the nations of the world; one act of recklessness, power grabbing, and abuse of power, waywardness of the highest order can change the whole world for ever like it did in the case of ***9/11***. If the perpetrators of ***9/11*** had good home training and the fear of God, they will be more responsible citizens. ***If we continue to neglect the re-introduction of Bible reading at schools because of a few that are bias against the gospel, for our children to learn knowledge and wisdom, for God to begin to do great and mighty things in their lives as youths and growing adults, the damage is enormous***, it can go on and on and on from generation to generation and the worst is yet to come until we learn wisdom; wisdom is the best choice wisdom is the principal thing with the best result in every situation; the pursuit of wisdom in all we do must come first and true wisdom we can ever come across is found in the Scriptures **The Bible**.

Why is the other religion radicalizing their children from their early stage teaching their children to read their book and there is nothing we can do about it? The adage says, "catch them young," it is to continue to carry on and carry out their agenda, to force the whole world into one religion, to introduce their demonic laws, to radicalize and control the world. While centuries ago, Christian nations sleep on, the enemy crept in to sow tars and the result is the invasion of every other god on planet earth and the nation became infested with paganism, and idolism. The Ten Commandments upon which the laws of the land are based have been ordered out of the courtrooms; people fight to remove **"In God We Trust"** from our currency. There are only two of them, **"God"** and **"Satan"** so if we don't want to **trust** in God anymore to control our economy, then Satan takes over and the result will be economic woes if that is who we want.

Jesus of Nazareth was presented at trial, Barabbas was presented, and they asked the people who they want to set free, they all chorused Barabbas who was a robber. Then we complain about the increase of armed robbers and robberies worldwide are on the increase. Have we forgotten that we were given a time of choice to choose, and we chose the robber? You either go to the left or to the right, no middle way, if we don't want God, Satan takes over, he takes over everything including the economy period! The same problem with our children, if they're not taught the way of the Lord, they will teach themselves the way of Satan, they will bully people, they will rape, they will commit murder, they will rob people, they will tell lies, they will take over the streets, they will be disobedient to both God and their parents even be disobedient to the law of the land. I mean, think about all the ways of Satan, they will graduate into it all.

The one-time eyes of the spirit became blinded, we prioritize non-priorities, when we should be training our children the way of the Lord. Gradually we began to snuffle churches out of strategic locations and we give or sell the properties upon which churches are built to developers, instead of creating or allowing more churches and encouraging growing up churches to help the oncoming generations we decide the location of churches by zoning, the other well-funded politically motivated turned religion are buying up our church buildings and turning them to their meeting places, places where they teach hate and violence while we left the worship of the Most High God to the worship of *the god of mammon*, we worship the dirty god of immorality, *we distribute condoms in our schools instead of the distribution of the Holy Bible*, we promote immoral teachings in our schools we call it sex education instead of promoting Bible Studies.

No wonder illegal sexual activities are issues of the day in our schools, our children wear dresses that are too short for comfort to schools and are getting raped, women, girls of under-age could spread their legs under any tree; we are too slack to instill discipline on our children in the area of illicit sexual appetites, we encourage them to engage in indiscriminate sexual activities by opening avenues where they can deposit their new born babies without questioning, some will wrap new born dump babies in dumpsters and we're not ashamed at the alarming rate at which all these are happening. When we sow a wind, we surely will reap whirlwinds!

Because we refused to train our children in the way of the Lord like Eunice and Lois trained Timothy we are under a curse; we encourage our children to watch and store up violent video games, violent movies and right on our watch our children became interested in everything evil and as such we gave the other people an upper hand to continue to radicalize our children male or female; our children became so violent and fearless, they can say anything because they know nothing will happen, they can chant any slogan aimed at anyone and nothing happens, then they die on the streets like chicken because of lack of honour and lack of respect for the law of the land; instructions of parents and teachers they will no follow; they respect nobody's opinion and behave above the law, no respect even for their parents at home and on the streets they behave like vagabonds, no an iota of respect and honour for God, teens male and female from Christian homes have gone far without their parents knowledge, they enlists themselves with the jihadists to kill innocent people around the globe but they call it a religion of love. People of God! Parents, what are we doing, isn't this going too far, are we losing our senses, must our children be left only to be trained at schools where immoral activities cannot be cubed or are encouraged?

Children go about terrorizing homes, they set fire to anything they can find and smoke like chimneys, they live under the influence of whatever they smoke or drink, our boys and girls will drink like fish and guess what? All kinds of immorality start from there; nothing is new to them anymore, rape, murder, arson, think of anything, it begins from there, babies given birth to babies; they disobey the rule of law. Are this what God wants from us as His children and from our children and our children's children? This is our fault as parents, we are responsible for the actions of our children and that disqualified us from walking uprightly and abiding with The Father of Love and of Peace!

Our children bully people everywhere, they shout and misbehave on the streets, vandalism of the highest order; our children take nude pictures of members of opposite sex without their consent and then posting them online to ridicule and disgrace the other party; consent or no consent it is an act of hooliganism and terrorism and it is evil. In all of these they think they are having fun, but it is not fun, and it is not funny. Children join gangs to prove a point, that they are also turf, that they also can brake bones that they can handle firearms; so they toy with guns, knives and all kinds of weapons they can lay hands on, they disrespect the police that are keeping the rule of law, they refuse every single instruction from their teachers even from the police, children armed themselves to schools and other places of recreation, they can harm anyone without regard for lives. Many are doing it to get popular, to make names, why don't they get serious at school and become successful, play basketball or be a footballer or a soccer player to get popular why cause harm, why take lives?

CHILDREN ARE GOD'S GREAT GIFT FOR OUR FUTURE LIVING!
Psalms 127:3-5
"Lo, children are an heritage of the LORD: and the fruit of the womb is his reward."

> ***Deuteronomy 6:6-9*** *says, "And these words that I command you today shall be on your heart. You shall teach them diligently to your children, and shall talk of them when you sit in your house, and when you walk by the way, and when you lie down, and when you rise. You shall bind them as a sign on your hand, and they shall be as frontlets between your eyes. You shall write them on the doorposts of your house and on your gates. Behold, children are a heritage from the LORD, the fruit of the womb a reward. Like arrows in the hand of a warrior are the children of one youth. Blessed is the man who fills his quiver with them! He shall not be put to shame when he speaks with his enemies in the gate."*

> ***Psalm 127:3-5***

People of God, the word of God contains so many great Bible verses about children. Anyone raising children knows how difficult things can get but also what a blessing the children are. Children are not casual guests in our home. They have been loaned to us temporarily for the purpose of loving them and instilling a foundation of values on which their future lives will be built. I believe that children are our future. Teach them well and let them lead the way. Show them all the beauty they possess inside.

> ***Proverbs 22:6*** *says, "Train up a child in the way he should go; even when he is old he will not depart from it:"*

Finally, Brethren, how you Train up a child will determine he or she end up, and who you are now is a picture of how your future will look like. **_Proverbs 29:15_** says, **_"The rod and reproof give wisdom, but a child left to himself brings shame to his mother:"_**

Life is divided into three terms - that which was, that which is, and that which will be. Let us learn from the past to profit from the present, and from the present, to live better in the future.

There is always one moment in childhood when the door opens and lets the future in. Therefore, our awesome responsibility to ourselves, to our children, to the community, to the nation and to the future is to create ourselves in the image of goodness, because the future depends on the nobility of our imaginings. They should be trained to honour all, respect and obey the law of the land even while on the streets.

The police in our communities are wonderful people, remember they decide in a split second what to do in a situation when they see someone breaking the law, they can escalate or de-escalate to use minimum or maximum force depending on the situation, they can as well do their job without extremes; we should respect, train and encourage our children to respect and obey them for putting their lives on the line as they're doing a great job all over the place, guess what will happened if we do not have these men and women in uniform to keep the law and order? We don't see the streets when we are at home relaxing, but we know how violent some of our children can be and how some behave at home, some can slap their parents, some will curse and abuse their parents, some misbehave under any kind of influences including satanic influence: then guess what happens on our streets when we're not there.

We then in turn blame the police, sue the police who are working tirelessly serving and protecting, while we are fast asleep; daily we see policemen and women risk their lives they are also dying while protecting others and while they rescue others from the troubled and turbulence waters of life; we forget that these men and women in uniform also have their own families who are waiting for them to come back home into their arms after the day's work; they put their lives on the line, in the rain, in the snow, at night, but they have their lives also to live. What we should be doing is to educate our children on what could happen when they disobey simple instructions given by the police!

Guess what? What if your dad, your mom is one of the men and women in uniform, what if your son, your daughter is one of them, would you want them to never return home to their loved ones, how do you feel when you see burial procession of police men and women on the street going to bury one of their own, how do we feel? Think about it, the Bible says, *".... come let us reason together!"* Eli's household came into God's judgment *[I Samuel 3-4]*, not because Eli himself as the prophet of God committed sin but because of the sins of his children that he was so weak to curb, for the lawlessness of his two sons, he and his house perished! When a child of someone commits murder, have we ever watched the court proceedings of murder cases, the agonies the parents go through even while trying to say *"good things"* about the accused child so they can *"walk"* as if they're really good?

The parents go through fear, torment, some cry their eyes out, it is a shame to take your parents through those agonies. Why would you? Some would even want to fake and plead insanity in other to escape justice, what if it's your life someone else took, would you want him or her to go free, to kill you and walk as if your life does not matter?

The Bible says: *"Train up a child in the way he should go: and when he is old, he will not depart from it:" [Proverbs 22:6]*

Do we even know how God feels about us not given our children proper training? Do we try to train them in the basic things of life? Once they hit the magic number 18, and are now on the streets, they become uncontrollable; children need direction, we shouldn't let it be like the story of *"who will bell the cat"* who will train my child for me, then why do we have them if we can't train them to become good citizens and responsible people in the community?

A teacher friend and a member of our church was so worried at the way children are going and growing wild everyday even at schools. He was saying how it becomes so difficult for him to control his class, he says, "he can't touch them, he can't give them instructions, so violent and wayward, they throw stones and objects at anyone: they can fabricate lies and make it stick like Jezebel:

My wife used to have a vitamin store somewhere around the route to and fro some schools and at the time of closing of schools, every day we must be ready to stand by the signboard rain or snow because when they come out of schools problems begin, they can carry whatever signpost in their way on the roadside, throw them, kick them or carry them along and when you try to pursue, they drop it as far as 2 blocks away, damage anything and it became a constant routine, they will storm some grocery stores in their numbers at a time, they vandalize, shoplift candies and other things. Does this look like those who will be responsible tomorrow; don't we have a case to answer with God?

Do we not leave our children to be trained only at schools where teachers have no say? Don't we leave them for TV sets to train where they learn all kinds of dirty games, immorality including violence and are not cautioned, do we care? We leave them to their friends to tame on the streets, friends who are also wayward while we are busy looking for what is not lost? Internet is the world's busiest street to cross, yet we allow our children to wonder and to cross that street un-accompanied without bothering what they're clicking on; so, what then do we expect? Should the police or any law enforcement agents be crucified for protecting their own lives, should the police look on while they are clubbed or shot to death and never return home any more to their loved ones? How are we faring parents? Think about it, are we not failing in our duties and obligations to God in training our children?

I know what you're saying, "What about the killings by the police, in what account do we put that?" Well, I am seriously against killings and everyone should, no one has any authority to take humans life when we are not at war, but can we use the yardstick of the mistakes of a few to judge the rank and file of the brilliant cops? The police are doing great jobs and we need to honour and respect them for their good work, we need not to assume that they are all bad. Are there not a majority of good cops out there as well as we have good and bad citizens in every society on planet earth? And so, if and when police kill unjustly, there is no justification for any kind of violence, excessive force or deadly force that results in killing, the man or woman who kills another person should be made accountable for the sin committed, he must also be ready to face the music and pay the price.

Let us all reason together, shouldn't we be training our children how to respect the law of the land? Shouldn't we teach them how to respect elders, how to also respect every human being young or old no matter the age or color and obey simple instructions; how uprightly then are we walking with the King when we leave our children to behave unruly? We are so afraid to correct or instruct them when they go wrong, and instead of us controlling our children the reverse is the case, it is the children that now control their parents, which is not the plan of God for us neither is it for them.

"..... that their days may be long upon the land which the LORD their GOD giveth them?"

What about you children teen or adult, are you a child to a parent? Are your parents still alive? Do you take care of your parents? Are you meeting their needs, especially if they're old? Do you live their needs to be met by others who are not members of the family? Do you let them live in lack and in want without care? Do you just throw them into some home like nursing home and neglect them while you spend their hard-earned money on riotous living or on your own family?

You're not walking uprightly with the Lord, you're not living and being truthful to yourself and as such, you have a case to answer. If you don't repent and make amends, no matter how spiritual you are, you may not see the beautiful gate of heaven. It's as serious as that for neglect of your parents. Also, the law of sowing and reaping is still very much in force, the law of repercussion is very much alive! Think about it.

"For I know him [Abraham], that he will command [train] his children and his household after him]:"

When they are trained in the way of the Lord, they will be responsible enough to take care of us when we become old and can no longer make a living, we will also have rest and not fear, we will be sure that when they go out either to schools or on errand, they are surely coming back home. God wanted us to walk uprightly with Him, train our children like He said of Abraham:

"For I know him, that he will command his children and his household after him, and they shall keep the way of the Lord, to do justice and judgment; that the LORD may bring upon Abraham that which he hath spoken of him!"

He wants us to live Holy, to be passionate after Him, to love Him passionately and love all, if and when we love all, we will respect all, we will always do His will and then we will be ready to 'Dwell' and 'Abide' with Him forever!

If it were not possible to live Holy, God would have not demanded holiness from us. God has a standard, and He demands for us to live up to that standard as God is not ready to lower or tailor His own standard in order for us to fit in; so, getting Born Again is the first and a step in the right direction which you have now taken, now you need to do more.

The Bible says in Philippians 2:12-16, "Wherefore, my beloved, as ye have always obeyed, not as in my presence only, but now much more in my absence, work out your own salvation with fear and trembling:"

What the Bible tells us here is true, working out your own salvation until it is completed; why fear and trembling if there is no possibility of a fall and a failure?

vs.13, "For it is God which worketh in you both to will and to do of His good pleasure:"

Suppose one will not obey in working out [verse 13] His own salvation, will God continue to work when man refuses to permit Him or remain in sin?

We are to shine as lights in the world: vs.12-13, Obedience is directed to God, not to Paul who hoped his potential death would not dampen Christian enthusiasm. Work out means to apply salvation, not to earn it.
In verses 12-18, three applications follow in this section: [vs.12-13], practical Christianity; [vs.4-16], positive steadfastness; and [vs.17-18], personal joy.

"Fear and trembling" means to have proper respect in response to God's blessing. True obedience comes from reverence, not fright. "God ... worketh" provides the deeper incentive: Christians are recipients of God's initiatives of motivation and empowerment.

vs.14 & 15, "Do all things without murmurings and disputing's: That ye may be blameless and harmless, the sons of God, without rebuke, in the midst of a crooked and perverse nation, among whom ye shine as lights in the world:"

> **_vs.16_, "_Holding forth_ the word of life; _that_, I may rejoice in the day of Christ that I have not run in vain, _neither laboured in vain._"**

Vs.17-18, *"Yea, and if I be offered upon the sacrifice and service of your faith, I joy and rejoice with you all: 18, For the same cause also do ye joy, and rejoice with me."*

<u>**Vs.14-16**</u>, "<u>**Murmurings and disputing**</u>" come from selfishness and vainglory; "<u>**Blameless**</u> *[complete Christian character]* and <u>**harmless**</u>" [inoffensive living <u>***Phil. 1:10***</u>

"That ye may approve things that are excellent; that ye may be sincere and without offence till the day of Christ."

Remember, as the *'Perfect Man,'* you must be willing to offer yourself for the sake of the gospel and for the sake of those who follow you!

"Who shall Dwell" and *"Who Shall Abide"* a selfish person, a wicked person, a dubious person? I don't think so!

God desires that we love, forgive and show kindness one to another; but we have allowed ourselves to become selfish and proud; selfishness is evil it is sinful to be selfish, it takes away our peace and joy. It is contrary to the nature of God and brings about spiritual death. The result is a life without hope, but God has provided a miraculous way to renew us, giving us eternal life through Jesus Christ our Lord and Saviour! The total concept of the ***Gospel*** is love and loving one another unconditionally which the Bible calls the *'Agape love.'*

Believers are to be straight models for lives that are distorted by their failure to understand the Word of God. They are to be highly visible examples of integrity and trust, we must be capable of loving for us to be loved.

<u>***Vs.17-18***</u>, These two verses recall the Old Testament sacrificial system. Paul was the substance of a drink offering being <u>***offered***</u> for these believers *[Num.15:5]*. Sacrifice is the burnt offering; service

performed the ceremony. All of this brought Paul and the Philippians believers-joy!

Man's power to will and to do as he pleases should not be puzzling, such power comes from God but the use of it lies with man. One who will not use this power to work out His salvation, will be held responsible. All men possess but all do not use it. It is through Him we can be made perfect when we allow Him to work in us.

> ***Psalm 15:1***, *"LORD, <u>who shall</u> abide in Thy Tabernacle; "Who shall dwell in Thy Holy Hill?"*

To be able to admit the response to these statements in question, we must be a born again child of God because what we are about to find out regarding God's demand can be frightening and shocking if you are a baby Christian; you will also wonder if really God demands that living holy is essential to our walk with Him.

The Tabernacle referred to here are not types, but realities themselves. The word *'<u>abide</u>'* means to dwell there continually, not to visit, not just to go there on vacation, or once a while visitor, not a guest who might one day leave, not to spend time in worship there and then go back to your old life. The ungodly might worship in the earthly tabernacle, as we will soon see other types of tabernacles, but This Tabernacle in question, one has to meet the conditions of <u>**vs.2-5**</u> of our text *[Psalms 15]* to go to God's house and dwell with Him forever!

> In <u>vs.2</u>, *"<u>He that</u> walketh uprightly, and worketh righteousness, and speaketh the truth in his heart."*

Can we be anything short of this as children of the Most High? Remember the text question:

> *"LORD, <u>who shall</u> abide in Thy Tabernacle who shall dwell in Thy Holy Hill?"*

Who Is A Perfect Man? Who Is A Perfect Woman?

It is the greatest question of man and guess what God's response was! "A Perfect Man:" He want us to be perfect in all! Listen people of God, I am not exonerating myself from any responsibility here, not from any obligation or task, here in this book myself and everyone inclusive Bible says, ".... All have sinned!"

"For All have sinned, and come short of the glory of God:" [Romans 3:23] *"If we say that we have no sin, we deceive ourselves, and the truth is not in us."*

If even as we have read, and strongly believe that:

"Every WORD of GOD is pure, He is a shield unto them that put their trust in Him; therefore, I receive the WORD of GOD, not as the word of men, but as it is in truth the WORD of GOD, which effectually worketh also in me that believe:"

"*Who Then Is A Perfect Man?*" This is the question!

Psalm 130:3 says, "If Thou, LORD, same here as before, [capital '**L**' capital '**O**' capital '**R**' capital '**D**'] "If Thou, LORD, shouldest mark iniquities, O Lord, who shall stand?"

This is why this study book is written and this is why we have this book in our hands, for us as children of God male or female, young or old to understand God's requirements; here we have two important questions on our hands that we should be asking ourselves, two important questions any serious Christian should be asking himself/herself: We should not lose the focus of this great question of man:

> *"LORD, who shall abide in Thy Tabernacle who shall dwell in Thy Holy Hill?"*

So, people of God, knowing us, ourselves and us *"Who shall Dwell and Who Shall Abide!"* May the Lord help us to measure up to *'Dwell and to Abide'* in Jesus name; because we know ourselves, we know what we are capable of doing, the more reason for us to get close to God by studying the Word of God, attending a Bible believing church, going to Bible Studies and attending service regularly: remember it says for us, "not to forsake the assembly of the righteous! ***"[So, faith cometh by hearing, and hearing, and hearing and hearing, and hearing by the WORD of GOD]***:

To understand clearly what the Bible is saying and what this question is all about is to understand the phrase of the Bible that says:

"Follow peace with all men and holiness, without which no man shall see the Lord," [Heb.12:14]:

This is talking about sincere holiness, this is talking about purity, it is talking about absolute perfection, it is also talking about walking in righteousness and believe it or not, we cannot see Him if He cannot control us, we cannot see Him if we cannot obey Him and walk in His commandments, if we have our focus on making heaven, this we must all take very serious. He is a just God who will not lower His standard because *"He is no respecter of persons!"*
It says, in **_Ps.15_**: here in **_vs.2_**:

*"**He that** walketh uprightly, and worketh righteousness, and speaketh the truth in his heart."*

Let us examine this statement right now by going into the Word of God and how it all started: Why did David asked this question? David knew God, he understands His character, he also knows His standard that He is a Holy God. David knows that God must have a place of habitation, and having called us all His people, and being His people, where will we be after the end of time. He then asked the LORD this question because of his tender heart and love for the LORD, David was so much in love with the Lord, his heart was so sold out that he became *"A man after God's own heart:" and so much that he wants to dwell and abide with the Lord after his tenor on planet earth!*

He must be wondering after all he went through in the hands of people he trusted and judging by his own way of life with the Lord, will they all both the good and the bad reside with the Father? The question means a lot more than we can imagine, because he was wondering whether he would see his persecutors and those who afflicted him here on earth at the feet of the Father?

What was God's answer or response to this great question; what is His expectation? ***"The Perfect man!"*** now I don't care how we slice it or cut it; I don't care how much we try to twist the *'statements and phrases'* of the Bible to suit our lifestyle; without perfection, we cannot *'dwell'* nor *'abide'* with Him. You say but, **"what is God's standard for righteousness?"**

We will soon come into that as we focus in the next pages reading the **"Ten Commandments"** because, how righteous are we or can we be when it comes to relating with other people of different ages, how righteous and just are we when it comes to the issues of sincerity, how righteous are we, even when it comes to the things of God, how faithful are we in our local assemblies, how loyal are we to the ministers of God, those whom the Lord placed over us, to be our spiritual fathers in our churches?

Again, "Who Is A Perfect Man/Woman" or ***"Who Is a Righteous Man/Woman"*** or we don't think a woman is inclusive in this, or can we contest that? That the Bible talks only of men and women not inclusive? What about when the Bible says that Jesus fed five thousand men, does it mean only five thousand men were present; what about their wives and children? We know in any crusade, women can outnumber men 3 times married or unmarried and, in many cases, they will also come with children, so we are looking at closely twelve to fifteen if not twenty thousand people here at this great gathering. It is the language of the Bible mentioning the number of men and not women nor children, so when the Bible puts the number as men, it includes men, many women, and children, so here we go:

"He that walketh uprightly, and worketh righteousness, and speaketh the truth in his heart."

- A man who walks uprightly without blame vs.2 Let us try to take them one by one so we can fully understand what we are dealing with in this study.

Ps.58:1 *"Do ye indeed speak righteousness, O congregation? Do ye judge uprightly, O ye sons of men?"*

We serve a just God that is so very sensitive and very loving: the Bible says He searches through the heart of man:

II Chronicles 16:9a&b, *"For the eyes of the LORD run to and fro throughout the whole earth, to shew himself strong in the behalf of them whose heart is perfect toward him ..."*

God rates you according to your heart for Him, He said to Saul, *"I've found a neighbour of thou that is better than thou,"* what makes him better? he said, *"I have found a man who is after mine own heart:"* so every time you have a heart for God, you make a mark on the earth automatically because God rates you according to your heart for Him: it says:

"For the eyes of the LORD run to and fro throughout the whole earth, to shew himself strong in the behalf of them whose heart is perfect toward him .... "
"I LORD search the heart, I try the reins, even to give every man according to his ways and according to the fruit of his doings." **Jeremiah 17:10:**

God checks your heart before He measures your act: so your heart is the foundation for God's reaction towards you, if you are going to fly high here on planet earth, you need a heart for God, and a heart for God will always translate to a heart for men: He says to love the Lord our God first and then love our neighbour as ourselves: so He's not just asking us to love and be upright for nothing, it's because of

His own nature and the benefits we stand to gain from Him for being righteous because His eyes cannot behold iniquity.

Look at **Ps.85:11**, *"**Truth shall** spring out of the earth; and **righteousness shall** look down from heaven:"*

What does this mean? It is our truthfulness here on earth, it is our faithfulness here on earth that bursts open the heaven, when we are faithful, loyal, honest and committed here in all things especially in the service of the Lord, our prayers will bring everything to fruition, miracles will then follow righteousness shall look down toward us from heaven!

God's Standard for Righteousness is hereby laid down for us in **'The Ten commandments:'** and it is here for us to follow precept by precept, line by line, word for word, since the Bible is our road map as children of God.

We will then read the Book of **Exodus 20:1-17** and explain each verse for us to know and fully understand the purpose of this book and what this book is all about. *Verse 1*, **"And God spake all these words, saying:**

vs.2, *"I am The LORD thy GOD, which have brought thee out of the land of Egypt, out of the house of bondage."*

First, God is telling us of His sovereignty over man as the Creator, The Elohim: To start with self-identification, as **the LORD** does here, was normal for a covenant document sent from a king and for royal proclamations and inscriptions. Delivering the Israelites *[you and I]* has become part of His identity, what people should think of when His name was mentioned. God's delivery of His people out of slavery in Egypt influenced stipulations about how slaves should be treated *[Exodus 20:2; Exodus 21:2-11]*. In the ancient Near East, Israel's system of laws was unique in that it came from God and obedience, or disobedience was oriented toward God; elsewhere rulers might present laws to a deity for approval, but the laws themselves were not given by the deity. In Israel, lawbreaking was first of all an offense against the LORD, not just disruption of order or an offense against other people.

Secondly, God wanted us to know how we became His children, He wanted us to know where we are coming from that He has authority over us as He brought us out of, *[the land of Egypt, the house of bondage, the land of magicians, the land of slavery, the land of sorcerer]:* Egypt translates the world with all her idols, images, demonic acts, cults, deceptions, bondages, oppressions and depressions.

Therefore, He warned in *vs.3*, judging by all He has done, the salvation, the deliverance from where we are coming from, to not be an ingrate, *"to walk with Him in righteousness:"*

> And here it is; *"Thou shalt have no other gods before Me:"* Meaning,
> *Vs.4*, *"Thou shalt not make unto thee any graven image, or any likeness of anything that is in the heaven above, or that is in the earth beneath, or that is in the water under the earth:"* Okay, what is God's point here?

God knows that as human beings, we're never satisfied with just One God, we have several other gods, everywhere we look there is a god that we may tend to serve and worship: *[the sun, the moon, the stars, stones, cow, etc.]* whatever we place in between us and the worship of Jehovah has become a god, whatever is competing with the service of the God of heaven in our lives in addition, many worship human beings like themselves; we often allow the blessing of God to be in the way of our worship; like our jobs, the boss at work, the bread winner at home, some worship their wives, some worship their husbands while some worship their sons and daughters but He says:

"Thou shalt have no other gods before Me:"

Vs.5, *"Thou shalt not bow thyself to them, nor serve them: for I the LORD thy GOD am a jealous God, visiting the iniquity of the fathers upon the children unto the third and fourth generation of them that hate Me."*

Vs.6, *"And shewing mercy unto thousands of them that love me, and keep my commandments."*

Vs.7, *"Thou shalt not take the name of the LORD thy GOD in vain, for the LORD will not hold him guiltless that taketh His name in vain."*

Vs.8, *"Remember the Sabbath day, to keep it holy."*

Vs.9, *"Six days shalt thou labour, and do all thy work."*

Vs.10, *"But the seventh day is the Sabbath of the LORD thy God: in it thou shalt not do any work, thou, nor thy son, nor thy daughter, thy manservant, nor thy maidservant, nor thy cattle, nor thy stranger that is within thy gates."*

Vs.11, *"For in six days the LORD made heaven and earth, the sea, and all that in them is, and rested the seventh day: wherefore the LORD blessed the Sabbath day, and hallowed it."*

Vs.12, *"Honour thy father and thy mother: that thy days may be long upon the land which the LORD thy GOD giveth thee."*

Vs.13, *"Thou shalt not kill."*

Vs.14, *"Thou shalt not commit adultery."*

Vs.15, *"Thou shalt not steal."*

Vs.16, *"Thou shalt not bear false witness against thy neighbour."*

Vs.17, *"Thou shalt not covet thy neighbour's house, thou shalt not covet thy neighbour's wife, nor his manservant, nor his maidservant, nor his ox, nor his ass, nor anything that is thy neighbour's."*

To continue our explanations of The Ten Commandments *[please open to all references and read in confirmation to statements]*:

Vs.5, *"Thou shalt not bow thyself to them, nor serve them: for I the LORD thy GOD am a jealous God, visiting the*

> *iniquity of the fathers upon the children unto the third and fourth generation of them that hate Me."*
> **Vs.6,** *"And shewing mercy unto thousands of them that love me, and keep my commandments."*

Not to make a **graven image** ran counter to every instinct of ancient Near Eastern Cultures, but to do so is an affront to **a jealous God**. God is concerned to protect the integrity of His relationship with His people *[Exodus 34:14]*. If the Israelites made idols to worship, it would be an act of hatred, disloyalty, and repudiation. When the Lord made Himself known to the Israelites, they did not see any form *[Deuteronomy 4:10-20]*. The best way to know and worship Him was to recall what He had already done and said and to be alerted to trust Him and see what He would do in the future.

Visiting The Iniquity of The Father Upon The Children involved penalties for successive generations who continued to commit the sin they learned from their fathers. This did not mean that in a court case a son would have to suffer the penalty for his father's crime *[Deuteronomy 24:16]*, nor that individual standing or fellowship with God was determined by the behaviour of one's parents *[Jeremiah 31:29-30; Ezekiel 18:1-32]*. It meant the excuse, *"The don't know any better; it's how they were raised,"* that excuse doesn't work with God. But the Lord's **mercy** would far exceed His judgment *[unto thousands; Leviticus 26:39-45; Isaiah 65:6-7; Jeremiah 11:9-12; 32:17-19; Daniel 9:8-16]*.

> **Vs.7,** *"Thou shalt not take the name of the LORD thy GOD in vain, for the LORD will not hold him guiltless that taketh His name in vain."*

In ancient times misusing **the names of the LORD** could have meant failing to fulfill a sworn oath or making an oath with the intention of deceiving someone. Those who swore an oath in the Lord's name called on Him to bring punishment if they did not keep the promise or tell the truth *[Genesis 24:3; Leviticus 19:12; Joshua 2:12]*. Those who do so **in vain** were acting as if His presence as a witness were not important *[Deuteronomy 6:13-14; 10:20; Isaiah 48:1-11; Jeremiah 4:2; 12:16; Zech.5:4]*. By extension, this command would also apply when a person attached the Lord's name to an activity contrary to His character or will, resulting in certain punishment *[Psalms 50:16-23; Jeremiah 14:14-16]*. In a sense, misusing the Lord's name misrepresented His character, His purposes and actions revealed to the people of Israel, which amounted to lying about who God is.

> ***Vs.8**,"Remember the Sabbath day, to keep it holy."*
> *__Vs.9__, "Six days shalt thou labour, and do all thy work."*
> *__Vs.10__, "But the seventh day is the Sabbath of the LORD thy God: in it thou shalt not do any work, thou, nor thy son, nor thy daughter, nor thy manservant, nor thy maidservant, nor thy cattle, nor thy stranger that is within thy gates."*
> *__Vs.11__, "For in six days the LORD made heaven and earth, the sea, and all that in them is, and rested the seventh day: wherefore the LORD blessed the Sabbath day, and hallowed it."*

The Sabbath day, introduced with the giving of manna *[Exodus 16:22-30]*; the term *"Sabbath"* being related to the Hebrew verb meaning *"to cease.,"* would be a perpetual institution, not just a day to observe while receiving manna in the wilderness. It would serve as a reminder of the Mosaic or Sinai covenant. In Exodus it comes up for discussion again in *[Exodus 23:12; Exo.31:12-17; Exo.35:1-3]*, *[verses 8 and 11]* use forms of the same Hebrew verb *'qadash,'* *"keep/declare holy;"* to speak of consecrating the Sabbath. The Lord had set this day apart *[hallowed it]*, so that the people of God should treat the day as *'holy.'* The list in *[verse 10]* makes the Sabbath command particularly directed to adults who had children and were wealthy enough to own slaves and livestock. If it applied to these people-the ones with the most influence in a community-it would apply to everyone.

Vs.12, *"Honour thy father and thy mother: that thy days may be long upon the land which the LORD thy GOD giveth thee."*

A stubborn and rebellious son who refused to listen or refused other discipline could be taken before the elders for judgment *[Deuteronomy 21:18-21; Leviticus 19:3]*. Eli's sons showed contempt for their father and for the Lord, which resulted in death *[I Samuel 2:12-17, 22-25, 29-30]*. The respect and kindness that Jacob and Ruth showed to their respective parents provide positive examples *[Proverbs 1:8; 19:26; 20:20; 23:22; 28:24; 30:17]*. **Days** that are **long** may also refer to the tenure of the nation in **the land**. Failure to honour parents was one of the sins that Ezekiel listed in a description of the people of Jerusalem before the city was destroyed *[Ezekiel 22:7; Micah 7:6]*. Long life for individuals is also a possible interpretation and is mentioned elsewhere as an outcome from the Lord for loyal obedience *[Exodus 23:26]*.

Vs.13, *"Thou shalt not kill."*

"Thou shalt not kill," is "thou shalt not kill," period, the word also translated *"kill"* is not necessarily a general word for killing, and it is not necessarily used for slaughtering animals or for executing humans in war or legal system. Cities of refuge were designated so that anyone who committed manslaughter could run to these cities to avoid being killed in revenge. This also meant that a case of homicide could be properly investigated to determine whether the killing was accidental or premeditated *[Exodus 21:12-14; Numbers 35; Deuteronomy 19; Joshua 20]*.

Vs.14, *"Thou shalt not commit adultery."*
Vs.15, *"Thou shalt not steal."*
Vs.16, *"Thou shalt not bear false witness against thy neighbour."*
Vs.17, *"Thou shalt not covet thy neighbour's house, thou shalt not covet thy neighbour's wife, nor his manservant,*

nor his maidservant, nor his ox, nor his ass, nor anything that is thy neighbour's."

These commands address the inner life, the source of wrong actions including murder, adultery and stealing. In the same breath Moses told the people to *fear not* yet to have *fear*. They should not fear that God might capriciously exterminate them. Nevertheless, the purpose of the frightening displays is that they might recognize God's power, His Presence, and His Holiness and be motivated to avoid *sin* and consequent judgment.

7 Things that constitute uprightness:

- Walking in the way of God's judgments:

"Yea, in the way of thy judgments, O LORD, have we waited for thee; the desire of our soul is to thy name, and to the remembrance of thee." Isa.26:8

On behalf of himself and the righteous, Isaiah expressed longing for God and specifically for His coming judgment on the wicked. But even in the context of passionate desire for God, they did not demand His actions but expressed confidence *[we waited]*.

People learn about righteousness when wickedness is punished. Otherwise, evil behaviour is encouraged:

"Because sentence against an evil work is not executed speedily, therefore the heart of the sons of men is full set in them to do evil. [Eccl.8:11]

Vs.9 of *Eccl.8* - chapter *9:1* is in focus - These passages focuses on God's governance of the world: it struggles with the question of why evil sometimes seems to triumph sometimes even in the church of Jesus Christ; some think others did it and got away with it, really, really, think they got away? *[Please read all references on your own].*

- Examples of this include: cruel people in the community, cities, on national levels, even in the leadership hierarchies of the church rising to power [8:9], wicked people being honoured in public [8:18], wicked people avoiding punishment [8:11], and good people suffering while the wicked do well [8:14].

  Against this, Ecclesiastes affirms that God does set things right [8:12-13] and asserts that a person should enjoy life and not always brood over evil [8:15]. More than that, we must acknowledge that God alone knows what He is doing and why He does it, and we must be content to let Him rule the world [8:19-9:1].

- Waiting for the Lord to lead us:
  Meaning in whatever we do or may want to engage in, we must seek the face of the Lord and then wait for His leading, it is un-Christian-like for us to take decisions without consulting with the Lord, knowing that we do not own ourselves, we belong to Him our life is in His hand; waiting for the Lord to direct our paths means we totally depend on Him ***He loves that***, and He will not let us down!

- Desiring the name of the Lord:
  In all that we do, wherever we may be, the name of the Lord is in our hearts, on our lips singing melodies and worshipping Him always, desiring Him always knowing that he delights in us.

- Remembering the Lord always
- Desiring God with your whole soul
- Seeking God early with your spirit
- Taking counsel from the LORD and allow to be led by Him.

"Woe to the rebellious children, saith the LORD, "that take counsel, but not of me: and that cover with a covering, but not of My Spirit, that they may add sin to sin." Isaiah 30:1

Who Is A Perfect Man? Who Is A Perfect Woman?

"Blessed is the man that walketh not in the counsel of the ungodly, nor standeth in the way of sinners, nor sitteth in the seat of the scornful:
v2, But his delight is in the law of the LORD; and in His law doth he meditate day and night.
vs.3, And he shall be like a tree planted by the rivers of water, that bringeth forth hi fruit in his season; his leaf also shall not wither: and whatsoever he doeth also shall prosper. Psalms 1:1-3

The Bible says when we neglect God to take counsel elsewhere and seek help where there is no help rather than from God Himself, we are rebellious children *[Psalms 1:1]*, expresses the sense of *"[Blessing]"* the sense of happiness, and of joy, and of satisfaction in one's state or circumstances for obeying and taking counsel from the LORD. It often is the result of blessing that comes from trust in and obedience to Jehovah *[Psalms 34:8; Psalms 40:4; Psalms 84:5; Psalms 89:15]*.

- Learning righteousness by chastening is actually what we need to accept to be able to allow for God perfecting us; the Scripture explains why and if we accept chastening from our earthly father, why cannot God the Father of spirits chasten us? But it is then we get more furious at the church, it is then we get more critical, it is then we want to fight, it is then we confront, it is then we get angry at the pastor, at the elders or anyone who mete out the correction, and rebelliously we live the church to 'a perfect church' as if there is any instead of seeking the face of God in prayer:

"And ye have forgotten the exhortation which speaketh unto you as unto children, My son, despise not thou the chastening of the Lord, nor faint when thou art rebuked of him.
vs.6, For whom the Lord loveth he chasteneth, and scourgeth every son whom he receiveth.

> *vs.7, If ye endure chastening, God dealeth with you as with sons; for what son is he whom the father chasteneth not? vs.8, But if ye be without chastisement, whereof all partakers, then are ye bastards, and not sons.*
>
> *vs.9, Furthermore we have had fathers of our flesh which corrected us, and we gave them reverence: shall we not much rather be in subjection unto the Father of spirits, and live?*
>
> *vs.10, For they verily for a few days chastened us after their own pleasure; but He for our profit, that we might be partakers of His holiness.*
>
> *vs.11, Now no chastening for the present seemeth to be joyous, but grievous: nevertheless afterward it yeildeth the peaceable fruit of righteousness unto them which are exercised thereby.*
>
> *vs.12, Wherefore lift up the hands which hang down, and the feeble knees:*
>
> *vs.13, And make straight paths for your feet, less that which is lame be turned out of the way; but let it rather be healed." Heb.12:5-13*

Familiar language appears throughout the Book of Hebrews. The First Person of the Trinity is **God the Father**, and the Second Person of the Trinity is **His Son**. The Son became a human being in order to unite Himself with His believing *"brothers."* The Son can then bring His brothers into the Presence of the Father, who will consider them His *"sons."* Citing *[Proverbs 3:11-12]*; the author argued that believers in Christ are children of God, they have a superior source of comfort. They are more than mere servants; God addresses them as sons; and yet, a father displays his love for His sons by disciplining them. Just as the readers have accepted discipline from their natural fathers, so too should they receive discipline from the Father of spirits. God does not discipline His sons to harm them, but to bless them. The benefit of the Father's discipline is participation in His holiness and receiving His peace and righteousness.

Who Is A Perfect Man? Who Is A Perfect Woman?

Many called believers didn't understand this concept, that it is of God to chastise, that it is of God to rebuke openly after several warnings, chastening is an act of love; but what we see in our churches today is frightening, we see it the other way round; the aftermath of chastisement then we see a few sympathizers, gathering around the offender we call them *'pity party' [the criers if you will]* when they should be praying a prayer of forgiveness with this fellow who is an offender and asking God for his or her restoration; but they gather around them in pity and lament. It is gossip! You are one of *[the Christian atheists]* who will reason with the offender that the rebuke is evil and cruel, the pastor should be crucified for his action.

What we are doing is making it difficult for the offender to realize his or her mistake, we fired them up to begin to assassinate the Man of God's character, to want to take a revenge, or to want to leave the church instead of repentance; the ambitious and rebellious and the proud ones will go and set up a church without being called instead of praying for restoration, and some group will follow him.

Spiritually, we have just joined hands with that fellow to dare God, we have used our mouths anyhow against the anointing, we are aiding and abetting spiritual evil against the anointing, against the church and against the gospel, we are not truthful, we're not walking in love neither are we doing the work of righteousness.

In _verses 14-29_ of **_Hebrews 12_**, The sovereign grace of the Father displayed in discipline is the source from which the Christian finds strength to move forward. Salvation is by grace, but it demands a human response. Loving discipline is evidence of the Father's grace, and His children should hold on **to grace** *[vs.28]*. Christians should move toward peace and holiness, and they should warn one another against falling short of God's grace or allowing a root of bitterness *[vs.15]* to spring up within them. The church does not exist on Mount Sinai with its terrifying law that commands and condemns. Rather, the church is moving toward mount Sion where it should dwell in the Presence of God, Jesus, angels, and the righteous people who have been perfected by the sprinkled Blood of Christ.

<u>Verse 14-17</u>, "Follow peace with all men, and holiness, without which no man shall see the Lord.
<u>vs.15</u>, "Looking diligently lest any man fail of the grace of God; lest any root of bitterness springing up trouble you, and thereby many be defiled:
<u>vs.16</u>, "Lest there be any fornicator, or profane person, as Esau, who for a morsel of meat sold his birthright.
<u>vs.17</u>, "For ye know how that afterward, when he would have inherited the blessing, he was rejected: for he found no place for repentance, though he sought it carefully with tears!"

"Follow peace with all men, <u>and holiness</u>," People of God, are we at peace with all men?
Don't we even go to our churches with pride, anger, jealousy, wrath and clamor in our spirits *"Follow peace with all men, and holiness,"* he says, are we living holy, are we striving to live holy lives, because the Bible says without *"peace with all men,"* the last time I check, *"all men"* means everyone who we may come in contact with; your neighbour, *"all men"* **our enemy,** *"all men"* your co-workers, *"all men"* our church members, well-dressed and not well-dressed, rich or poor, *"all men"* with car or foot-wagon, *"all men!"*

"Follow peace with all men, and holiness, without which no man shall see the Lord."

The Bible says, *"be not deceived,"* when we as members of a congregation or any local assembly don't like the angel of the Lord that God puts at the helm of the affairs of His church the pastor, we don't like his wife, we always complain about them, *"to you and to you alone,"* they're always wrong, they're not *"spiritual enough to lead me;"* we want to draw other people to us in other to pitch tent against the man and the woman of God in our local assemblies and plot against them especially the pastor, what we are failing to realize is that God saw us before they were chosen to lead.

What we are doing is, if we cannot defeat the message of the servant of God, then we discredit the messenger, we accuse the servant of God, we sow seeds of discord in the heart of the brethren and in the hearts of them that are still babes in the Lord, we call for meetings upon meetings in order to divide; whoever is not joining us is isolated and that fellow has become our enemy, every time we brand that person as an offender, we lash out at that person in many ways, with our eyes and with words indescribably, we are bias in anything they do yet we come to church and sit under his anointing thinking we have come to pray and be blessed, to which god if I may ask?

> ***"Now I Paul myself beseech you by the meekness and gentleness of Christ, who in presence am base among you, but being absent am bold toward you."***
> ***vs.2, But I beseech you, that I may not be bold when I am present with that confidence, wherewith I think to be bold against some, which think of us as if we walked according to flesh. II Corinthians 10:1-2***

'Now I Paul,' marks the most important transition. The only other place he used his own name was in salutation. The first nine chapters have been warm and encouraging. Here the language dramatically changes to a hash, threatening tone, because Paul was on the defensive against charges made by the false apostles, *[the leaders [11:13] "For such are the false apostles, deceitful workers, transforming themselves into the apostles of Christ."*
Paul planned *to be bold against some* who had accused him of behaving in an unspiritual way--that is, according to human standards.

The so-called *"super apostles"* were not simply believers who disagree with Paul in motive or method; they were agents of the devil, agents of Satan who had gained access and a hearing in the church. This is the only place the phrase false apostles occurs:

> ***See Revelation 2:2, "I know thy works, and thy labour, and thy patience, and how thou canst not bear them which are***

evil: and thou hast tried them which say they are apostles, and are not, and hast found them liars."

These are members of the faith that could be in our churches and on our pulpits today, they can so frustrate the good works that the Lord is doing in His church, when you get up on the day of the Lord to go to the house of God, when you feel so happy to present yourself before the Lord, everyone in the house is ready and all are going on smoothly, happy and excited and you all look great for the service and the worship of Jehovah.

Probably some of those that are incensed against you are already waiting to spoil your day. Remember in ***Psalms 55:12-14***, the psalmist says, *"For <u>it was not</u>,"* *[please see and notice all underlined words and phrases in the references]* of the Bible, in my study Bible all underlined, *"<u>it was not</u>,"* is underlined to emphasize the gravity of this issue in discussion;

> *"For <u>it was not</u> an enemy that reproached me; then I could have borne it: neither was it he that hated me that did magnify himself against me; then I would have hid myself from him:"*
> *vs.13, "<u>But it was thou</u>,"* underlined again for us to understand what is going on here; *"<u>But it was thou</u>, a man mine <u>equal</u>, my <u>guide</u>, and mine <u>acquaintance</u>:*
> *vs.14, "<u>WE</u> took sweet counsel together, and walked unto the house of God in company:"*

Satan rides into our churches on our complaints and criticism; he rides into our churches on the critical opinions we voiced out, even negative things in our minds about something. He then launches his attack through angry and manipulative words issued from a carnal heart. We must beware of some of the members we sit with together, take counsel together, deliberate together in the house of God because Satan does not use an outsider against the church, to sow discord, to manipulate, to cause confusion, to scatter and to divide the church of Jesus Christ, he uses an insider in most cases, ***leaders*** in the church. When we come to Christ, our spirits are saved, but our minds are still in Egypt *[so is the case of many]*, and if we remain in Egypt under the pretext of being saved, we cannot **'Dwell' and 'Abide'** with **the Father**; how did I know this? Come with me to the one of the most miss-understood but most glaring and very clear chapter and verses of the Bible!

> *vs.14* *"Be ye not unequally yoked with unbelievers: for what fellowship hath righteousness with unrighteousness? and what communion hath light with darkness?*
> *vs.15, "And what concord hath Christ with Belial? or what part hath he that believeth with an infidel?*
> *vs.16, "And what agreement hath the temple of God with idols? for ye are the temple of the Living God; as God hath said, "I will dwell in them, and walk in them; and I will be their God, and they shall be my people.*
> *vs.17, Wherefore come out from among them, and be ye separate, saith the Lord and touch not the unclean thing: and I will receive you,*
> *vs.18, "And will be a Father unto you, and ye shall be my sons and daughters, saith the Lord Almighty!"* **II Corinthians 6:14-18**
>
> *"Love not the world, neither the things that are in the world. If any man love the world, the love of the Father is not in him!"* **I John 2:15**:
>
> *What will you do with this verse of the Bible? If you are a lover of a worldly group?*

Any Christian *[... talking about he that believeth]"* who is a member of a worldly group, union group, township group, any Christian who professed to be **Born Again** who frequents towns' meetings, worldly meetings who joins himself or herself and sit at such meetings with unbelievers and at such worldly meetings, with the township rituals of the which they may never know the origins and all of their operations, is still in Egypt. They can never be good Christians neither can they ever be good leaders in the church of Jesus Christ: *[they are called Christian atheists they don't understand the things of the spirit].* They are still in Egypt!

They are used to drinking and winning with demons *[towns' ruler spirits]*, pouring libations, incisions on their bodies, eating of food dedicated to their town gods, *[idols]*, bathing in rivers and making sacrifices with demonic costumes; you may think you're not doing all those with them but in the spirit realm you are; even listening to them at the town's meeting in itself alone is sinful because the town's ruler spirits will be there, the meeting is dedicated to them they cannot be absent; just like we are in church meetings that the Spirit of God is in our midst it's the same; once we're born into the family of God, we have no more business parading their shores, it is the shores of evil because knowingly or unknowingly to you, you will be initiated into the worlds of evil and nothing anyone preached or teach in the church will go well with you except you're a pretender, pretending that whatever the preacher says is well with you, going with the crowd in pretext: your dreams will confirm to you that you are a part of them and that you are still in Egypt!

> ***vs.15,*** *"And what concord hath Christ with Belial? or what part hath he that believeth with an infidel?"*
> ***vs.16,*** *"And what agreement hath the temple of God with idols? for ye are the temple of the Living God;"*

If we are in what I've just described, we are being deceived or we are yet to be convinced; if *[II Corinthians 6:14-18]* is not explanatory enough and we're yet to understand the concept of the Gospel, we're not Born Again.

> *"[.... for what fellowship hath righteousness with unrighteousness? and what communion hath light with darkness?"]*

Our salvation is questionable my dear, we need to pray and go for deliverance for all those demonic spirits to come out of us, if we believe in transference of spirits as the Bible puts it, then association matters and some spirits may have entered into us, blind folded us *[it's in the Bible]*; so we can see the light, after we've seen the light our eyes will then clear and we will strongly believe the above five verses of the Bible; and the Lord will receive us unto Himself.

When we don't renew our minds according to the Word of God, we can never do anything to please God, our mind stays carnal and as such, we are **'Christian Atheists.'** Some of those carnal tendencies sit in the pews of our churches; we will want to bring the ideas of our towns' meetings and worldly meetings into the church, we want to introduce worldly agendas into the church, we want to introduce ***idol*** worshipping into the church, the Bible says, **"[Ephraim is joined to idols: let him alone:" Hosea 4:17]**; and when as individuals we cannot get our ways, we begin to criticize the preacher, we criticize other leaders in the church; we voice our **"concern"** about the issues we wish to manipulate to our favour.

The world calls this *"pressure;"* the sanctified call it *"concern:"* what was *"gossip"* in the world becomes a *"conversation of concern"* in the church; the result and the sources are the same, whether it is inside or outside the body of Christ. I am not asking us to believe the evils that are associated with these worldly meetings, adultery goes on there because adulterers and fornicators are the leaders, drunkenness, jesting, backbiting, gossip, tale-bearings and all of what the Bible condemned are manifesting in their midst. **"Come out from among them, that I may receive you:"** He says!

> *"For dogs have compassed me: the assembly of the wicked have inclosed me: they pierced my hands and my feet."* **Psalms 22:16**
>
> *In **Philippians 3:2**: "Beware of dogs, beware of evil workers, beware of the concision."*

I know what you're saying, "but we are all Christians many from other churches or at least the majority are Christians; well, you are all birds of the same feather who don't know the Bible: most of you don't attend Bible studies in your churches so **no WORD** and none of you have Christ in you *"[the BIBLE says "a little leaven']"* so you lie, they are all there and a lot are happening in your midst all of which the Bible condemned! Trust me or at least trust the Bible, wrong association. They are demonic!

Some strange characteristics of the last days that should in no wise be mentioned among children of God are revealed in us; unfortunately, many of these behaviours dominate our lives such as being a lover of self, we blaspheme, we live unholy lives, treachery and loving of pleasures beyond loving God, more accurately describe us as ungodly *[atheists]*. But because professed Christians are found among those who openly manifest and defend such behaviours today, the designation **"Christian Atheists"** has become necessary. Christian atheists are therefore professing Christians who believe, act and defend behaviours and characteristics that are contrary to Christian values as recorded in the Bible.

The most noticeable error of a Christian atheist is commitment to the philosophy ways of the world. They profess to be Christians but find it easy to identify with the world principle, in the way they speak, do things and where they frequent even in their general worldview. It is contrary to the word of God in the reference below: The saints that will go with the rapture are different from the saints that will be left behind; the saints that will be left behind are the Christians that are falling and rising, in and out of sin and clinging to grace, they are weak and cannot abide with the Kings of Kings!

> *"Ye adulterers and adulteresses, know ye not that the friendship of the world is enmity with God? whosoever therefore will be a friend of the world is the enemy of God." James 4:4*
>
> *And in Titus 2:12: "Teaching us that, denying ungodliness and worldly lusts, we should live soberly, righteously, and godly, in this present world."*

Who Is A Perfect Man? Who Is A Perfect Woman?

He says for you to come out from among them "Wherefore come out from among them, and be ye separate, saith the Lord and touch not the unclean thing: and I will receive you."

You know what I think? I think you better leave that church if we're not getting along with the pastor *[the angel of the church]*, we're not getting along with the people in the church, and we're not coming out from among the demonic worldly meetings *[our town's meetings]*. Who we are is, we're serving two masters and we're not walking uprightly with the Lord so He cannot receive us, nor will He receive our offerings. We're not also with the church nor with the leadership spiritually, we're there in their midst only as a figurehead.

Once we are in enmity with the head or with anyone in the church of Jesus Christ, we have become principalities in the church and are not walking in love amongst the brethren and as such, no matter what, we may not prosper in that church under the servant of God's anointing, we are against them which in other words means that we are against their prayers for us, their blessings upon our lives is rejected, their spiritual guidance over our life is refused in the spirit realm and we may remain the same, because we rejected them in our spirit then everything they have to offer is refused:

[when Israel rejected God from being a king over them and demanded an earthly king like other nations in I Samuel chapter 8, things didn't go well with them anymore, they are on their own outside of God's umbrella to do their own thing by themselves, and they began to live in fear of the nations around them]!

Anything we reject physically is also rejected in the spirit realms; remember the Bible says, *[.... anything we bind on earth is bound in heaven and anything we lose on earth is also loosed in heaven]:* It is a spiritual thing; we are under the umbrella as like under a shade, when we move away from under that umbrella either physically or spiritually, we are no more covered, that's as terrible as our actions are; the pastor himself and, his wife nor the leaders have no control over that no amount of prayer, except we accept them in our spirit and ask God to forgive us, ask them to forgive us, and love them genuinely before their prayers over us can have any meaning: otherwise we may be losing, and losing a great deal except we repent!

CHURCH DISCIPLINE: *IS A MUST*!

Jesus Christ founded and purchased the church with His Blood *[Acts 20:28]*, and He builds it upon acknowledgement and faith in Him as Messiah *Matt.16:18]*. This means the church belongs to Jesus and represents Him to the nations. In light, the purity of the church is vital. Rightly practiced.

TWO CATEGORIES OF CHURCH DISCIPLINE:

Two categories of church discipline describe ways a church may teach its members right living and right beliefs.

- *Formative Discipline*: Formative discipline is a preventive measure. It includes the positive, direct teaching of Biblical truth through sermons and Sunday School lessons, New member's class or Maturity class. It also includes modeling godliness and mentoring new believers.
- *Corrective Discipline*: Corrective discipline is used when trouble arises. It can include contradicting, challenging, rebuking, and excommunicating a member for impenitence or erroneous teachings.

    Corrective discipline may seem controversial, but Jesus clearly taught that if a believer continues to sin despite the call to repentance, the church should treat him as if he were **"an heathen man and a publican" [Matt.18:17]**. This exclusion from church membership is generically called **"church discipline."** It is also called **"excommunication"** because those under discipline are not permitted to participate in Communion **[The Lord's Supper]**.

CORRECTING MISCONCEPTIONS ABOUT CHURCH DISCIPLINE:

Excommunication is the *final* stage of church discipline. It is undertaken only if other corrective measures fail to bring the sinner to repentance. Tough, painful and traumatic, excommunication is not an unloving act. One of the obligations of love is not to leave someone in their sin. *"Open rebuke is better than secret love. Faithful are the wounds of a friend; but the kisses of an enemy are deceitful." [Pro.27:5-6]*

Excommunication does not mean that the person should stop attending the church. Except in rare cases, the congregation desires the disciplined sinner to continue attending and sitting under the preaching of God's Word. By this the sinner is confronted by Scripture and his life are observed by the faith community that has disciplined him. Church discipline needs to be permanent. One of the goals is the repentance of the sinner. Paul rebuked the Corinthians church for not readmitting into membership a repentant member whom they had disciplined *[II Cor.2:6-7]*. Finally, church discipline is not an infallible assessment of the eternal state of the person discipline. It is instead a fallible but serious warning about an evident lack of regeneration.

WHY CHURCH DISCIPLINE IS IMPORTANT:

Church discipline presents to the world and believers a clarifying picture of what it means to follow Christ. It is important to make sinners aware of their sin *[e.g., I Cor.5]*. By confronting persistent sin, the church may reveal hypocrites-both to themselves so that they might repent, and to the church so that the church might distinguish sheep from wolves *[see Matt.7:15-20]*.

The practice of church discipline is also an important part of glorifying God, for the church is to reflect God's holy character in a fallen world *[I Pet.1:14-16]*. God is both merciful and holy. To neglect either aspect of His character is to distort His image and lie about Him.

Furthermore, preoccupation with the things of this world is incompatible with holy living. the commitment of the Christian atheist to the world is especially seen in the area of materialism and worldliness, which the Word of God warns against in *[see I John 2:15]*. This commitment to the world leads to disappointment, failure physical and spiritual loss, and untimely God's judgment *[see Luke 9:25; Ephesians 5:6]*; perilous times are here! The right attitude to take in times as these is to heed the admonition of the Word of God in *[see Romans 12:1-2]*, by resisting the temptation to conform to the standards of this world. Rather, we should seek to be transformed into the image of Christ by the renewing of our minds.

Jesus Christ in **Matthew 17**, had some apostles with Him on the mount of transfiguration Peter, James and John, they are the members of His inner circle, they knew His calling but they probably don't understand how important His calling was for mankind and the generations after, I can figure it out this way if permitted, *"Master, it is good for us to be here, why do we have to go back into that sinful world? I mean, nobody cares, let's stay here and damned the rest of the world if they die in their sins, let it be! After all they hate you!"* had Jesus consented and agreed to be manipulated into staying put, where will you and I be today?

Look seriously into many of the churches that are divided or are no more today, we will not look far before we find a leader behind the division through craftiness.

You say, *"but the pastor has offended me,"* the Bible says, *"Follow peace with all men, and holiness,"* **the Bible says!** *"That sister didn't say hello to me,"* **well why don't you now go and be the first to say,** *"hello to that sister?" "Follow peace with all men, and holiness,"* I don't care how spiritual you are, how much you give on Sunday, your case cannot be different because Cornelius case was not, there is a vacuum somewhere that needs to be filled because he says, *"without which no man shall see the Lord:"*

If the pastor offended you through the sermon or by the way he speaks, or that sister or that brother offended you, why don't you see them and let them explain their actions, because the grace may not cover your enmity, your wrath, your anger, behaviour nor will the grace cover your insinuations against those people, these may stand in your way, and that is not living holy, **you cannot *"Dwell"*** neither can you *"Abide"* and you cannot *"see the Lord!"* this is not me saying this people of God, this is what God Himself says in *verses 2 & 3* of our text *Psalms 15:* The truth is, if we're lost we need to stop, listen and hear correction and if we do, there is hope of retracing back our steps. But if we say, *"all men are created equally, I don't have to listen to you, this is a free country, I am free to choose which way I want to go:"* of course we're free, but we may remain lost! I pray that God will help us not to remain lost but to be more abiding in Him in Jesus name. Amen!

> *vs.2, "He that walketh uprightly, and worketh righteousness, and speaketh the truth in his heart.*
> *Vs.3, "He that backbiteth not with his tongue, nor doeth evil to his neighbour, nor taketh up a reproach against his neighbour."*

Talking about us *"looking diligently,"* very important for us to note, he says, *"to not fail the grace of God,"* which is why I said that grace may not cover many things like the *"root of bitterness springing up in us,"* without repentance, when we are chastised, all these acts of unrighteousness defiles; it is the Spirit of God, the Jesus in our lives that give the grace; grace cannot manifest outside Jesus, that life in us is what propels us to good works and with good works, we won't be looking to hide behind grace to commit sin, it is an abuse of grace: he also talks about *"lest there be any fornicator, or profane person,"* let me explain a little more here. When we are chastised and corrected in a particular church as children of God and we don't like the way we were chastised, instead for us to pray and seek God's face and desist from whatever is making us to backslide, we take our Bibles if we have any, if we're not always depending on the pews Bibles, we take an offence, we take our Bibles and we leave the church for another place, we are committing *"spiritual fornication,"* ever heard of that? A *"profane person"* means: *[not concerned, irreverent toward God, not caring about holy things, speaking, acting or doing things in contempt of sacred things]*; it means we're blasphemous and we're not hallowed nor consecrated!

> *<u>Hebrews 12 vs.15</u>, "Looking diligently lest any man fail of the grace of God; lest any root of bitterness springing up trouble you, and thereby many be defiled."*
> *<u>vs.16</u>, "Lest there be any fornicator, or profane person, as Esau, who for a morsel of meat sold his birthright."*
> *<u>vs.17</u>, "For ye know how that afterward, when he would have inherited the blessing, he was rejected: for he found no place for repentance, though he sought it carefully with tears!"*

Unbelievers refers to the false apostles, whom Paul considered to be Satan's servants. Unequally yoked pictures two different kinds of animals plowing a field under a single yoke *["Thou shalt not plow with an ox and an ass together." Deut.22:10]*. To hitch an *ox and an ass* up as a team was to invite all kinds of difficulty because of their different natures and habits. Paul chose this law to illustrate how Christians must not marry outside the faith *[II Corinthians 6:14-18]*. Under such circumstances the objective cannot be reached. Paul emphasized spiritual incompatibility by nothing the impossibility of Christ and Satan being friends. But you say, *"When we marry, I will convert him, or I will convert her:"* what if he or she is stronger than you and converts you?

Because you are still a babe in the Lord after so many years in Christianity. In the first place if we are genuinely born again, what are we doing marrying a Buddhist or a jihadist or a necromancer or a stargazer or a magician when the Bible says to *"marry only in the Lord"* are we reading our Bibles at all? What does the undermention Bible reference mean to us?

Who Is A Perfect Man? Who Is A Perfect Woman?

"Be ye not unequally yoked with unbelievers: for what fellowship hath righteousness with unrighteousness? and what communion hath light with darkness?
vs.15, "And what concord hath Christ with Belial? or what part hath he that believeth with an infidel?
vs.16, "And what agreement hath the temple of God with idols? for ye are the temple of the Living God; as God hath said, "I will dwell in them, and walk in them; and I will be their God, and they shall be my people.
vs.17, Wherefore come out from among them, and be ye separate, saith the Lord and touch not the unclean thing: and I will receive you,
vs.18, "And will be a Father unto you, and ye shall be my sons and daughters, saith the Lord Almighty!" II Corinthians 6:14-18

Belial is Hebrew term found elsewhere in an Old Testament phrase, *"sons of Belial,"* sometimes translated *"wicked,"* or *"ungodly"* *[Psalms 101:3; Proverbs 16:27]*. The plural *"ye"* *"ye are the temple"* points to the corporate entity of the local congregation or *[the body of Christ]* as a whole; I Peter 2:5 rather than to be individual *[for which,] see I cor.6:19; [read all reference here]*.
These verses assemble a number of OT texts. *Verse 16b* is stated first in **Leviticus 26:12** and repeated in **Jeremiah 31:33; Jeremiah 32:38**. this was God' promise of His Presence to His covenant people, now fulfilled in the new covenant instituted by Christ *[Heb.8:7-13]*. **Verse 17** cites **Isaiah 52:11**, referring to Israel's' future holiness when they will be restored to the Lord's **favour**. *Verse 8* is found first in **II Samuel 7:14** in God's covenant promise to David, but it is echoed in **Isaiah 43:6; Isa.49:22; 60:4; Hos.1:10**. In these passages *[please open them all, it is Bible Study remember?]* The Lord promised a family relationship between Himself and His people.

But we want God's blessings, we want His miracles, we want long lives, we want prosperity, we want our children to grow old and be useful to us, be useful to the community, in the city, in the nation as a whole, to be someone of importance; but we are not training them for these assignments, we ourselves are not disciplined parent both spiritually and otherwise; how can we want to have it both ways without doing His Will?

> *"What shall we say then? Shall we continue in sin, that grace may abound?"*

This is New Testament for those of us who hide behind grace to commit sin and we say, *"grace covers it all, both of my sins past present and future"* without confessing them repenting of the sins, coming out of them and never go back to our vomit? I don't think so! And as such may perish in our sins; so why don't we please grow up and not remain in self-deceit?

The answer then comes in **vs.2**:

> *"God forbid. how shall we, that are dead to sin, live any longer therein?"*
> **vs.3**, *"Know ye not, that so many of us as were baptized into Jesus Christ were baptized into His death?*
> **vs.4**, *"Therefore we are buried with Him by baptism into death: that like as Christ was raised up from the dead by the glory of the Father, even so we also should walk in newness of life."* **Romans 6:1-4**

You may be going to *a place* of worship for service for weeks even months and the word 'sin' is not mentioned for once. And so if you are in a church where the messages are not life-changing, the messages are not messages of repentance and consecration; if the messages that are coming from the pulpit are only messages of prosperity, messages of *"grace, God understands"* kind of messages that keeps you perpetually in sin that *"His grace is sufficient"* and you are a serious Christian with heavenly focus, that church is not a place for you! You need a Bible believing church where the truth of the Word of God is taught, where the doctrine of our Lord Jesus Christ is emphasized precept upon precept, word upon word. The Bible says,

"[.... come out from among them ...]" except you are birds of the same feather, then you can be comfortable there, and then you can flock together.

Many of us wants to be comfortable in any church we attend, we want the pastor to preach about prosperity, we like to hear pampering words, and things that give us a momentary joy that is why we are not growing in the things of the spirit. What you hear is *"I took the pen, I took this, I borrowed that;"* no, you stole it" did the owner know? *"He slept with me, I touched her, we had an affair,"* Oh no, you committed fornication together, you committed adultery with someone else's wife or husband, you sinned, you are sinful partners.

I read my Bible over and over, except where I'm missing something, I've never come across the term we now use today even in our churches, *"boyfriend and girlfriend, I'm now dating so and so"* I don't remember seeing any of those in the Bible, but I see courtship, I see espoused in the Bible, it doesn't sound like *boyfriend, girlfriend, dating or sleeping together of a thing!* By the time we look up we have so many exes here and there, many would have had up to 10 exes to the extent of moving out of town and guess what?
In our new location, we started lining them up again. Why don't give our hearts to God first before we give it to any, man or woman and they soon disappoint us and break our hearts. Bible says, *"[God is a jealous God:]"*
Moving in to live with a boyfriend as one body without being married is wrong, premarital sex is sinful, it is not of God. If you are a good Christian who is rooted in the Word of God, you will know it's all wrong; your marriage may not last because Satan is a legalist he fights on legal ground.

What do I mean? Here it is, what you do before you marriage determines how long you stay in marriage because Satan will accuse you of infidelity before God who is supposed to be your Father guiding you in your affairs: he will tell God why He should quit guiding you and lay off protecting your affairs, he will contest why you should not remain married and then you may not know what is causing arguments, turbulences and all sort of unwanted issue that will eventually lead to divorce, and *"God* hates *divorce"* but we are too quick to get in and out of marriage. God said for us to submit one to another especially in marriage: but we say our common slogan *"I'm old enough to reason by myself, nobody tells me what to do and what not to do"* because of this sin of lack of submission, we are missing the mark. There are so many married women in this age of civilization whose husbands have no control over them which also indicates that God cannot control them. Such women are violating God's rules, thereby, they can't stay in marriage; they will be shuttling from one husband to another, and their *land will be polluted.* I didn't say that the Bible does!

"They say, If a man put away his wife, and she go from him, and become another man's, shall he return unto her again? Shall not that land be greatly polluted? But thou hast played the halot with many lovers; yet return again to me, saith the LORD." Jeremiah 3:1

We are complicating our lives and those of our children, we are too proud to stay married, that is why we have more single parents than married couples in our society; this then brings curses upon ourselves and upon our children because of our pride. If we as parents are too proud to stay in our marriages, how then do we expect our children to last in their respective marriages? That is not *perfection*, and except we break the curse and go for deliverance, or the child who knows his or her Bible where it says:

"….. the fathers have eaten sour grapes, and the children's teeth are set on edge? Behold, all souls are mine; as the soul of the father, so also the soul of the son is mine:" here it is in *verse 20,* *"the soul that sinneth, it shall die! The son shall not bear the iniquity of the father, neither shall the father bear the iniquity of the son: the righteousness of the righteous shall be upon him: And the wickedness of the wicked shall be upon him." Ezekiel 18:2b&20:* also go for deliverance and be delivered from the *spirit*

of Nebuchadnezzar for the curse to stop operating in our lives and that of our children.

We can as well read the whole chapter to understand more, what this is saying is in ***[John 832***: *"Ye shall know the truth, and the truth shall make you free:"*** which in other words means the truth that you know is what you apply. If you are an offspring of a separated home you need to do this by exonerate yourself from the curse by taking the Word of God back to him that your own home cannot suffer separation because of the sin of divorce in your lineage that **"the son cannot be put to death because of the sin of the father or mother, the soul that sinneth it shall die"** it is a spiritual thing and a spiritual battle **"*[warfare]*"** that we need to understand how to fight otherwise it will continue in our lineage from generation to generation except the curse is broken but then in order to keep your own home too, you must be submissive as the Lord commands.

We see women lose their health to plastic surgery to get rich, to look more attractive, to win more men and they are in the church, youths lose their virginity like child's play in the church and we're saying all is well when it is not; we live as if there is no God, we live like we are never going to die; men and women live together as one like being married, partners in crime friendship, we put anything on to church and our dressing is not reflecting who we are because the messages on our pulpits are messages of comfort, *[when there is no comfort]* it's always about prosperity and making us comfortable in our mess; how about teaching and preaching on **spiritual prosperity?** But we are used to hearing messages that will not bring tears to our eyes and bring us to repentance and bring us closer to God.

The truth cannot be taught on our pulpits anymore, we are insanely aligned with errors and hereditary teachings, and we are happy about it, we jump, we shout, we look in amazement at the preaching's of show and emotion!

> **"The prophets prophesy falsely, and the priests bear rule by their means; and my people love to have it so: and what will**

you do in the end there of?" Jeremiah 5:25-31, [explains the activity and the corruption of them, false teachers and false prophets that are doomed for hell].

"But ye put on the Lord Jesus Christ, and make not provision for the flesh, to fulfill the lust thereof. <u>Romans 13:14</u>

What are you wearing? If you are God's representative, a child of God and a member of a **Living** church, God is very much interested in your dressing, what you are wearing to the church. You must be clean and must not ridicule the Name of the Lord Jesus whom you represent. No dress that exposes your nakedness is appropriate for you to put on to His Presence. If you are fuelling lust in the hearts of the opposite sex by virtue of your dressing, then you are representing something else other than the Lord. Before you put on any dress, you must ask yourself: will this dress please the Lord? Does it cover my nakedness? Would Jesus approve that I put on a dress like this, would He put this on while He was on earth? Will people who see me wearing a dress like this glorify God or Satan? Do I have inner peace wearing what I am wearing? You are assessed by what you're wearing, if you dress like a free woman who has something to sell and like who is available for catch, you will be assessed as such, and you are tarnishing the name of the church.

God's concern about the clothes of His children did not just start; it started from the beginning. You are addressed by the dressing you put on. If you are dressed up in earthly clothes, you can only influence the earth. It takes putting on Jesus to influence Heaven and earth; what kind of clothes are you putting on? The Scripture below describes the special dress the bride of Jesus will wear on the last day. It is going to be a white, clean and beautiful linen dress.

"And to her was granted that she should be arrayed in fine linen, clean and white: for the fine linen is the righteousness of saint.:" <u>Revelation 19:8</u>

Who Is A Perfect Man? Who Is A Perfect Woman?

From this scripture, we see that there is a link between one's state of righteousness and the dress one is wearing. In heaven and in eternity, your dressing will speak of your righteousness; in those days, Christians were known not necessarily by their verbal confessions and claims, but by their dressing and modest adornment. Today, you can take some ministers for street urchins and take some minister's wives for women of easy virtues. Sister, if you attract rapists to yourself by your indecent dressing you attract such to you, don't blame God.

Churches where it does not matter how you dress to church leaving sensitive areas of your bodies uncovered like Jezebel, we dress immorally and sit on the front pews to seduce the preachers of the *gospel* even seduce men in our churches and you're not cautioned, some when cautioned in connection to their way of dressing they leave the church to where their immoral sin is condoned; churches where anything goes, where Jesus is not represented; no wonder self-proclaimed ministers commit immorality with them ***[just mark the register and show your face, give offerings and no commitment]***, no regard, no consecration yet we still think grace covers all of our sins after knowing the truth, that we can live together marriage or no marriage without genuine repentance? I don't think so! We have become a generation of adulterers and fornicators, it goes on in our churches, our acts are unclean, our behaviours are unclean, our thoughts are unclean, our utterances are unclean; just what was the sin of Sodom and Gomorrah in the Bible before they were destroyed?

It is pretty difficult to catch an eagle because of the altitude at which it flies. If we fly high spiritually, it will be very difficult for us to be caught by Satan's traps. Eagle hunters occasionally become successful in ensnaring and capturing eagles, how? They clear a space in the jungle open enough for the eagle to see when flying ahead, they hide so they can monitor the place and the eagle, the space also gives a clear view of the bait set for the eagle, eagles love chicken as we also love chicken, so a chicken will be used as a bait with a rope tied around its neck so it can only move within the circle created, as soon as the eagle sees the chicken, it will zoom with speed downwards to pick its prey and the rope will not let the eagle escape with the chicken, in its struggle, the eagle will be entangled and be caught with the ready set net. This is how Satan gets his prey amongst the Christians, he always uses what we love most to entangle or snare us into his net; ***[remember carrot or the red pottage in the Book of Genesis that made Esau sold his birthright]?*** What is your own carrot or red pottage that can easily make you fall?

May the Lord open our eyes to see Satan's bait before we get caught in it in Jesus' name, food that will lead to our destruction as it is presented to us may we not near it. Satan knows that Samson loved strange women, so he used Delilah as bait to capture him. Samson was a highflier like the eagle, but sin reduced his divine ability, into a powerless, blind and mocked captive. Gehazi had the opportunity of becoming the greatest eagle of the Old Testament but his love for money stood between him and his God. It is sin that stops highfliers. If you are flying high for God, run as far away from sin. If you are winning several souls for the Lord, run away from sin. Be careful with converts of opposite sex because Satan does not mind getting you into sin with your converts, your converts may very well become your regular sex partner whenever you are sex starved by your wife or your husband.

We engage ourselves in filthy behaviours and yet we want God's blessings, we want His miracles, we want long lives, we want prosperity, we want our children to grow old and be useful to us, be useful to the community, in the city, in the nation as a whole, to be someone of importance, listen to this:

> ***"What shall we say then? Shall we continue in sin, that grace may abound?" Absolutely not! The Bible says: "God forbid. How shall we, that are dead to sin, live any longer therein?"*** <u>***Romans 6:1:***</u>

Paul rejected the invalid inference with the strong expression ***"God forbid."*** Phillips aptly translated it, ***"What a ghastly thought!"*** Paul argued that believers are *"dead to sin."* He did not mean that our sin nature was eliminated at the cross or at the moment of our conversion or baptism. Instead, as he said elsewhere. God ***"delivered us from the power of darkness and hath translated us into the kingdom of His dear Son" [Colossians 1:13].*** Having experienced such a transfer, dare we go on living in sin? How can we be disobedient to Him and still want His blessings?

> ***"But he answered and said, It is not meet to take the children's bread, and cast it to the dogs." Matthew 15:26***

Comparison of the Canaanite woman to a dog sound like a racial slur to modern readers, but the word *"dogs"* **[Greek *kunarion*]** was diminutive used as a term of endearment. It typically referred to house dogs that slept in the master's lap. Jesus' metaphorical statement merely implies that He had a higher obligation to serve His fellow Jews, not that He despised Gentiles. The woman replied that Jesus need not neglect Jews by meeting Gentiles needs any more than children go hungry because *crumbs* that fall from their *table* are eaten by their dogs.

The question is, *"are we children or dogs?"* Food for thought if we're looking for any kind of blessing from the Lord and if we are seriously looking to *'Dwell and 'Abide* with Him.

Jesus in His discussion with the Syro-phenician woman whose daughter was possessed by evil spirits, Jesus expounded that those who belong to the Kingdom of God are children of the Kingdom, while those outside of the Kingdom are viewed as dogs: this truth is further established in:

> ***"For without are dogs, and sorcerers, and whoremongers, and murderers, and idolaters, and whosoever loveth and maketh lie." Revelation 22:15***

And Jesus said that miracles, such as healing, promotions, and blessings as mentioned above are meant for the children of the

Kingdom and not for dogs. So, are you a child or a dog? You are a candidate for blessings, miracles of all sorts if you are among His children and it will be unfortunate if you remain in the position of a dog! Unless we repent and believe we may not see His face!

The thing is, enjoying divine blessings is conditional. We must be ready to honour God with our lives and all it contains if we want to enjoy divine blessings *[Deut.28:2]*, If we claim to belong to God and yet we are flouting his commandments, we deceive ourselves because God is not a magician. God's blessings can only be enjoyed on the condition that we obey Him.

JEHOVAH TSIDKENU-- THE LORD OUR RIGHTEOUSNESS:
Jesus is the King who would come from David's line, and He is the One who imparts His righteousness to us!

- **A man who works righteousness vs.2:**

    "*He that* *walketh uprightly, and worketh righteousness, and speaketh the truth in his heart.*"

Acts That Constituted Righteousness:

[The life of Job is actually a great challenge to all of God's children, all who claimed to be Born Again, Christians that profess and name the name of Christ.
We must try to understand something here about righteousness through the life of Job, his integrity, his commitment, his patience, his endurance and his faith in the Lord.
What he went through, physically, emotionally, and spiritually yet he remains solidly faithful to the end. And as we read each account, let us line it up with our lives and ask ourselves questions in each instance. What will I do if I am Job, will I still be faithful and righteous]?

Who Is A Perfect Man? Who Is A Perfect Woman?

The Book of Job tells the story of a righteous man. The first two adjectives **used to** describe the character of Job are ***"blameless"*** and ***"upright."*** Next, we are told that he "feared God and turned away from evil," as a wise man should. The Book of Job is part of the wisdom literature of the Old Testament, a literature that praises righteousness over wickedness, diligence over laziness, wisdom over folly. Job is a kind of test case of the wisdom worldview.

[What if I am used as a test case, and I lost everything like Job, will I still be standing, will He still be my God?]

The English rendering of Job's name comes from the Greek translation of the Old Testament. The Hebrew form reflects a name that is common in the ancient Near East, meaning "where is the [Heavenly] Father." The name carries a double significance for the story. Not only will Job wonder whether God has abandoned him, but it suggests the deeper question: is God really sufficient for every aspect of life? Will He be there when I need him? Is He aware of what I'm going through? Does God care?

Job's devotion to God was wholehearted. He <u>was perfect and upright</u> and walked wisely before the Lord [Job 28:28]. This indicates that Job had a consistent spiritual walk with God, not however though, that he was sinless.

<u>A BLAMELESS AND UPRIGHT MAN</u>:

There is no doubt about Job's integrity and from that has flowed life's blessings. We are told in the prolog of his seven sons and three daughters and then of his great wealth, measured *[in patriarchal times in which the scene is set]* in numbers of sheep, camels, oxen, and donkeys, all of which need servants to tend them.

[The numbers seven [<u>seven sons</u> and 7,000 <u>sheep</u>], three [<u>three daughters</u> and 3,000 <u>camels</u>], and 1,000 [500 <u>yoke</u>

of oxen, where a yoke represents a pair; and 500 <u>she asses</u> symbolizes perfection and completeness, Job's impressive family, servants, livestock, and material wealth made him the <u>greatest</u> man in <u>the east</u>, where "east" could designate "virtually any place from Damascus to Arabia and as far east as Persia."

Job is described here as *"greatest of all the people of the east."* This may be a hint as to his location, combined with the reference in ***Job 1:1*** to the land of Uz. The likely position of Uz is to the south of Israel, in Edom. This is supported by possible Edomite connections in the names and locations of Job's three friends who appear later in the book. Traditionally, the east was where wisdom was said to reside.

We are then told of the feasting of Job's children--possibly referring to the celebration of birthdays or of other important ceremonial days. This sets the scene for the later calamity which happens during one such feast, but it also serves to show us more about Job's piety. Job used to sacrifice on behalf of his children, in case any of them had sinned. *[To ensure his family's purity Job regularly acted as priest].* This is to stress the full nature of his righteousness--it is not just for himself that he is concerned, but for others too.

SATAN'S CHALLENGE

[Please open to the references and read].
The scene now changes from earth to heaven, and we are shown a glimpse of the heavenly council *[the sons of God are the angels, [Job 2:1] the heavenly setting],* held by the LORD. Among the council members, although not necessarily one of their number, is "Satan." *[the accuser Zech.3:1-2 also came to the heavenly council; he always opposes the work of the Lord [Matt.16:23; Rev.12:9 but is limited in his power [Job 1:12; Job 2:6]. LORD translates the Hebrew name of the covenant God of Israel [Jehovah or Yahweh].* God remarks on how proud He is of Job and describes him as a model of wisdom and piety.

Who Is A Perfect Man? Who Is A Perfect Woman?

Satan questions Job's motivation for being such a God-fearing man. *[the Lord's questions suggest that Satan came to the meeting uninvited but do not indicate that God was ignorant of Satan's activities. God's omniscience is attested throughout the Scriptures [Ps.139:7-12]. Instances in which He asks questions are acts of accommodation that allow Him to relate to humans via dialogue.*

The key phrase is *"for nothing."* Does Job fear God for nothing? Or does he fear God because he hopes to gain from it? This question raises the theological issue of disinterested righteousness. Why believe in God? Is it for the hope of blessings, or is faith the sole motivation?

Satan accuses God of putting a fence around Job and his property and of enumerating his blessings.
God has offered such protection to Job that it is no wonder Job fears God! What would happen if all that protection was taken away? What if his children and his possessions were all lost? Would Job then maintain his fear of God? This is the challenge that Satan issues to God--take away the fence and see what happens.

So, the scene is set. Satan wagers to God that Job will curse God if all he has is taken away. God is sufficiently trusting of Job's integrity that He is prepared to let Job become the test case. He therefore allows Satan to take away all that Job has, but He makes one proviso and that is not to touch his person. So, the heavenly scene ends with finishing of the interview between God and Satan, and we infer that the worst is now going to happen.

> <u>*SATAN*</u>*: The Satan figure here in Job is probably one of the earliest depictions of the character that went on to become a personification of evil in later thought. Here he is simply one who challenges God ["the Satan" means "the accuser"] but in later thought he becomes God's adversary, even God's antithesis, and the embodiment of evil.*

SCENES OF CATASTROPHE:

We are now returned to the earthly scene, and to the feasting of the children of Job. This time they are feasting in the house of their eldest brother. Job is not there--he first hears of what happens via four messengers who escape each situation to give him messages of calamity.

First of all, calamity strikes the oxen and donkeys and those tending them. They are attacked by a group of Serbians *[possibly a nomadic tribe from the south]*, the herds are carried off and the servants killed. Just as this messenger is relaying his message, another comes, that a natural disaster has struck. This time it is lightning, known as the fire of God, which has consumed the sheep and those tending them.

Then the third message comes that more human enemies, this time the Chaldeans *[a tribe from the north]*, came and raided the camels *[a source of real wealth in such a culture]* and took them away, killing the servants tending them. Finally, the climax comes with the fourth messenger who brings the devastating message that another natural disaster--a great wind from across the desert *[probably the sirocco]* -- caused the house of the eldest brother to fall upon all of Job's children so that all are dead.

Not surprisingly, Job is devastated, and he performs a number of mourning rites. He tears his robe, shaves his head, and falls prostrate on the ground. His reaction, in line with the earlier description of his character, is a remarkably accepting one. He realizes that we are born with nothing, and we die with nothing. he knows that life does not just consist of blessings from God, despite appearances to the contrary in his own life.

He says that the Lord gives His blessings and takes them away, as He wills. it is up to the Lord--human beans cannot **"expect"** anything from God; all they can do is bless Him. We are told at the end of this scene that Job never charged God with wrongdoing; he never blamed God for this misfortune that had come upon him. His reaction to such tragic event is exemplary--he reacts as a righteous man should in accepting his fate, whether good or bad, and continuing to bless God.

IN BONE AND FLESH:

The heavenly council is again the center of attention. The scene is again set with God asking Satan where he has come from and Satan replying that he has been walking the earth. Then the exemplary Job comes into discussion once again. God reveals that Job has maintained his integrity in the face of the unwarranted punishments that Satan persuaded God to inflict upon his righteous servant.

Satan's reply now is to challenge God to allow him to afflict Job in the bone and flesh that is to make him ill with disease. Then Satan argues, Job will curse God. Satan's theory is that people will do anything to save their own lives--if Job feels that God has abandoned him to death then he will give Him up. God allows Satan to afflict Job but with the proviso that Job's life be spared.

Job, of course, does not know that he is the victim of a test or wager. Only the reader is being given an insight into what is going on in heaven, the outcome of which is inevitable. Satan smites Job with sores from head to foot, possibly open sores that never heal, a skin disease that may resemble leprosy. The sores are clearly itchy because Job takes a potsherd with which to scrape away at them.

We are also told that he is sitting among the ashes. This may be because he is still mourning the deaths of his children, although it may indicate a heap of burnt ashes [usually dung] just outside the town walls. These heaps would be tall and would be home to outcasts whose uncleanness would not allow them to be a part of town life. However, we don't have any precise location for Job in a town or city, only having been told of the land in which he resided, so we cannot be certain about his location.

Job 2:3, "And the LORD said unto Satan. Hast thou considered my servant Job, that there is none like him in the earth, a perfect and upright man, one that feareth God, and eschewed evil? and still he holdeth fast his integrity, although thou movedst me against him to destroy him without cause!"

God denounced Satan's motives as pure hostility, first against God and then Job. Although Satan ***movedst*** God to afflict Job, this does not mean that God can be manipulated against His will. Job was not a mere pawn in a superhuman struggle.

Satan's second test suggested that Job was callous and concerned only for himself. The proverbial saying ***skin for skin*** could indicate Job's willingness to give up all he had, including his family, in order to save his own life; or that if the Lord allowed Satan to afflict him bodily, Job would in turn deny the Lord. Again *[Job 1:12]* Satan's power to afflict Job was limited by the Lord. The severity of Job's condition would convince his friends that Job was being punished for sinning *[Deut.28:35]*.

JOB'S WIFE HAS HER SAY:

At this point we are introduced to Job's wife. Of course, the calamity of losing their children happened to her too. Her character, however, is not to have developed greatly in history. She only appears here to advise Job to give up on his integrity and curse God. She is perhaps angry and upset in her bereavement and cannot understand Job's pious attitude toward the misfortune heaped suddenly upon him. She is ready to blame God and to give up on Him, and Job rebukes her for it, calling her foolish. He reiterates his believe that one has to accept good and bad alike from God. It is God's will, not ours. Again, we are told that Job did not sin, an important point in maintaining his status as a righteous man.

THREE FRIENDS ENTER INTO DEBATE WITH JOB:

Three friends now come from their homes to comfort Job. They are described as being from Teman, Shuhar, and Naaman respectively, all arguably areas in or around Edom. Their names--Eliphaz, Bildad, and Zophar--can be related to Edomite genealogies. They join forces and then go to console Job. We are told that when they saw Job from a distance, they did not recognize him--maybe they were too far away, or perhaps the idea is that Job is so changed that they did not realize it was him.

On seeing him, they too adopt mourning rituals--they weep, and rend their clothes in sympathy with Job. They sit in comforting silence with Job for seven days and nights out of recognition of the gravity of his suffering.
But then a dialog ensues in which the friends speak in turn and are far from silent! This is a curious reversal of their previous forbearance. Each friend speaks to Job in three rounds of speeches which take up the body of the book *[Zophar's third speech disappears in the third cycle and scholars have attempted to reconstruct it from some of Job's own words]*. Job replies to each in turn.

Here, then, the story itself is put on hold as a theological debate ensues on the principle of retribution. This is the belief, from the wisdom tradition, that good people are rewarded by God while the wicked are punished. This principle is the one that Job had also assumed until the calamities struck him. So, the friends consistently maintain that the only reason Job is now being treated as a wicked person, with all his sufferings, is because of sins he must have committed.

[Do we not do the same today, we judge someone who is going through some situations in his or her life, and we conclude it is because of their sin, and we say "well, God is not unjust to nail it in].

We know *[from the heavenly scene],* and Job knows because he really is blameless and upright, that this is not the case as he has not sinned. We know that he is the victim of a test, but neither Job nor the friends know this. The friends are individuals, but all three argue the same point of Job's guilt using varying illustrations. Eliphaz claims divine visions in the night for his insight that no one can be innocent before God *[Job 4:12-21];* Bildad asks if God perverts justice, the answer clearly being no, and he chides Job to seek God and learn from the wisdom of old *[Job 8:1-10];* and Zophar suggests that job is actually suffering less than his guilt probably deserves and urges him to repentance *[Job 11:1-20].*

There is a certain amount of banter between friends and Job--they accuse him of not listening and refusing to see the truth, and Job sees the friends as persecuting him. Their basic argument is that God operates according to the principle of retribution and cannot do otherwise. Job, therefore, must have sinned otherwise he wouldn't be suffering, so if Job repents of his sin he will be forgiven by God.

JOB QUESTIONS GOD'S JUSTICE:

In the dialog with the friends, we are introduced to a rather less accepting Job who questions God on a more profound level than his initial response indicated. Here we find a more realistic description of a person suffering immense torment. A great deal of the dialog is simply lament on Job's part. In *chapter 3*, for example, Job wishes that he had never been born--then he wouldn't have had to experience such suffering. He tries to wish away the day of his birth and night of conception, such is his torment.

He would like to wipe the day of his birth from the calendar, so that all memories of him are lost. This contrasts strikingly with his children's celebration of their birthdays. Job calls upon evil powers that can evoke the chaos monster, overcome at creation by God. He longs for darkness rather than light in a reversal of creation itself. Job then wishes he had died at birth or been an untimely birth *[a miscarriage or abortion]* which would not have survived.

He is now a man suffering great torment, with old certainties removed. He sees God's protective hedge, as described by Satan earlier, as oppressive. His physical torment means that sighing and groaning are all he can do, and he can't even rest because of pain. At times Job longs for death as a release, but then he realizes that in death he cannot continue the debate with God, and he wants more than anything for his innocence to be vindicated by God Himself. he calls for a redeemer or a mediator who will judge him independently of God, who appears to have become his prosecutor.

There are moments of optimism, such as a vision of vindication by God *[Job 19:23-9]* with God on his side, and also moments of despair *[Job 14:1-17]* in which he reflects on life and its brevity, and on God's oppressive presence.

Through this process of lament, despair and complaint, Job gradually comes to a deeper understanding of his relationship with God. The dialog ends with a final lament *[Job 29-31]* in which Job, in legal mode, presents his case to God. It is now up to God to reply!

GOD'S APPEARANCE IN A WHIRLWIND:

Before we come to God's reply, we discover a fourth friend. this is Elihu, a young man who had not liked to speak out before in the face of older wise men, but who now feels it is his moment to speak with Job. Elihu reiterates the friends' repeated points that Job must have sinned and anticipates some of what God goes on to say in His speeches about His Greatness and otherness.

Finally, God does appear in a whirlwind, ostensibly to answer Job, although His words do not answer Job's questions directly. Rather, a series of rhetorical questions asking where Job was at creation and describing God's actions in creation and nature have the effect of putting Job in his place.

God's power and greatness are stressed here. he is involved in every detail of the creative process; He maintains order against the monsters of chaos that threaten to overcome Him; He creates wild animals, each species according to its own type and behavioral patterns, Job's situation seems petty by comparison. Yet, the very fact that God appears to Job is in itself an answer of sorts. It shows that God is not absent for Job or for humanity. The encounter with God is perhaps what influences Job to humble himself before the grandeur of the Almighty.

The relationship between God and man is the main theological issue here--how can human beings relate to God in the face of suffering? Does God care or notice? Does God act according to principles of justice that human beings can know? Or are we in danger of inventing too small a sphere of activity for God? Rather, we need to understand His power and otherness, and accept that He may have His own reasons for acting in ways which we do not understand.

RIGHTEOUSNESS REWARDED:

The Book of Job ends with an epilog that appears to overturn much of the previous debate about whether the righteous and the wicked get justice--in the epilog it seems that they do, whereas in the dialog it was far from certain. We are told at the beginning of the epilog that Job was right while the friends were not. Does this refer to Job's protest? Is it better to argue with God than to simply repeat traditional formulas as the friends [appeared to do? Or is it Job's initial, more pious reaction in the prolog that is being praised here?

Job is then asked by God to offer a sacrifice on behalf of the friends--<u>a sign of forgiveness</u> and healing. He is then restored with a new set of children, camels, sheep, and so on--an exact doubling of numbers of animals as he had before. What if Job had refused to forgive? Would he have been restored? Absolutely not! God cares about the ministry of forgiveness that is why Jesus said, ***"If you refuse to forgive, neither will your heavenly Father forgive you!"***
One might wonder how satisfactory a new set of children might be--not so easily replace as working animals, perhaps. Job's wife does not reappear at this point, nor, interestingly, does Satan. Rather, the restoration of Job's fortunes is left entirely to God. The message here

is that righteousness ultimately has its reward. Job lives to a ripe old age, seeing fresh generations of children descended from his line.

His three daughters are known for their beauty and are given an inheritance alongside their brothers *[an unusual detail and an uncommon practice at the time]*. Job has survived his trials, learned from his experience, and been doubly blessed by God.

IN RIGHTEOUSNESS IS THE MINISTRY OF FORGIVENESS:

If we want to live in righteousness, to fully operate like a child of God, you need to learn how to forgive even your worst enemy. This book is also to learn about 'The Ministry of Forgiveness:' especially if you are a minister who minister to others--a Pastor, a Christian Leader, a Teacher of the WORD, Bible Scholars--The Evangelistic Ministry--Workers in the Church of Jesus Christ. If you harbor the spirit of un-forgiveness, you cannot go far in the ministry, neither can you succeed!

On the relational level, it has been observed that it is not doctrine, it is not discipleship, interestingly that put more people out of ministry, sin of unforgiveness takes the lead; most of the time, we reach a place where in our lives we think it is too much to forgive others, to forgive whatever wrong done to us, the injury others caused inflicted on us: "Too much to let go what he did, too much to let go what she did, what they did and most people end up in the ditch out of ministry because of the failure in the area of forgiveness.

Forgiveness means to release someone from the obligation that resulted when they injured us; we are fully convinced that, *"That's just right for him/her to do all that he/she did, that's unfair, look at all the evil they did to me, to us;"* okay, alright we know and agree that it's unfair and not right but through forgiveness we can release them from the obligation that resulted when they injured us.

Again, what is forgiveness? Let us see the Book of **Philemon 1;** there are three characters here in this important Book of the Scriptures we will see the culprit, which is the offender *Onesimus*, we will see the offended, **Philemon**; and we will see the peacemaker Paul himself who is on the sideline bringing both together.

The Offender or the Offended? *[Setting Your Captive Free]*

Let me tell us a story from the Bible and I believe this story will do something in both of our lives as we read this book and as children of God who want to 'Dwell and Abide" with the Lord.

How would you answer this question: "Do you have any relationships that are currently broken or estranged?" Someone you've wronged, or someone who has wronged you, but the relationship is not right.

Maybe it's been severed totally, or you're just managing to have a truce [that is a temporary suspension or a temporary cessation of hostilities, either for negotiation or other purpose], but there's not real peace and a right relationship between you.

Probably two or more people, or families that are supposed to live harmoniously in peace and be happy together and relate together and do stuff together without any reservation; but along the line, you suddenly found out that you can't pick up the phone and call that person; maybe you're afraid to run into them.

The thought of that person maybe stirs up negative emotions in your heart. Is there anyone like that in your life? Think about it or think about that fellow.

While I will ask you to open your Bibles to the book of Philemon; *[read the whole chapter right now and then continue your reading of this book]!* It is a little one-chapter book, and this one-chapter Book is a story; Philemon is found right before Hebrews, just toward the end of the New Testament; let me just give us an overview of the story line.

Philemon was a man who lived in a city of Colossae. He was apparently wealthy, he was influential; he and the Apostle Paul were friends. Philemon had actually come to know the Lord years earlier under Paul's ministry.

He was a devoted believer; he was commended by Paul in this letter for his love; Philemon was a man who gave all to the course of the gospel and always want to give more; the Church in Colossae met in Philemon's home. So, he was a devout man of God.

Now one of Philemon's slaves, named Onesimus, had run away. And apparently, he had robbed Philemon before he ran away. He ran from Colossae to Rome, which was approximately *1,200 miles* away, to get lost in the crowd, as thousands of runaway slaves did in those days.

Somehow Paul, who was under house arrest in Rome while awaiting trial, met Onesimus, who had run to Rome. And after they met, Paul led Onesimus to Christ. Paul discipled this young man, and Onesimus actually became a good friend and a useful assistant to Paul.

Let me say something here. The institution of slavery, as we know, was an accepted way of life in the Roman Empire. Paul never actually directly attacked the institution itself, though he did condemn the abuse of slavery.

But what he did was to preach the gospel, both to slave owners and to slaves. And as their lives and their relationships to God were transformed, their relationships to each other were also transformed, and ultimately the whole system was overthrown.

Now Paul knew that Onesimus, as a runaway slave, had a responsibility to his former employer, Philemon; and that he needed to make restitution for what he had stolen. So, Paul sent Onesimus back to Philemon.

It was too dangerous for Onesimus to go by himself; why? Because there will be slave catchers who might kill him before he ever got back to Colossae. So, he sent Onesimus with a man named Tychicus, who was carrying letters from Paul to the Churches in Ephesus and Colossae.

He also sent along the letter to Philemon, telling him what had happened and – urging him to do something that was absolutely radical in that culture, as it is in ours, and that is to forgive the man who had stolen from him, who had offended him – to lose an employee, to lose a slave, was to lose something of great value.

Remember we're saying something about **"The Ministry of Forgiveness in Righteousness:"** Learning and practicing the art of forgiveness and how to keep forgiving others!

That is a little bit of the backdrop of the story. So let us pick up the reading text in *vs.10*. Paul says:

> *"I beseech thee for my son Onesimus, whom I have begotten in my bounds:"* another version says, *"I appeal to you [Philemon] for my child, Onesimus, whose father I became in my imprisonment."*

I became his spiritual father – I led him to Christ. "[Formerly he was useless to you, but now he is indeed useful to you and to me]. I am sending him back to you, sending my very heart.

> *"I would have been glad to keep him with me, in order that he might serve me on your behalf during my imprisonment for the gospel, but I preferred to do nothing without your consent in order that your goodness might not be by compulsion but of your own free will."*

> *"For this perhaps is why he was parted from you for a while,"* to be renewed, to become a new creature, a new man in Christ, *"that you might have him back forever, no longer*

as a slave but more than a slave, as a beloved brother – especially to me, but how much more to you, both in the flesh and in the Lord" [verses 11-16].

Vs.17-19, "So if you consider me your partner, [Philemon], receive him as you would receive me. If he had wronged you at all, or owes you anything, charge that to my account. I, Paul, write this with my own hand:" [now talking about integrity]; "I will repay it – to say nothing of your owing me even your own self."
And then vs.21, "Confident of your obedience, I write to you, knowing that you will do even more than I say."

Now there are three main characters in this story as I've earlier said. There is the offender: that is Onesimus, the man who stole from his employer and ran away. There is the person who was offended: that is Philemon. And then there is the peacemaker: that is Paul, who seeks to bring these parties together.

Now at any given point in our lives, chances are we are in at least one of those three categories. At times you may be the person who's been the offender; at times you may be the person who's been offended; and at times you may be the person on the sideline trying to bring together two people who are estranged in their relationship.

Isn't it interesting, when there's been an estrangement, how hard it is to sort through who's the offender and who's the offended? Because if you talk to the person on one side, they say they're the offended party. If you talk to the other party, they say no, they're the offended party.

So, we're not generally willing to call ourselves the offender. We usually think the other person is the offender, and we are offended.

In each case, whether you've been offended or you're an offender or whether you're the peacemaker, you have some responsibilities. The offender, in this case Onesimus, was to humble himself, to take the initiative, to go back and seek forgiveness. He had to make restitution.

He needed to accept the consequences for his sin, even though that sin was before he became a Christian. He had to go back and make it right. That was his responsibility. And when you are the offender that is your responsibility.

Now, Philemon was the man in this case who had been wronged, who had been offended. What was his responsibility? Well, it was to forgive. Not only to forgive, but to restore the one who had offended him.

Now I know what you're saying, *"How can I forgive someone who did all that, to me? Common ......, you know how it is ......"*

He had to be willing now to look at this runaway slave, who had stolen from him, in a different light. To see him through the eyes of Christ's love; to see him as a brother in Christ now. When you've been offended, what's your responsibility?

To receive, to forgive to restore, to be willing to absorb the loss, to look at that person in a new light, knowing that we have once wronged someone in the past, even wronged God; but isn't it hard sometimes?

Once we've seen a person and the way they've wronged us, we always see them through those eyes. And God says, no, we need to be willing now to look at them through different eyes.

And what was Paul's responsibility, as the man in between these two? He was responsible for doing everything he could to bring these estranged brothers together. So, he challenged the offender to repent and seek forgiveness; and he challenged the one who had been offended to forgive – even though it cost Paul himself.

Remember the family of God getting together in *"Our Lord's prayer."* Remember it's being called *"The Lord's Prayer."* It's been called "<u>The Disciples' Prayer</u>." It's been called the *"Family Prayer."* That is the family of God getting together and saying, *"Our Father which Art in Heaven, Hallowed be Thy name, Thy Kingdom come, Thy Will be done on earth as it is done in heaven, Give us,"* not just give me, that will be selfish, but *"give us this day our daily bread, and then forgive us our debts as we forgive our debtors."*

You know in the family especially in the family of God, we need to forgive one another. We who are children of God sometimes we intentionally or un-intentionally, foolishly or ignorantly step on one another's toes, but then we forgive one another in the family, and as the family of God we're telling God to forgive us our debts; the key here is *'as we' forgive those that trespass against us;"* now if we are not forgiving others, how do we want God to forgive us?

Forgiveness is very important as well as restitution; Paul said, putting his integrity on the line, that **"I am willing to pay a price,"** to see these two brothers reconciled. So in **<u>vs.18</u>** he says to Philemon, **"If he has wronged you at all or owes you anything, charge it to my account."** It can be costly to be a peacemaker, can't it?

If care is not taken, you can be accused of what you didn't say nor do, they can bring the whole thing on you even though you're trying to bring them together, to bring them to live together in peace, you can be accused again.
Yet no matter the cost, that is what God expects of us as His children if we are truly His children and are genuinely born again, and the thing is, to whom much is given . . ., much is also required.

The question is, are we truly His children, are we born again? But you say, "I am born again, but in this matter, it is do or die, over my dead body will I reconcile with that fellow, God forbid that I should sit together again with him/her."

So where does God find us today, as it relates to these three categories? Maybe in more than one of those categories. Is there someone that we have wronged, someone that we have offended? Have we been angry and sin when the Bible says, *"be angry and sin not:"* have you sinned as a result of your anger? Many get angry at the drop of a hat: anger is a big giant in their lives; it is unfortunate that believers nurse the terrible demon of anger and they can hold in the offense of others for ages with malice but they tell you *"anger, me? no, I'm not angry, what will I be doing with anger:"* and they swallowed up in anger and are dying of it! We probably are forgetting that as meek as the Bible described Moses, anger was what robbed him off of the Promised Land, with anger, you cannot *"Abide"* nor *"Dwell"* with the Heavenly Father. With all of your sacrifices and labour in the vineyard *"anger"* alone can drop you as it did in the case of Moses. Beware!

Think about that estranged relationship, have you created any offense in that relationship? Have we said things that are not, right? What do we need to do to seek forgiveness, to make restitution? If you have offended that person, if we've wronged them, we need to go back and make it right.

Well, I know what you might be saying, "I didn't offend him /her, I am not the offender," because we can easily put ourselves on the defensive, perhaps someone has wronged you, what can you do to show the grace and the mercy of Christ to that person?

Don't wait for them to come to you, by the way. See if you can be the first to get to the Cross, to initiate reconciliation of that relationship. If you are indeed a child of the Father! You can do it! You can really be the first to make a move.

Now, it won't always be possible, but **_Romans 12:18_** says,

> *"If it is possible, as much as lies within you, live peaceably with all men."*

But are we not living a life of segregation; if it is possible, and it is possible, the Bible says all things are possible.
So, I think it is possible to be the first to move to the path of reconciliation, it is possible to be the first in all matters to be the first to get to The Cross.

In **_Mat.6:12_**, there is a clause in your prayers to God, that, God should forgive you as you forgive your debtors; **_vs.14_** says:

> *"For <u>if ye forgive</u> men their <u>trespasses</u>, your heavenly Father will <u>also</u> forgive you;" <u>Lk.11:4</u> [read]; <u>Lk.6:37</u> [read]; <u>Lk.17:3</u> [read]; <u>Eph.4:30-32</u> [read].*

Or then ask yourself, "do I know two people who need to be reconciled to each other? What can I do to bring those two together? Did you notice that Paul didn't take sides in this estranged relationship?

Paul didn't pick up an offense for Onesimus; he didn't pick up an offense for Philemon *[as some of us will engage in divide and rule game playing eye service or playing the one against another]* because we are good at doing that.

Paul didn't do any of those, he just said, *"they're two brothers who have been estranged, and they need to be brought back together; what can I do to bring them together?"* not what can I do to separate them more? Playing one against another.

What Paul did is what is expected of us if we want to be sincere, we shouldn't go and be putting fire or pepper into it, we should also be careful to not pick up an offense, we will never be part of the solution if we take sides or we pick up an offense against someone else.

So, as we think of those people, we know who need to be reconciled, ask God, "How can I be an instrument to bring those people together?"

Remember, the Bible says,

"If any of you lack wisdom, let him ask of God that giveth to all men,"

Ask God to use you as an instrument of peace in between them and not an instrument to scatter or put them apart the more.

Paul knew how much God had forgiven him; and he knew that God had forgiven Philemon; and he knew that God had forgiven Onesimus; and he knew that it was important that these men extend grace and mercy to each other.

Permit me if you will, to say that the illustration in this story makes it so clear that we need to understand and we need to practice forgiveness – seeking forgiveness and extending and expressing forgiveness.

And we need to help others practice seeking and extending forgiveness, whether you're the offender, the offended, or the person on the sidelines saying, "What can I do to see the grace of God extended in this situation.

Our relationships have spiritual significance. If we want to 'Dwell and Abide' with Him, we must also be willing to establish ourselves in the ministry of reconciliation!

Trying to change someone is a waste of time. The very thought of changing someone is saying that they are not good enough as they are, and it is soaked with judgment and disapproval. That is not a thought of appreciation or love, and those thoughts will only bring separation between you and that person. You must look for the good in people to have more of it appear. As you look only for the good things in a person, you will be amazed at what your new focus reveals.

"Who Is A Perfect Man:"

Read further and see one of the things that matter to God and what the Lord wants from us concerning one another then to conclude within ourselves if it needn't matter to us as well as His children who want to 'Dwell and Abide' with Him!

Reconciliation I want to suggest that the Christian life is about relationships: our relationship with God and our relationship with each other. There is no Christian faith without the relational element, because as we look through this book of Philemon, we see this whole issue of the importance of relationships.

Look with me in *vs.1* and see how many relational words are there;

> *"Paul, as a prisoner of Jesus Christ, and Timothy our brother, to Philemon our beloved fellow worker."* People of God, those are relational words. *"And to Apphia, our sister,"* that is a relational term, *"and to Archippus our fellow soldier,"* [vs.2]
> Look at vs.7, *"I have derived much joy and comfort from your love, my brother, because the hearts of the saints have been refreshed through you."* Those are relational terms, people having positive, healthy, godly relationships.
>
> Vs.10, *"I appeal to you for my child, Onesimus, whose father I became in my imprisonment."* The Christian life is a relational life.
> Vs. 20, Paul calls Philemon his brother and says, *"Refresh my heart in Christ."*
> Vs.23, *"Epaphras, my fellow prisoner in Christ Jesus, sends greetings to you, and so do Mark, Aristarchus, Demas, and Luke, my fellow workers."*

Paul had friends. He considered them partners in the ministry, partners even in his imprisonment, *"my fellow prisoners, my brothers, those I love dearly."*

Just looking at that little glimpse of Philemon, not to speak of the whole rest of the Scripture, I would say it is clear that relationships matter to God. And they need to matter to us.

God never intended that we should be a lone ranger Christian. You have a need, as I do, to cultivate and nurture relationships with other believers and to safeguard and protect those relationships from falling apart........ to promote love ......

It is unfortunate that our natural selfishness, our natural sinfulness works against relationships. But as we're being sanctified in Christ, we need to be moving toward healthy, godly, committed relationships.

Yet the fact is, relationships do get strained. We live in a fallen world. We're sinful people. We live with sinful people. Your mate is sinful a person. Your friends are sinful friends. You say, "I knew that." But you're a sinful mate too.

Your children are sinners; your parents are sinners. Your pastor is a sinner; your co-workers are sinners; your boss is a sinner the Bible says, we have sinful nature; in the book of Romans, it says,

> ***"If we say we have no sin, we deceive ourselves and that there's no truth in us;"***
> ***I Jn.1:8***, confirms the same statement, ***"If we say we have no sin, we deceive ourselves and there is no truth in us."***

So, it's not a question of whether you believe what I'm saying that we are all sinners or not; the Bible says so, period.
And because of this sinful nature, sinner by birth, the Bible says,

> ***"In sin did my mother conceived me."***

Sinner in utterances [our tongues], sinner in deeds, in actions even in everything; and because of this; relationships sometimes get frayed. All these we need to understand and then get into the process of righting the wrongs in our lives, to begin making amends and getting right with the Lord.

So, as we look at the story of Philemon, we see several principles in this whole matter of relationships. The obvious thing to me is that God is a redeeming, restoring God. He's always seeking to reconcile relationships, vertically and horizontally.

He wants to make sure that we're right with Him, and God cares about our being right with each other. As children of God and imitators of God, we're supposed to be doing the same thing. Actively, proactively, pursuing relationships; and where necessary pursuing reconciliation when the relationship is broken.

So, when God brings people into our lives who are estranged or they have broken relationships, what is our role? What is our responsibility? It is to do what Paul did in this broken relationship between Philemon and Onesimus.

It is to help those people move toward reconciliation and restoration. We're responsible to do everything we can to help them move toward that. But the adamant ones are the proud, they are those who will resist reconciliation, they may claim to be born again, holy and spirit fill, but God is far from them.

I can't tell you how many times I have encountered in churches, in ministries, on the mission field, people who are not getting along together in the same ministry, people who are on the mission field together.

They say, one of the biggest problems on the mission field is missionaries who can't get along with each other at times, so which god are we working for if we are in enmity with one another?

It is one of the biggest problems in our churches today; it is a tragedy that in our churches we should have people going to the same church, sitting under the same anointing; working together in the same church that cannot get along with each other. It is a shame, because then, who are we preaching, God of love or god of hate?

And I tell you, it is even a bigger tragedy that we should have it in our own homes, and our gospel is not believable to this world when we can't get along with each other. How should we expect people to want to know Christ, The Peacemaker, when we can't get along with each other?

We have a responsibility to help those with broken relationships and let me say this applies in the whole area of marriage. It means rolling up your sleeves and doing the hard work, whatever it requires. We're going to stand with you.

We say, "one more divorce, what's the big deal?" Well, I'll tell us what the big deal is. The big deal is, #1 God hates divorce; secondly, God is a reconciling God, He is also a God of love, that's what the big deal is. If there is any kind of conflict in our marriages, we should seek reconciliation and there if there is this same unconditional love no conflict is irreconcilable, we are children of The Most High God!

We cannot stand by and let those marriages go the way of the world. We see marriages here in America that are lasting 3 days, 1 - 4 weeks, we see also here 6 months in marriage on and on, the story I witnessed of a couple who didn't get home from the wedding and began to fight and ended up in divorce: it became so easy here to get in and out of marriage at will; you can get in one today and get out of it tomorrow, before the sun goes down you're in another one is that how God designed it? What you did before marriage determines how long you stay in marriage! That's what the big deal is. We can't afford to do it, we cannot fold our arms, we've got to be pursuing reconciliation, and that's always God's heart desire.

Restoration begins in our relationship with God. Before we can be right with others, we have to be right with God. Before Onesimus could be right with Philemon, he had to be right with God. So that's where it starts. We need to be helping people to get reconciled with

God. And then remember that God will go to any length necessary to bring about reconciliation. Think about the story of Onesimus and Philemon.

Onesimus fled into Rome some 1200 miles away thinking he could get away from his situation, only to meet Paul the Apostle under house arrest in Rome who introduced him to Christ. Paul, who happened to know Philemon by leading him to Christ too, said, "I am going to send you back to get you guys reconciled." I mean who but God could have orchestrated that story.

So, for us to think God does not care about relationships, about reconciliation, think again. God is more concerned about us being right with Him and with others than we are. God will go to incredible lengths to help us be reconciled to Himself and to others.

The question is how far we are willing to go to be reconciled. I mean, think about Onesimus having to go back 1200 miles to be right with his former employer. What a price! He knew it was a great risk under the Roman law.

Philemon could punish him harshly. But he was willing to go back because he had met Christ and to say, "that the man I formerly hated is now my brother, and I want to be right with him, I want to be reconciled."

Another question is, have we met Christ or we're still trying to meet Him; is He in our lives at all or we're just trying to seek Him; have we declared that old things in our lives, the spirit of hatred, envy, anger and jealousy, strive be gone?

Then if so; how can we not be in talking terms with sister B or brother A in the same house of faith; how can we not be in talking terms with any one and we sit under the same anointing; why do we want to be a lone ranger Christian? Christianity is not supposed to be that way and can never be. If we really believe we are Christians and are truly serving the Lord and we want to "Abide" and "Dwell" in His tabernacle, we need to be willing to go back and face the people that we have offended and face the people who offended us even without knowing the outcome.

It may be risky; it may be costly. It will take faith because they may not forgive you, but if you've taken the steps God wants you to take, you will be free.
Listen to me. We cannot be right with God if we're not right with man, in so far as it depends on you, if you're not right with every other human being.
You cannot be right with God and be estranged from your husband unless you have done all that you can to pursue reconciliation.

A woman sinned greatly against her husband and the husband doesn't know it yet, and she's scared to death to tell him the truth about what she had done. The minister said to her, ***"you can't be right with God until you're honest with your husband."*** You can't be right with God until you seek His forgiveness and pursue reconciliation.

And let me just give us the good news of the gospel, that God is a God that can "restore the years that the locusts had eaten." He's a redeeming God, who is making all things new, and it can be better than before. That is the hope we have in Him.

<u>Vs.16</u>: Paul says to Philemon,

> ***"Receive him now, no longer as a slave, but more than a slave, as a beloved brother."***

You're not just going back to the way things were, he says. God is a God who can redeem the situation, turn it around and make it more wonderful than it ever was. Now listen to what happened next!

A few decades after the book of Philemon were written, one of the early church fathers, whose name was Ignatius, wrote a letter to the Church in Ephesus in which he referred to the pastor of Ephesus as Onesimus, a man of inexpressible love.

He paid a price and God promoted him. Everyone has a past, but the question is, are we willing to put our past behind us, are we willing to pay a price in other to be right with God?

God can restore your husband/wife, He can restore that parent, God can restore that son or daughter who has decided to go the way of the world; following bad friends and never at home; God can restore that person you live with or work with, that roommate.
God can restore that person. God can restore you no matter what you've done or how you've sinned or offended others to a place of greater fruitfulness than you ever dreamed possible, that is the Good News of the Gospel!

What does it require? It requires the offender to be willing to pursue reconciliation, to seek forgiveness. It requires the one who has been offended being willing to extend mercy and grace and forgiveness:

If you've ever seen anyone who is constantly sick and from one sickness to the other; check very well, un-forgiveness, keeping of offenses of others is playing a prominent role in that situation; that person may never be well until he/she forgives; it is a spirit.

And it requires peace makers who are committed to the ministry of reconciliation; to also play their part to reconcile both the offender and the offended.

Jesus Christ calls for total, unilateral immediate forgiveness:

- Total means you have to forgive everything no matter what it is.
- Immediate means, you need to do it right quick, today, forgiveness with immediate effect.
- Unilateral means, you need to do it to everyone involved, to forgive everyone and forget like it never even happened.

That's what the Bible says! In fact, Jesus says on forgiveness, *"so will My Heavenly Father do to you if you do not forgive your brother who err against you."* Failure to forgive puts more people out of ministry.

Failure to keep forgiving--so we make the decision to forgive but overtime past the crisis of forgiveness we slip back into unforgiveness; when we say, *"we have forgiven, oh, that's gone,"* but after one week, one month, one year and many years after, we are still going through the pain, the injury because we will not let go! Because we have not totally forgiven what was done to injure us or what was done against us; many of us are still keeping the sin of ten - twenty years at our fingertips; when there is any issue arising in between us, we quickly bring it up as if it's a fresh wound; guess what? You only think you know Christ; you have not met Him if you can't forgive.

You say, *"I can't forgive if I can't forget,"* it is completely wrong, you will never forget until you forget, the thing is to now make the decision again and keep it out of your mind. You will make the decision not to bring it up to them, the decision not to bring it up to others and most importantly not to bring it up to myself. That is the commitment, the offence, not to them, not to others and not to myself ever again!

When we fail at that, we have to go and repent of our unforgiveness back to the crisis then into the process of treating them as though it never happened; that is what God does with our sins once we ask Him to forgive and forget, **that is a command**, we even go to the extent of asking Him to wipe it off, guess what He does; He's wondering what we are talking about because to Him, after we asked for forgiveness and stated our request for Him to wipe it all off, He doesn't know what we are talking about there is nothing to wipe off because it's like it never even happened! If we are created in His image, we should be like Him!

Failure to express forgiveness: when someone comes to us, they've sinned against us, they've offended us and they say, *"will you forgive me?"* immediately you need to say *"yes, I do forgive you,"* not *"I will not agree,"* not superficially, not something vague, look them eye ball to eye ball, say it from your heart, this is the commandment from Jesus Christ, this is the doctrine of Jesus Christ, it is the most Christian thing we do, we must say, *"I forgive you,"* and mean it! Failure to express forgiveness, let's look at the Bible, you can't believe how many times Jesus Christ Himself said, *"Father forgive them,"* as we are following and Awesome Saviour, let's pattern our lives after His Total, Immediate, Unilateral forgiveness.

> **_Ephesians 4_ says, "Be kind one to another, tenderhearted, forgiving one another," here it is, "even as God in Christ has forgiven you."**

In our deep heart awareness that we have forgiven people--when you practice forgiveness and you deeply understand all you've been forgiven of and it is a part of us to forgive and forget what is done against us or the injury they caused us, it is not as hard to extend that message to others, teaching the art of forgiveness--so by focusing on the Saviour the Lord Jesus Christ who has forgiven all of our sins, we can make the life changing decision to keep on forgiving others. Jesus Christ asks the disciples *"how many times must you forgive others?"* One said, *"seven times,"* so we can begin to count and when it is up to seven times then we say, *"done! You're through, it's already seven times, no more."* But Jesus said, *"I say not to thee, until seven times, but, until you seventy times seven:"* which means until you lose count! Forgive because He forgave all, all of your sins!

Is there unforgiveness in your heart over some hurt or offence done to you by anyone, a wife, husband, your friends, a church member or a relation? If you love yourself, forgive today, not tomorrow in fact as we read this book, begin to recollect as many as have erred against us and we're holding them captive and not letting go, forgiveness must be communicated to as many as you have forgiven in sincerity. Some will say, *"I have forgiven my offender, but I will not let him know,"* it is wrong, let the person know that he or she is forgiven.

When a person is offended, it is like being owed some kind of debt. It is when forgiveness is released that the debt is paid. Refusing to forgive your offender sustains the debt, and we are commanded to not owe any man anything but love *[see **Romans 13:8**]*. The irony of unforgiveness is that the one who refuses to forgive hurts himself or herself the most. The offender may be going about with a free mind, but the offended cannot move forward. The pain in his or her heart is so heavy and drawing him or her backward; unforgiveness ties the offended to the same sport. Do not peg your rise by not releasing your captive.

CHAPTER THREE

"THE LORD WHO SANCTIFIES"

JEHOVA MEKADDISHKEM *- THE LORD WHO SANCTIFIES:*
God sets us apart as a chosen people, a royal priesthood, holy unto God, a people of his own, He cleanses our sin and helps us mature in Him!

PSALMS 15:3

Vs.3: ***He that*** backbiteth not with his tongue, nor doeth evil to his neighbour, nor taketh up a reproach against his neighbour.

Ephesians 4:26 says, "Be ye angry, and sin not: let not the sun go down upon your wrath:" ***vs.32****,* And be ye kind one to another, tender-hearted, forgiving one another, even as God for Christ's sake hath forgiven you:"

Paul offered five examples of what living the new life means in the context of relationships with others. Each example includes a negative command, a positive command, and a spiritual principle on which the commands are based. At the core of all Paul's command is a God-centered spiritual foundation. In ***verse 32***, Paul used a play on words to illustrate his point. Believers are urged to be kind one to another because of Christ and if we want to walk uprightly according to God's commandment, we will love all unconditionally.

The Bible talks about *'Agape love'* an unconditional love: we mistake love for something else, what you love to do is not in question here.

I love traveling, I also love and enjoy traveling Business Class, I have travelled to many parts of Europe in the eighties during my trade business days, being in London over twenty-five times, Belgium, Paris, Rome many times, once in Dubai, a stop-over at Bombay each of the three times I traveled to Hong-Kong, travelled through under-water tunnel from Hon-Kong to Cocoon Island, a city on the outskirts of Hong-Kong; then I realized how Great and how Creative our God is, our God is a God of adventures and I applaud His awesome sense of humor! What we love to do has nothing to do with this kind of love I am talking about, I am talking about *'The AGAPE Love!'*

What is **AGAPE LOVE?** *[We will discuss that]!* But okay first, here is a little bit of explanation. Have we ever wondered why there is **AMERICA**, why there is **ASIA**, why there is **AFRICA**, why there is **EUROPE**, and other parts of the world? Every Country, every City, Towns and Villages with each and everyone their kinds and cultures have we wondered? It is because God wants to promote love and adventures within and amongst His people. Listen, we are all His people, **White People, Black People, Yellow People, Green or Blue People;** We are all His people and He created us in love because God is love. God wanted us to live in love together as one people under God Almighty.

During my globetrotting days, I met people I never thought for one bit I would ever meet, people I've never set my eyes on ever, as I came down to the lobby of Empire Hotel in Hong-Kong with my other two friends in a particular instance, we met some business men, citizens of that country and the moment we met, they were so excited to see us and we immediately blended like old friends who have been away and have missed each other, they took us to the sea-side restaurants that are all built in tents by the sea shore; there they have life fishes of all species, shrimps and life lobsters of all kinds, crabs just name it from the ocean were all there life; we were asked to point to any of the life animals of our choices and in minutes, our food is ready hot and served. If you've seen one of **CNN** program called ***"Anthony Bourdon Parts Unknown,"***

Who Is A Perfect Man? Who Is A Perfect Woman?

The Travel Channel Program called "Bizarre Foods" by Andrew Zimmer you will agree with me that these are showing us God's intention for creation. You will also know and understand what I'm talking about. These men go from one continent to another, from one nation to another, to the cities and cultures of the world, mixing with all kinds of people, tasting their delicacies, dancing with them, enjoying their cultures; very interesting that's exactly what God has in mind for all people of the world. God bless **CNN and Travel Channel** for letting us know how beautiful it is to dwell together in love and harmony! What about **David Letterman's** show and the likes after Night News, **Oprah Winfrey Show** and the likes, plus all other beautiful programs that brings people together sitting under one roof as one family, whites, blacks, all peoples of the world of all colors mixing and laughing together, relating together like one happy family without reservations. That is the mind of God for us that is what God created us for!

It is so very exciting traveling to places you've never been or dream of going, meeting all kinds of people, enjoying their company with their beautiful and colorful cultures, attires and costumes of colorful dyes and paintings, even paintings on people for special occasions, beautiful architectural designs and places of interests: but unfortunately, the cultures, the places of interest, the people, assorted foods, costumes are all still there and are still the same, but sadly enough, everything is not the same anymore, everyone is afraid of everyone!

What God in His great creative sense of humor wants us to experience and enjoy was what I described above, He wants us to experience the beauty of friendship and togetherness, that was what He had in mind, and then He created us into this abundance, friendly magnificent Universe to proclaim His glory to show and exhibit His beauty and love for mankind but soon we threw the freedom, the liberty, the beauty of all to the winds as we refuse to relate and dwell with one another:

Here on this planet earth *[directed to all planet earth citizens regardless ...],* the reverse of all I've just mentioned is the case with us, instead:

- *There is mistrust everywhere.*
- *Extortion of The Highest order.*
- *We demonize each other.*
- *We vandalize homes and properties of other people.*
- *We marginalize ourselves.*
- *We promote hate.*
- *We embrace and peddle lies at the expense of TRUTH.*
- *We tell lies so many times to make it stick and stay.*
- *We pervert justice.*
- *We promote injustice.*
- *We incite violence.*
- *We condone and organize terrorism worldwide.*
- *We execute human beings in different [mob styles and the rest].*
- *Imagine humans being holding butcher's knives to the neck of another.*
- *Mass graves are being discovered yet known and unknown everywhere.*
- *We turned our land into sepulchers.*
- *We promote racism.*
- *We war against one another.*
- *Nations against nations, kingdoms against kingdoms.*
- *We turned the cities of the world into war zones.*
- *World powers spy on one another.*
- *We are suspicious of one another.*
- *We put the lives of innocent children in danger.*
- *Women, children and the feeble ones are at risk.*
- *Lives has no meaning, abductions, kidnapping, rape, killing of teens and pregnant women are the order of the day!*
- *We cannot travel one city to another without fear of being killed.*
- *We cannot go from one country to another without suspicion.*

Who Is A Perfect Man? Who Is A Perfect Woman?

- *Not able to go from one continent to another without being labeled.*
- *We create tension here and there.*
- *We messed up God's good intension.*
- *We isolate ourselves.*

Just where is the world going, are we not insane turning the world upside-down?

We should be ashamed and weeping right now for the inhabitants of the earth, and for these calamities that has befallen us; a cry of repentance to our God for this shame and recklessness including all I've just described without fear of God!

> **"[And it repented the LORD that He had made man on the earth, and it grieved Him at His heart!]"** <u>Genesis 6:6</u>

Should we not be grieved that we made Him grieve over us for the creation of man; people of God should we not grieve over what and who we have become?

In every village of the earth, towns and cities on planet earth, we live in fear. Fear infects souls, it taints peace, fear is a disease, fear is an illness, and so we're destroying ourselves. We contaminate the most beautiful, magnificent friendly environment that God created for us and our children, for everyone to enjoy and experience and live therein in peace and in harmony: while we look on, every other pagan gods invaded our territory; they performed their rituals, they influenced the people of the land because of their thirst for blood to commit abortion randomly; the issue of abortion now becomes a thing of controversy and contest, *[which shouldn't be]* it became an issue of political debate that must influence our vote *[this is holding people to ransom and it is wrong],* we refuse to believe that abortion is murder, we eat up our babies and drink their blood; invasion of other gods influenced our minds and stole our hearts away from the service of the Living God: *we followed them to ban the reading of*

the Holy Bible in our schools of learning, and as we speak, there are agitators going to the court of law agitating to take down

The Ten Commandments upon which the laws of the land are based on our courtrooms; others are fighting to remove ***"In God We Trust"*** from our currencies; no wonder the land is in distress as we buried the beginning of wisdom for us and for our children!

> *"And they served their idols: which were a snare unto them:*
> *vs.37, Yea, they sacrifice their sons and daughters unto the devils:*
> *vs.38, And shed innocent blood, even the blood of their sons and daughters, who they sacrificed unto the idols of Canaan: and the land was polluted with blood:"* <u>Psalms 106:36-38</u>

Then we became a people under gun when we should be a people, and ONE PEOPLE under God! One people, regardless of color; one people, regardless of race; one people, regardless of sexual orientation, regardless of where we came from; one people, Under God! We neglect the worship of Jehovah The Living God, for the worship of mammon [the demon god of money]; we forget our heritage; owning a fire arm has become a thing of importance to us because we think with arms we are secured, but guess what, those who have the power of the gun are using it to murder their wives, murder their husbands, murder their children, we get angry and gun people down at will, some line-up their family on firing squad and end innocent lives, lives we cannot give we take; we forget and we didn't teach our children, also not letting them know that the only security we have is in the Lord Jesus Christ; we affected our children so badly that they also believe in the security that knives, guns and all kinds of weapon can give; we set the world adrift we thirst after wealth, we thirst after power, we thirst after blood, no regard for life, the life of another human being means nothing as people are dying in their thousands every day, execution gangster-style every day, because of our greed and lawlessness, because of our recklessness, our selfishness and lack of control; no fear of God from top to the least, no wonder the Bible says that:

> *"But they that will be rich fall into temptation and a snare, and into many foolish and hurtful lusts, which drown men in destruction and perdition:*
> *<u>vs.10</u>, For the love of money is the root of all evil: which some coveted after, they have erred from the faith, and pierced themselves through with many sorrows."* <u>I Timothy 6:9-10</u>

When we understand the magnitude of what money can do and can cause, we will understand what the Bible says about the love of money, we will also understand why the Bible says, *"it is the root of all evil,"* it ripples homes, money brings arguments, strive between a mother and her daughter, between a father and his son; war between husbands and wives. Mothers, fathers, husbands, wives, sons and daughters, siblings, each take themselves to the courts of law over money, we swindle one another, we kill one another for insurance benefits, no regard for life anymore because we want to take either by force or by any means what belongs to another fellow.

Just what is going on? *"The root of evil!"*

What is condemned here though is hurtful lusts, not the possession of things: the warning is not simply that love of money can be harmful, but that this craving has led some people to deny the faith and show themselves to be unbelievers even though they carry the Bible, many of the world's politician even preach the gospel to deceive the people but their faith is in their possessions, that is why they are so reckless in so much that they have no regard for the poor and the problem is, they're never satisfied:

> *"If thou seest the oppression of the poor, and violent perverting of judgment and justice in a province, marvel not at the matter: for <u>He that is higher than the highest</u> regardeth: and there be higher than they:*

vs.9, Moreover the <u>profit of the earth is for all: the king himself is served by the field:</u>
vs.10. <u>He that loveth silver shall not be satisfied with silver;</u> not he that loveth abundance with increase: this is also vanity." Ecclesiastes 5:8-10

The teacher here tells us not to be surprised at political corruption. But note what he says *[He that is higher than the highest regardeth] in other words, the God of heaven the Highest Judge sees it all, and there will be a recompense]*. Layers of government bureaucracy are supposed to ensure that every official is accountable to someone higher and is behaving properly, but all these layers of government can make for more layers of corruption. If that is the case, should we abandon the idea of government and embrace anarchy? No! Government is not something we can do without: The lengthy passage on wealth says, that a life spent pursuing wealth is futile:

"For what is a man profited, if he shall gain the whole world, and lose his own soul? or what shall a man give in exchange for his soul?" <u>Matthew 16:26</u>; <u>Mark 8:37</u>

People of God, God's desire for us is to make heaven, for us all to 'Dwell and Abide' with Him if really that is our focus as we walk with Him: but He cannot beg nor force us to do so against our will, He is not a forceful God neither will He lower His standard for every ***Tom, Dick and Harry*** to fit in!

"The Lord is not slack concerning his promise, as some men count slackness; but is long suffering to us-ward, not willing that any should perish, but that all should come to repentance." <u>II Peter 3:9</u>

But we can have a change of heart worldwide and disengage from all these corruptions and irresponsible behaviour and begin to walk uprightly with the Lord; we can be tenderhearted towards one another. Just as a negative heart transplant is possible so also is a positive heart. No matter how stony our hear is God can operate on our heart and replace it with another if we let Him Ezekiel 36:26. A stony heart is a dead insensitive and spiritually incapacitated heart. The Spirit of God cannot dwell in a stony heart because it cannot receive spiritual transmission from the heavenly radio station. God can exchange our stony hearts for a heart of flesh, a soft, sensitive and living heart which can respond to the spirit of God.

The type of heart we have is a reflection of the spirit that dwell in us: we cannot have a negative heart and expect that Spirit of God to reside in us: for God to come into our sinful heart, we must realize that we are sinners, we must confess and forsake our sins and invite Jesus Christ into our heart. In addition, there is an appropriate heart we must have in order to serve God in any heavenly task. Without this heart, service will be such a struggle and will be incapable of eliciting heaven's expectations and goals *I Samuel 10:9-12*. This is why we must never lobby for positions: no, we cannot, the positions for which we are not called hence we get there and begin to fumble and misbehave: we are children of God, our focus should be on Him.

The Bible says, *"Love ye therefore the stranger: for ye were strangers in the land ...."* *[Deut.10:19]*: loving all and shunning all act of wickedness against the strangers and the needy, embrace the Lord and embrace the poor regardless of race, age, or sexual orientation knowing that our God loved us regardless of who we are, where we came from or what we look like, by creating us as such in different species or form, He is making a statement that He is the God of all! Then why should we hate, why should we discriminate against one another: loving all unconditionally is *"AGAPE"* God created us in love this is the whole story in the Book of *I Corinthians 13*, we will be looking into this chapter about love in *chapter eight* of this book: he created us in love and as such He wants us to live in love; *"to love Him with all our hearts, with all our soul and with everything in us, then to love our neighbours as we love ourselves:"* with this kind of love to our neighbours, we will not be able to harm anyone deliberately or otherwise because we love them like we love ourselves: if we love others the way we love ourselves we will be His children as He is our Father:

Psalms 15.2-3: *"He that walketh uprightly, and worketh righteousness, and speaketh the truth in his heart."*
Vs.3: *"**He that** backbiteth not with his tongue, nor doeth evil to his neighbour, nor taketh up a reproach against his neighbour."*

- ***JEHOVAH TSIDKENU-- THE LORD OUR RIGHTEOUSNESS:***
Jesus is the King who would come from David's line, and He is the One who imparts His righteousness to us!

Other Acts That Constituted Righteousness:

1. Keeping the Sabbaths *[all Sabbaths, not only weekly services but all not once a while service, but constantly]*:

"For thus said the LORD unto the eunuchs that keep my Sabbaths, and choose the things that please me, and take hold of my covenant:
vs.5, Even unto them will I give in mine house," isn't that telling us something about 'dwelling' and 'abiding?' "and within my walls a place and a name better than of sons and daughters: I will give them an everlasting name, that shall not be cut off." Isa.56:4-7

Eunuchs were typically excluded from worship *[Deut.23:1]*. The law pointed out that gender and sex were divine gifts that should not be intentionally altered. However, this verse describes an obedient eunuch and thus one who had become a eunuch accidentally or who had converted to worship of God after becoming a eunuch. Such devout eunuchs were invited to join in the worship of God.

Eunuchs could not have sons who would perpetuate their name, but God will provide them an everlasting name. God will not turn away anyone who desires to worship Him, even foreigners and eunuchs. His house, the temple will be a place where anyone can come to pray.

[Please be informed that the church has never been under obligation to keep any Sabbath. Christians are free to keep any day].

> *"One man esteemeth one day above another; another esteemeth everyday alike. Let everyman be fully persuaded in his own mind:*
> *vs.6, He that regardeth the day, regardeth it unto the Lord; and he that regardeth not the day, to the Lord he doth not regard it. He that eateth, eateth to the Lord, for he giveth God thanks; and he that eateth not, to the Lord he eateth not, and giveth God thanks." [Rom.14:5-6]*

The observing of special days is complicated. Luther believed Sunday was not the Sabbath but a new day of worship, whereas Calvin believed the Sabbath was changed to Sunday. Some Christian groups believe on Friday/Saturday Sabbath observance. In thinking through this issue, we should consider the implications of Christ's Sunday-morning resurrection and the new covenant: Our religious practices are to be done out of conviction before God. How we live and die must come from the conviction that we belong to the Lord: we do not have to condemn or disown them that believe otherwise to our own belief and as the Book of Romans 14 puts it, everything we do or believe is unto the Lord.

> *"How be it then, when ye knew not God, ye did service unto them which by nature are no gods:*
> *vs.9, But now, after that ye have known God, or rather are known of God, how turn ye again to the weak and beggarly elements, whereunto ye desire again to be in bondage?*
> *vs.10, Ye observe days, and months, and times, and years:*
> *vs.11, I am afraid of you, lest I have bestowed upon you labour in vain." Gal.4:8-11*

Paul's readers had established a true relationship with God through faith in Christ. He asked how they could turn back again and be in bondage to a viewpoint of justification by works that was as weak and beggarly as the elements they had worshipped before, **"Even so we, when we were children, were in bondage under the elements of the world:"** *[vs.3]*. The presence of the Jewish teachers in Galatia makes it likely that the days were Sabbath observances, while months and times had to do with longer seasons of the Jewish calendar [e.g., *the time from Passover to Pentecost*]. Years would be sabbatical years or the year of Jubilee. Since those in the Galatians churches were back where they started before Paul arrived-enslaved spiritually-he feared that his best efforts had been in vain.

"Blotting out the handwriting of ordinances that was against us, which was contrary to us, and took it out of the way, nailing it to the Cross:
vs.15, And having spoiled the principalities and powers, he made a shew of them openly, triumphing over them in it:
vs.16, Let no man therefore judge you in meat, or in drink, or in respect of an holyday, or the new moon, or of the Sabbath days:
vs.17, Which are a shadow of things to come; but the body is of Christ." Col.2:14-17

The handwriting of ordinances [lit "certificate of debt consisting of decrees"] is referring to a written document or to the Mosaic law. Paul typically viewed the law's purpose as revealing the guilt of sinners *[Deut.27:26; Rom.7:13; I cor.15:56; Gal.3:10 read all]*. Some Jewish writings, likewise, speak of God keeping records of people's sins as debts against them. God, however, like it never happened God has abolished those records through Christ's substitutionary atonement that was accomplished when He died on the Cross. God humiliated these spiritual rulers in a public spectacle of shame and defeat.

The word 'triumphing' to explain the verse, *[In antiquity, victorious generals paraded into their capital city toward the king's palace with human captives and treasure displayed behind them. Sweet incense was offered. The citizens saw and smelled evidence of victory. Here, Christ is leading Paul and all other believers into eternal city where God is King!]* It evokes the imagery of a victorious general leading a parade to display the booty and prisoners of war from His conquest.

The Colossian believers were apparently pressured by some in the church to observe Jewish dietary laws and holy days. Because God has completely reconciled believers to Himself, they are free from condemnation and from practicing customs required for God's covenant people in the past *[Rom.8:1] [read all references]:*
Paul used the words shadow and body to contrast the incomplete nature of these former obligations with the fullness brought about by Christ. God instituted the dietary laws and holy days as a means to foreshadow the coming reconciliation in the Messiah. this is another way of saying that He is the fulfillment of the law *[Rom.10:4; Heb.10:1].*

> *"For thus said the LORD unto the eunuchs that keep my Sabbaths, and choose the things that please me, and take hold of my covenant:*
> *vs.5, Even unto them will I give in mine house," isn't that telling us something about 'dwelling' and 'abiding?' "And within my walls a place and a name better than of sons and daughters: I will give them an everlasting name, that shall not be cut off."* <u>Isa.56:4-7</u>

2. Choosing the things pleasing to God: simply means to observe His law and His commandments; to believe in His existence, to trust, honour and obey Him always in everything: preview of His commandments in *Exo.20:1-17*, are the Ten Commandments that were written by the Fingers of God Himself hewn on two tablets of stones, handed over unto Moses. Didn't the people *[The Israelites]* see it done, didn't they know and witnessed it? Yes the people saw it, the Bible reference below confirms that; yes the people knew it, and yet they went a whoring, yet they carved out another god, the

calf in distrust of God, yet He was denied, yet they would not have Him rule over them, yet He was spoken against, yet they crucified Him: After His giving of the Ten Commandments, what happened? **vs.18** says:

"And all the people saw the thundering, and lightning and the sound of the trumpet, and the mountain smoking: and when the people saw it, they removed, and stood afar off."

That was the effect of God's Presence: the confirmation, that they witnessed what happened! After they saw all the LORD did, after they saw and witnessed all the miracles; yet they carved out another god in the form of a calf: why did the people rebel against the LORD? The reason is not farfetched, they've never seen God, they've never known God, they've never had an encounter with Him, they only saw the miracles, signs and wonders, they had no relationship with the Father; *"the people who knew the LORD will remain but those who saw His power will abandon and forsake Him because they are miracle seekers:"* The saints that will go with the rapture are different from the saints that will be left behind, these are those who are falling and rising from-in-and-out of sin and are clinging to grace; soon they go back to their vomit sinning again rising and falling. They cannot *"Dwell"* and *"Abide"* they will be left behind.

They were not totally sold-out to the LORD in their hearts, and they never believe the miracles of keeping them alive, supplying their needs, feeding and well-being were coming from a God that remained elusive and as such they saw Moses as the god that is performing all the miracles; so when Moses went to the mountain to receive The Ten Commandments and was late in showing up, they immediately thought that Moses their almighty god, the miracle worker is dead after all, so there isn't any more god to look after them and to perform miracles since people love miracles; the next thing is to cave out another god: this is exactly what is happening in our days today.

Who Is A Perfect Man? Who Is A Perfect Woman?

There are so many gospels that are not the Gospel of the Bible. When you read the Bible, God of the Bible will speak to you: you cannot find truth anywhere in the world neither can you find where truth is spoken except in the Bible. Also, there are many professed Christians who don't know who the real God is even though there has been miracles and testimonies in their lives, yet they are confused as to who is behind it all; the reason is we have too many objects of worship before us. The Bible says, *["…. My people perish for lack of knowledge … Hosea 4:6]*. Such people we put in a category that we call *[Chr-is-lam-herb]* what does this mean? Like I said, there are so many gospels that are not the Gospel of the Bible. ***Chr-is-lam-herb* is a religion, *a little bit of Christianity here; a little bit of Islam over there; we are so confused and are in crisis instead of being in Christ, a little bit of visitation to herbalists; a little bit of Buddhism, a little bit of Hinduism; some visits to the star-gazers, some to the magicians, another visit/s to the sorcerers; are we in Christ at all or in crisis?*** I have seen some of those who go to church and still consult and carry **Crystal Bowls** and **Ouija boards** Christians that are ***meditating or consulting through Yoga***; this is wrong, **meditation that is not through the Word of God is not of God** and so they are confused. These are not Christians, they belong in the category of the so "called *[Chr-is-lam-herb] religion,"* they claim freedom of religion, of course there is freedom of religion, but Christianity is not one of those. To many of them, whoever says *"god,"* they don't want to check to know which of the gods, they just run after them when the Bible says to *"[… test all spirits whether they be of God ..]"* and so they are confused and are deceived as to who the real god is, they are unstable as water and they don't know the truth; they cannot dwell with The Father *Matthew 7:23* says: *"[And then will I profess unto them, I never knew you: depart from me, ye that work iniquity!]"*

If we read from *verse 21* of *Matthew 7*, He says, *"Not every one that saith unto me 'Lord, Lord,' shall enter into the Kingdom of Heaven; but he that doeth the will of my Father which is in Heaven:"* this speaks the mind of God. By referring to Himself as *Lord* and depicting Himself as the ultimate Judge of humanity. Jesus asserted His deity. True disciples affirm Jesus' lordship, submit to His authority, and obey His commands. Jesus insisted that a person is confirmed as a true disciple not by prophecy, exorcism, or working or working miracles but by living a transformed life made possible by God. The disobedient lifestyles of evildoers are inconsistent with genuine discipleship. Jesus words, *I never knew you*, show that these were never truly disciples.

Many of us have some kind of objects and paintings hanging in our homes that we don't know their origins, where they came from nor the spirits behind them, and as such, some of these paintings or objects may be dedicated to ***idols; [the facts of which we may not or never understand, this is the truth but it's hard to believe];*** they create open doors thereby giving the devil or demons a legal permit entry into our homes, they are satanic properties and Satan and his cohorts operate on legal ground: ***[illustration: a divorced, separated couple, one of them has the custody of the children and the other party has a right of visitation, simple]:*** That is what happens in this situation, Satan has a right to go into any home or places wherever his property is located and before we know what, bad dreams, evil thoughts, strange movements in the house, demonic activities including hearing of voices, murders, immorality and all kinds of evil happenings ***["…. My people perish for lack of knowledge … Hosea 4:6].*** Unbelieving Christians!

So, the children of Israel were like that, that was why they were so quick to make a replacement of their god; they thought the more beautiful that god looks, the more solid that god is, and so they thought the more powerful it will be, so they caved it out in gold! And gold is solid and beautiful, but it is the handiwork of men, and it cannot save neither can it talk, so they that made it are like unto it!" ***[Psalms 115:4-8]:*** read.

3. Taking hold of His Covenant: Taking hold of the covenant means to consecrate to obey; to be the doer of the Word not only to hear.
4. Joining to the Lord, ***vs.6*** of ***Isa.56***

5. Serving the Lord with your whole heart: This includes evangelism, some are saying, **"but we don't know our ministry"** guess what? Every born again Christian is born with the ministry of evangelism.

> **"The harvest is past, the summer is ended, and we are not saved!" <u>Jeremiah 8:20</u>**

This is a proverbial saying meaning that all opportunities have passed, and no hope of rescue exists: which in other words is, there is room for us, the harvest is waiting for us, the people of God are waiting to be harvested, how dare we say that **"we do not know our ministry"** when the evangelism ministry is waiting!

> **"Therefore said He unto them, the harvest truly is great, but the labourers are few: pray ye therefore the Lord of the harvest, the he would send forth labourers into His harvest." <u>Luke 10:2</u> "Labourers are few, why can't we fill the vacancy and enlist in the army of God to do exploits?**

6. Loving the name of the Lord:
7. Being His servant:

- A man who speaks truth inwardly: There is a lot the Bible is saying here, and it is important for us to see, read, and hear from the Bible as we see some references about lying and not been truthful! When we speak lies or when we tell a lie about something, it always leads to a chain of lies why? Because when we tell a lie, and we know or sense we will soon be found out, in order for that not to happen, we have to tell another lie, and another lie, and another lie, a chain reoccurrences of lies will happen and we are going to see what the Bible says about lies, and about lying, and about liars, we belong in all of these categories: lying is a terrible thing, some say, *[lying is and emergency help in the time of trouble]* the Bible says, in the Book of and according to:

Revelation 21:8 *"all lairs, shall have their part in the lake which burneth with fire and brimstone: which is the second death."*

People of God, may that not be our portion in Jesus' name! His desire for us is to have our focus on heaven, to make heaven so as to *'Dwell'* and *'Abide'* with Him forever because He is our Father and our Creator, He is our hope and our Glory. [See and read the references below].

- **Proverbs 17:4**   *"A wicked doer giveth heed to false lips; and a liar giveth ear to a naughty tongue."*
- **Proverbs 19:22** *"The desire of a man is his kindness: and a poor man is better than a liar."*
- **Proverb 30:6:**   *"Add thou not unto his words, lest he reprove thee, and thou be found a lair."*
- **Psalms 116:11**   *"I said in my haste, all men are liars."*
- **Jeremiah 50:36** *"A sword is upon the liars; and they shall dote: a sword is upon her mighty men; and they shall be dismayed."*
- **John 8:44**   *"Ye are of your father the devil, and the lusts of your father ye will I do. He was a murderer from the beginning, and abode not in the truth, because there is no truth in him. When he speaketh a lie, he speaketh of his own: for he is a liar, and the father of it."*
- **I Timothy 1:10**   *"For whoremongers, for them that defile themselves with mankind, for men stealers, for liars, for perjured persons, and if there be any order thing that is contrary to sound doctrine."*
- **Titus 1:12**   *"One of themselves, even a prophet of their own, said the Cretians are always liars, evil beasts, slow bellies."*

- **Revelation 2:2**   "I know thy works, and thy labour, and thy patience, and how thou canst not bear them which are evil: and thou hast tried them which say they are apostles, and are not, and hast found them liars."

- **Revelation 21:8**:   *"But the fearful, and unbelieving, and the abominable, and murderers, and whoremongers, and sorcerers, and idolaters, and all liars, shall have their part in the lake which burneth with fire and brimstone: which is the second death."*

All of the above are talking about the degrees of carnality, lying, deceit craftiness and pretense: talking about false witnessing and they didn't make us at any time any righteous: Taking about deception combined with lying one to another and all the rest of it: but the Bible reveals the mind of the Father toward us in this next verse and chapter:

> *"For I know the thoughts that I think toward you, saith the LORD, thoughts of peace, and not of evil, to give you an expected end." **Jeremiah 29:11***

That is why Timothy said to us to study to *shew ourselves approved of the Father* and in Ephesians also below, *"That we henceforth be no more children, that will be carried about with every wind of doctrine,"* it is one of Satan's craftiness to either seal our ears from the truth or send the *false teachers* that will teach error in other to miss the mark and come short of His glory.

Let us see **Eph.4:14**: as you keep in mind this important question, **"Who Shall Abide, Who Shall Dwell:"** In thy Tabernacle? 'A Perfect Man:' **Who Is A Perfect Man?** That is our topic of Study!

> *"That we henceforth be no more children, tossed to and fro, and carried about with every wind of doctrine by the*

sleight of men, and cunning craftiness, whereby they lie in wait to deceiv.:" <u>Eph.4:14</u>

When gifted people equip the church, the community of faith will evidence stability in precept and practice.

"Study to shew thyself approved unto God, a workman that needeth not to be ashamed, rightly dividing the word of truth." [II Tim.2:15]. Study here means, 'Study, it means, to be 'Zealous; it also means, to Handle Scripture correctly!

Please be reminded that we cannot be innocent, innocence and excuse cannot keep anyone from the punishment due unto sinners, because He gave us each and every one of us wisdom, and we can hear the **Gospel** been preached day in day out, the teachers that are teaching errors then cannot be called as witnesses before God for confirmation of their erroneous teachings so we can be spared, everyone will answer for himself and herself! That is why we are advised to be sound in ***doctrine: [There are four kinds of pastors]***.

[1]. Those that are called by-self: they will do the things of self.
[2]. Those that are called by people: they will watch the countenance of the people and preach and do the things that will please the people.
[3]. Those who are called by the devil: they will not preach the doctrine of Jesus Christ rather they will preach what the devil wants them to preach to enrich his kingdom and they will do the things that please the devil.
[4]. Those who are called by God: they will be committed to the Lord, they will teach and preach the doctrine of the Lord Jesus Christ; when we are sound in the ***doctrine of The Lord Jesus Christ*** we will not remain as babes that can be ***"carried about with every wind of doctrine;"*** like new born babes, believers are to avoid acts of dissention and feed on the sincere milk of the Word of God, which refers to the divine sustenance drawn from the gospel. ***<u>II Peter 2:2</u>***: when we have the Word in us it will be difficult for those who teach error to deceive us and give us wrong interpretations of

7 Blessings of Perfection or What It Means to Be Perfect:

1. **Maturity**: We are no more children who took to 'evil teachings of the prince of the power of the air; *Eph.2:2* referring to various activities of the world as organized and run by Satan and man:

   "Now the spirit speaketh expressly, that in the latter times some shall depart from the faith, giving heed to seducing spirits, and doctrines of devils." I Tim.4:1

   It has already been predicted that this will happen, many of us have heard series of teachings that not in conformity with the Word of God most of which I cannot mention here in this book but that you have heard from them that are compromising the Word with the world but be not deceived.

   Please read the references below, study and digest:

2. **Established in the Faith**: No more of doubtful mind or tossed to and fro like the waves vs.14 of Eph.4: Jas.1:5-8.
3. **Rooted and Grounded in Truth**: No more carried about by winds of doctrine: *vs.14; Jn.8:32-38; Eph.3:17; Col.2:6-7; II Pet.1:2* [read].
4. **Freedom From Deception**: That is, you are able to discern truth from error: *vs.14* of *Eph.4; II Tim.2:15; Heb.5:11-14; Jn.8:32-36:*
5. **Ability to Speak the Truth in Love**: *Eph.4:15; Rom.15:14; Col.3:16:*
6. **Constant Growth in Spiritual Things**: *vs.15; I Pet.2:2; II Pet.3:18:*
7. **Harmony with All Others in Christ**: *vs.16; I Cor.1:10; II Cor.13:11:*

Are we still doubting these facts of the Word of God after reading all the above references? Then we are crafty! Craftiness is of the devil Bible says in:

> ***Gen.3:1** "Now the serpent was more subtle than any beast of the field which the LORD <u>GOD hath made</u>." "For thy mouth uttereth thine iniquity, and thou choosest the tongue of the crafty." <u>Job 15:5</u>. [read]*

When we talk about subtlety it's all over the place in the Bible, talk about deceit and deception:

> *"And Jacob said to Rebekah his mother. Esau my brother is a hairy man, and I am a smooth man:*
> *<u>vs.12</u>, My father peradventure will feel me, and I shall seem to him as a deceiver: and I shall bring a curse upon me, and not a blessing:*
> *<u>vs.13</u>, And his mother said unto him, upon me be thy curse, my son: only obey my voice, and go fetch me them:*
> *<u>vs.14</u>, And he went, and fetched, and brought them to his mother: and his mother made savory meat, such as his father loved:*
> *<u>vs.15</u>, And Rebekah took goodly raiment of her eldest son Esau, which were with her in the house, and put them on Jacob her younger son:*
> *<u>vs.16</u>, And she put the skins of the kids of the goats upon his hands, and upon the smooth of his neck." <u>Gen.27:11-16</u>*

We can read the account of this deception in the family; following Near Eastern tradition *[read Gen.18:9-10]*. Rebekah could not be in the immediate company of males-even family members-who were conducting business. However, she was listening to the men from nearby. After learning of Isaac's intentions for Esau, Rebekah came up with a scheme to overturn the plans. Perhaps she did it because she remembered the decades-old prophecy about Jacob dominating his older brother *[read Gen.25:23, ".... and the elder shall serve the younger:]"* with this, the Bible painted a picture of a troubled family: Rebekah using her son [not "their son"] to destroy her husband's plan, and Jacob agreeing to lie to his father and cheat his brother. A curse of an unexpected sort did result for both Jacob and Rebekah: their scheme force Jacob out of their family home, leave his father and mother *[Gen.28:5]*, and the Bible gives no indication that Rebekah ever saw her favorite son again. Every sin has its own consequences, you say "but God forgives," yes, He does, but you still pay a price, after you pay the price, He then forgives!

Gen.27:1-16, Like father like son. Jacob also was deceived about Rachel: **Gen.29:14-30**: *[Read all references see the chains of deception and the results]*.

> *Vs.3, He that backbiteth not with his tongue, nor doeth evil to his neighbour, nor taketh up a reproach against his neighbour.*

- Someone who is free from backbiting vs.3 of Ps.15: Let us go over it ...

God is intolerant of those who maliciously destroy other people with their speech *[Psalms 101:5-8]*:

> *"Whoso privily slandereth his neigbour, him will I cut off: him that hath an high look and a proud heart will not I suffer:*
> *vs.6, Mine eyes shall be upon the faithful of the land, that they may dwell with me: he that walketh in a perfect way, he shall serve me:*
> *vs.7, He that worketh deceit shall not dwell within my house: he that telleth lies shall not tarry in my sight:*
> *vs.8, I will early destroy all the wicked of the land; that I may cut off all the wicked doers from the city of the LORD."*

These verses focus on the King's promotion of righteousness in the community *[God's Kingdom]*. This wise ruler rejects slanderers and the proud but surrounds himself with those who are *faithful and blameless*. The moral standards of the king should be reflected by those who serve him; therefore, the ruler *[God the Father]*, will remove from His palace anyone who deceives and tells lies. Evildoers would be exiled from the precincts of Jerusalem.

["Great is the LORD, and greatly to be praised in the city of our God, in the mountain of His Holiness: Beautiful for situation, the Joy of the whole earth is Mount Zion, on the sides of the North, the City of The Great King!] <u>Psalms 48:1-2</u>

I don't know about you, the statement above sets my eyes on tears, if we read very well all the underline phrases without deceiving ourselves, God is telling us His mind and what He will do to as many as do His Will and what will befall those who are doing their own will, two things we see here pointing to our study; He says, when we slander our neighbour either openly or secretly, even with all ***that telleth lies***, He will cut off, do we even know what that means? 'Spiritual death' no communication of any kind with that fellow, their prayers will not be heard, no fellowship with the Father; that's what it means, He will not spare the proud and as many as are wicked will He also cut off from **"The City of GOD" please read it, it's there**; but the faithful of the land *[on planet earth]* and all of those that are walking in perfect ways shall **'Dwell' and 'Abide'** with the Father and serve the Father; you say, **"well He cannot destroy all the millions of people"** try Him! How many people were on earth in the time of Noah in Genesis chapter nine? It was the whole planet that was destroyed because of their abomination, their selfishness, wickedness and lawlessness save Noah and his household! Has God ever been a liar and say what He's not capable of doing?

12 Uses of The Tongue The Bible Condemned:

We will see the lists and Bible references of sins we commit with our tongue below after reading **_Ps.15:1-5_**:

In this family of the use of tongue, we see, **_'Gossiping,' 'Talebearing,' 'False Witnessing,' 'Whispering,'_** they are the same family in **_Lev.19:16_**,

> *"Thou shalt not go up and down as a talebearer among thy people: neither shalt thou stand against the blood of thy neighbor. I am the Lord."*

> *"They are all grievous revolters, walking with slanders: they are brass and iron; they are all corrupters."* **_Jer.6:28_**

In *[Jer.6:28]*, the people are described as grievous and stubborn in their rebelliousness, does that describe you and me?

> *"Take ye heed every one of his neighbour, and trust ye not in any brother: for every brother will utterly supplant, and every neighbour will walk with slanders."* **_Jer.9:4_**

Every brother will utterly supplant. Jeremiah argued, punning on Jacob's name *[Ge.27:36]*. *"Utterly supplant"* could be translated *"will supplant [like] the supplanter/Jacob" [read Hosea 12:2-4]*.

> *"In thee are men that carry tales to shed blood: and in thee they eat up mountains: in the midst of thee they commit lewdness."* **_Eze.22:9_**

Leviticus 19:16, contains the only other occurrence of the legal word "talebearer" in the Bible. There it is also associated with bloodshed. Thus, it is clear that Ezekiel was alluding to a legal stipulation that would have been well known to his audience. Ezekiel's use of the Hebrew word *zimmah* [lewdness] to denote un-chastity *[9:11;*

16:27,58; 23:21,27,35,44,48] followed the tradition in the Mosaic law [Lev.18:17-18; 19:29; 20:14] respectively.

This is talking about those who trade in words to shed innocent blood, the peddlers, it is used of those who peddle scandal, obtaining the secrets of others and retailing them as gossip wherever they go, they mess other people up with their mouth, always in a hurry to get to the next person so as to release the secret of others, they have problem in the area of how they use their tongue.

In the same company of gossip is where we see *'False Witnessing,'*

> *"A talebearer revealeth secrets: but he that is of a faithful spirit concealeth the matter." Pro.11:13: A talebearer spreads slander [Lev.19:16; Jer.6:28; 9:4; Eze.22:9] read all references!*

> *"Thou shalt not bear false witness against thy neighbour." Exo.20:16,*

[This prohibits false testimony in courts of justice, and lying about the acts, words, and property of another; to not invent a false report against another man].

> *"Thou shalt not raise false report: put not thine hand with the wicked to be an unrighteous witness:*
> *vs.7, Keep thee far from a false matter; and the innocent and the righteous slay thou not: for I will not justify the wicked." Exo.23:1&7,*

Slaying here does not necessarily mean with a knife or gun or other deadly weapon as we do slay *[kill the innocent]* with our mouth: *'Whisperings,'* is another deadly sin, it is an unrighteous thing to do; may the Lord help us!

"Being filled with all unrighteousness, fornication, wickedness, covetousness, maliciousness; full of envy, murder, debate, deceit, malignity; whisperers:
vs.30, Backbiters, haters of God, despiteful, proud, boasters, inventors of evil things, disobedient to parents:
vs.31, without understanding, covenant-breakers, without natural affection, implacable, unmerciful:
vs.32, Who knowing the judgment of God, that they which commit such things are worthy of death, not only do the same, but have pleasure in them." Rom.1:29-32

They're all in here **'Slandering,'** having read all of the above, someone is saying in his or her heart that *"[hey you writer, don't be too serious, as God is a merciful God, He can't be this serious, He forgives;]"* Oh yes, He very well does but not when we continue in all of the above and not willing to repent and turn away from whichever applies to us we
cannot see the Lord, the Bible says, *"God is too Holy for His eyes to behold iniquity:"* you cannot *'Dwell'* and *'Abide'* with Him!

"Even so must their wives be grave, not slanderers, sober, faithful in all things." I Tim.3:11

Paul talking to us as leaders in our respective ministries *[I think if you are a leader, a deacon, or a worker or even a member of a congregation]*, here we need to point this verse to our wives to let them see the importance of the doctrine of our Lord Jesus Christ as Ministers wives and if you are a wife or one of the leaders in the church this applies to you also.

Amongst which are, **'False Accusations,'** *Tit.2:3*, why is he talking to the aged woman? The *'why'* is in *vs.4*, *"that they may teach the young women,"* for the young women also to learn how to bridle their tongue, to be sober, to love their husbands, their children, also to be discreet because children especially girls love to tend after their mothers and they behave alike, they grow up to the same as they see their mothers do.

'__Vain Talking__,' __Tit.1:10__, [especially they of the circumcision, meaning even the teachers of the Word, the children of God; '__Defaming__,' it's a bad habit for any preacher of the Word or teachers of the Word to pull other preachers down, to promote ourselves in front of our congregation, what do we want to prove or gain in doing that? He says to us in:

> __*Psalms105:15*__, *"Touch not mine anointed, and do my prophets no harm."*

It's never appropriate to make oneself seem more important, knowledgeable or smarter by demeaning others to prove whatever point we might want to prove; God said, **"Touch not mine anointed and do my prophets no harm,"** I don't care how right you are about the issue. God's anointed ones would include the ministers of the Gospel regardless of their ages, young or old, kings, priests, prophets, all who received anointing in a dedication ceremony, not only that, all people regardless of color, race, orientations must be respected; God has not called us to be judges over ourselves.

When the children of Israel sinned against God, the Lord was slightly displeased with them, so to teach them a lesson, God allowed the heathens to invade and destroy their territory, but when prayer was engaged on their behalf, God suddenly became grossly displeased with the same heathen who dealt with His people, no matter how right we may be about any servant of God, please let us beware of how we touch them; any quarrel between God and His children is short-lived. An enemy may take advantage of such rift to torment God's people and may seem to get away with it, but it is only temporal. In the long run, that enemy will become the item of settlement between God and His children, we cannot use any child of God as an object of our evil discussion to pull him or her down. It is dangerous to touch the anointed of God, even when the fellow has sinned against God!

We cannot do it, period! Besides, it doesn't make us any good as Christians and as preachers of the WORD to pull others down on our pulpits,' who made us judges of others? Here is the implication, if the Man of God in question or the brother or sister have made their ways right with God in their quiet hours, have repented of whatever was wrong, and God has forgiven them; and here we are broadcasting it, peddling it, trading with it, defaming the other person, we shall not be innocent, we are guilty of defaming others, so can we ***'Abide' and 'Dwell*** with Him? No! Unless we repent and ask to be forgiven! God will always defend His anointing on His anointed. Why don't we try lift someone up instead of tearing them down and we will be happy in the long run.

One Bible character who had a good understanding of this was King David. He was on the run for his life from Saul for so long until one day, he found himself in a vantage position; he could kill his oppressor where he found him *[Saul]* sleeping. David's men wanted to jump at the opportunity they heaved a sigh of relieve, they wanted to kill Saul and put an end to the struggle, but David refused in ***I Samuel 24, and said "how can he touch the anointed of the Lord"*** David refused to kill his brother--turned enemy. We must not easily speak against, hurt or violate any genuinely anointed of God irrespective of his or her present spiritual standing. If you disgrace or hurt in any way a man of God who has done wrong, beware because one day, you will face the God of that man of God and He will have more than a pound of flesh. ***the most dangerous people to oppress are those who believe in Jesus. Either now or later, you will surely pay dearly for what you did against them!"***

Jer.20:10; 'Tattling,' I Tim.5:13; 'Lying,' Pro.6:12-14 & 17,

[people gossip with all kind of gestures, with the eyes, with some sarcastic signs, with the leg, even with their shoulders, women you know what am talking about, don't act like you don't]: ***"[once I do like this....and like that, you know what I mean and who I'm talking about ....]"*** Come on, let's quit that, it is evil!

1. *[Gen.31:24]* We see here where God protects Jacob from the tongue of man:

"And God came to Laban the Syrian in a dream by night and said unto him, take heed that thou speak not to Jacob either good or bad."

Why? God knows that whatever will come out of his mouth will be full of self-justification for his pursuit of Jacob: we might spend some time in this area of gossiping because we see it every time as it grows among believers.

Learning of Jacob's secret departure, Laban gathered a posse and set out to catch the group *[Jacob, his wives, the children, the herds of sheep and goats];* Laban intended to harm Jacob, probably because he believed Jacob had stolen his household god, but the God of Jacob's father kept the promise of protection made 20 years earlier *[Genesis 28:15]*, and warned Laban in a dream not to harm Jacob. Laban was also frustrated because he had no opportunity to kiss his daughters and grandson's good-bye and send the group off with a joyful celebration. *"The earth is the LORD's and the fullness thereof!"* God will always fight and protect His servants from whoever even from the scourges of another minister, we must beware how we use our tongue, even our thoughts against the anointed, remember God searches through the heart, God rates us through our heart, whatever is in our hearts is not hiding from Him. Our heart is the foundation for God's reaction toward us; if we practice love, we will not fall into practicing hate.

In *I Thess.4:11*, The Bible tells us to mind our own business, *"And that ye study to be quiet,"* **[stop]** what does that mean? *"To be ambitious, pursue eagerly, strive emulously and aspire to: prize above measure."* Talking about Christian behavior.

To learn not to be talkative! We are already a carrier of something incredible, something great, something that cannot be purchased with money, something the people of the world do not have, a gift of a lifetime, we carry the Spirit of God The Father in us, talkativeness cannot be joined to it, no room for both; we should have self-respect so that people who come in contact with us will honour and respect us.

To learn to be a keeper of the secrets of others that have been given to us in confidence; to learn not to be a brawler, to learn to be meek and gentle, to not be a noise maker anywhere we are, a man of God must be reserved, must not do all these things, a child of God must be respected where he/she goes.

We're talking about decency here, we're talking about spiritual discipline as well as self-discipline here, we're talking about integrity here, we're talking about honouring the God in us, the God that we serve here.

Not when we appear anywhere and people sight us from afar off, then they begin to check themselves, "he/she is coming, better mind what you say now, better mind what you do now, you don't know where the news carrier will carry the news; CNN, is coming, radio station, radio/network/vendor, is coming:" See why they tag us as such as a Christians: we probably have problems in the area of speaking, no control of the mouth:

If we read the Book of Samuel in *[chapter 22 from verse 6-12]* downward we will discover the obsession of Saul as it spreads to as many as had contact with David including his priests and his servants as Ahimelech was accused of conspiracy by Saul in order to find an occasion and be justified in killing the priest and all members of his household in verses *[13-16] Saul summons the priests*:

Vs.13, "And Saul said unto him, Why have ye conspired against me, thou and the son of Jesse, in that thou hast given him bread, and a sword, and has inquired of God for him, that he should rise against me, to lie in wait, as this day?
vs.14, then Ahimelech answered the king, and said, And who is so faithful among thy servants as David, which is the king's son-in-law, and goeth at thy bidding, and is honourable in thine house?

> ***vs.15**, Did I then begin to inquire of God for him? Be it far from me: let not the king impute anything unto his servant, not to all the house of my father: for thy servant knew nothing of all this, less more:*
> ***vs.16**, And the king said, Thou shalt surely die, Ahimelech, thou, and all thy father's house.*

Because of an indiscipline mouth of a servant, because of loose tongue of a man, tongue that is not tamed, the Book of James put it this way in ***James 3:5-6:***

> *"Even so **the tongue** is a little member, and boasteth great things, Behold how great a matter a **little fire** kindleth! **vs.6**, And **the tongue is** a fire, a world of iniquity: so is the tongue among our members, that it defileth the whole body, and setteth on fire the course of nature; and it is set on fire of hell."*

Like horse bits and ship rudders, the size of the tongue is disproportionate to the influence or holds. The tongue that teaches false doctrine is a world of iniquity it pollutes the whole body *[an individual or a congregation]* and determines the destiny of all who follow it. Did we see what the tongue of that man caused?

> *"And the king said unto the footmen that stood about him, Turn, and slay the priests of the LORD; because their hand also is with David, and because they knew when he fled, and did not shew it to me. But the servants of the king would not put forth their hand to fall upon the priests of the LORD:*
> ***vs.18**, And the said to Doeg, Turn thou, and fall upon the priests. and Doeg the Edomite turned, and fell upon the priests, and slew on that day fourscore and five person that did wear a linen ephod."*

Eighty-five priests died, along with every other living thing in Nob, because of Saul's misguided wrath." People use their tongue any how to destroy other people's lives, we just open our mouth, and we utter anything that cares to come out of those unbridled mouths and before we know it, it's a killer speech! We don't care on whose toes we're stepping on as long as we have our ways; people see some of us as news carriers. Listen to what David said here:

> ***I Sam.22:22***, *"And David said to Abiathar, I knew it that day, when Doeg the Edomite was there, that he would surely tell Saul: I have occasioned the death of all the death of thy father's house."*
> ***vs. 23****, "Abide thou with me, fear not: for he that seeketh my life seeketh thy life: but with me thou shalt be in safeguard."*

David in ***verse 23*** suggested that he and Abiathar could trust each other because they had a common enemy *[Saul]* from whom they needed to protect themselves. Thus, David aligned himself with the priests of the Lord, even as Saul further alienated himself from God.

Saul had an obsession to kill David so he ran away from Saul, Saul wanted to kill him not because of anything but because of envy and jealousy that aroused when God hath promoted David and that David would be king. David had his suspicions that **Doeg** would betray them, give them out and tell Saul *[to curry favour from Saul]* about David's visit to Nob when David was hiding and running away from Saul who sought to kill him, but failed to deal with **Doeg** when he had the opportunity and because of what **Doeg** did, Saul accused the priests of conspiracy against him.

The people we relate with day in day out already know us, they know what we are capable of doing, we probably have done something in that area of gossip in the past, we have revealed secrets before, you have betrayed the confidence of others before, because we don't have integrity, because we are news carriers, a private journalist; *[a freelance]*; ***Pro.6***, reading to us from ***vs.12***,

And only <u>vs.12</u> now *"A naughty person, a <u>wicked man</u>, walketh with a forward mouth."* Now let me tell us what that means in my Bible, and I will ask us to also read it: …… it means *[a good for nothing, a man worthless]:* so, tell me, if people or the Bible classify us as described, can we *'Abide' nor 'Dwell'* with the Lord? When we are caught doing something or we said something that didn't go right with the other person and are confronted, smartly we quickly twist it, and turn it around to favour us and to confuse the other person in order to prove our innocence and smartness, we use our earthly wisdom pointing an accusing finger at the other person even when we are wrong, but we know what we're doing; sometimes we never admit to anything because to us we're never wrong and so we don't take corrections, that is pride, but the eyes of the Lord is looking at us! We shall not be innocent!

<u>Vs.13</u>, *"He,'* now, I've taught us of the language of the Bible, so we do not say **the Bible says**, *'he' not 'she'* the Bible is talking to all of us, mostly women, okay: so, let's go, *"He winketh with his eyes,"* we commit sin of gossip with every member of our body, and Bible explains how we do it:

"He winketh with his eyes, he speaketh with his feet;" hello! *"He teacheth with his fingers."*

These three means, 'gestures', they refer to sign language to convey evil intentions and sinful practices of partners in sin while the next <u>vs.14</u>, talks about:

"Frowardness in his heart, he deviseth mischief continually; he soweth discord."

How do we sow discord? We tell this to that and that to this then confusion erupts, because of our mouth, we bare false witness, people begin to fight each other, we've sown hate, envy and jealousy; must we say it out, why are we so eager to divulge other people's secrets in our hands? To cause confusion?

'Continually' means, we don't ever change, it will take the finger of God for us to change, why? It's in the blood! We continually plot, schemes, and plans **evil; in _vs.18_** of the same Book of **_Pro.6,_** *[read],* they sow discord in families, in churches, in communities or nations: **_vs.20-23_**:

Let us go back now to see **_I Thess.4:11_**, where the Bible tells us to mind our own business:

> *"And that ye **study to be quiet**, and **to do** your own business."*

Talking about the behaviour of a true Christian, the truth is, we hide behind the grace to violate every rule in the Bible; the question is, are we true Christians, can we not try to be good for goodness sake?

The thought is that of a disposition and life of peace, and contentment; even temperament; to be meek, and learn self-control in all things, not to permit anything to disturb or cause a display of temper tantrums or disturb the peace of others.

Evidently there are a few idle, tattling people in the church all over, who instead of working, studying or reading their Bibles, minding their own business, went from place to place carrying on religious gossip, meddling with the business of others and causing divisions in places as mentioned.

> Hence, the commands to quit such practices, *to do their own business, let others alone, "to hold their peace, walk honestly toward the world, and to work with their own hands so they would have no time to gad about and gossip."* *[I Thess.4:11-12]*

The reference to brotherly love seems to govern the content of these verse in encouraging fellow Christians to lead a quiet life, mind owns business in the church and outside the church, and work with one's hands. To do otherwise places a burden of dependence on the community of faith and gives a poor testimony to outsiders, you hear people say, *"but he's a Christian, she's a Christian, I see her carry the Bible on Sundays,"* because they know that you are only a Sunday, Sunday worshipper: *"how can he/she do things like that, like this, how can she say things like this?"* by our actions we have cause an occasion by which the name of God in us is blasphemed: Bible says, *"such as is not common among unbelievers:"*

FOOD FOR THOUGHTS:

"Take ye heed every one of his neighbour, and trust ye not in any brother: for every brother will utterly supplant, and every neighbour will walk with slanders." Jer.9:4

"In thee are men that carry tales to shed blood: and in thee they eat up mountains: in the midst of thee they commit lewdness." Eze.22:9

"A talebearer revealeth secrets: but he that is of a faithful spirit concealeth the matter." Pro.11:13, A talebearer spreads slander [Lev.19:16; Jer.6:28; 9:4; Eze.22:9]. Read all references!

"Thou shalt not bear false witness against thy neighbour." Exo.20:16,

"Thou shalt not raise false report: put not thine hand with the wicked to be an unrighteous witness: vs.7, "Keep thee far from a false matter; and the innocent and the righteous slay thou not: for I will not justify the wicked." Exo.23:1&7,

"Even so must their wives be grave, not slanderers, sober, faithful in all things." I Tim.3:11
Psalms105:15, "Touch not mine anointed, and do my prophets no harm."

It's never appropriate to make oneself seem more important, knowledgeable or smarter by demeaning others to prove whatever point we might want to prove; God said, *"Touch not mine anointed and do my prophets no harm,"*

> *"Even so <u>the tongue</u> is a little member, and boasteth great things, Behold how great a matter a <u>little fire</u> kindleth! vs.6, And <u>the tongue is</u> a fire, a world of iniquity: so is the tongue among our members, that it defileth the whole body, and setteth on fire the course of nature; and it is set on fire of hell."*

Let us Pray!

Dear Heavenly Father, having read all these things about us and the way we have violated all rules, it is evident that our unseemingly attitude to You and to the gospel hiding behind the grace to perpetuate evil and committing sin is daring You O Lord, the Bible says:

"If I shut up heaven that there be no rain, or if I command the locusts to devour the land, or if I send pestilence among my people: vs.14, If my people, which are called by my name, shall humble themselves, and pray, and seek my face, and turn from their wicked ways: then will I hear from heaven, and I will forgive their sin, and will heal their land:

Father, it is evidently obvious that the world at large have turned away from You which is why we are going through all that is said in the first verse above: it is like heaven is shut against the inhabitants of the earth and heaven above is turned to brass that is why millions are suffering, confusion everywhere and many are lost, there is hunger everywhere, many are in debt these are the interpretation of heavens being shut and there is no rain! The locusts are devouring the land, there is pestilence amongst the people of the land, that is why there is war and shedding of blood everywhere, Satan is taking his toll on the people of God!

Dear Heavenly Father, please look down from Your Holy Habitation as we humble ourselves before You the God of Heaven, The Elohim, The All-Powerful we pray; The ADONAI, The Lord our GREAT LORD, we pray; Jehovah YHWH the Self-Existent One, we pray; Jehovah EL-ROI, The GOD who see Us, we pray; we humble ourselves before YOU; we seek YOUR face O LORD, we repent of all of our sins, O Thou, Mighty God, of Heaven forgive us and heal our land, bind the wounds of the broken-hearted ...... comfort those that are mourning right now and touch all that we may begin seeking you all of our lives In Jesus name ..... AMEN!

CHAPTER FOUR

JEHOVAH ROHI - THE LORD IS MY SHEPHERD:
The Lord protects, provides, directs, leads, and cares for His people, God tenderly takes care of us as a strong and patient shepherd!

PSALMS 15:4

Vs.4: In whose eyes a vile person is contemned; but he honoureth them that fear the LORD. He that sweareth to his own hurt, and changeth not.

<u>*I Thess.4:11*</u>: the Bible says for us to:

"And that ye <u>study to be quiet</u>, and <u>to do</u> your own business, and <u>to work</u> with your own hands, as we commanded you."

Study in this instance means to be ambitious: to pursue eagerly: strive emulously and aspire to: prize above measure: this is not the same <u>**Study**</u> as in <u>**II Tim.2:15**</u>, 'study,' 'study' here are two different words:

"Study to shew thyself approved unto God, a workman that needeth not to be ashamed, rightly dividing the word of truth;" [II Tim.2:15]. Study here means, 'Study', it means, to be 'Zealous; it also means, to Handle Scripture correctly! While the other 'study' in [I Thess.4:11] tells us to, here it is: "And that ye <u>study to be quiet</u>, and <u>to do</u> your own business:" to not be a talkative, to not engage in slander, to mind our own business!

This is the same with the Sanhedrin, they have their own doctrine and so the teachings of the Lord Jesus are a threat to them; it didn't go well with them, they thought if they find reasons to kill Him then He will not be able to teach His doctrine again, but they forgot that getting rid of Him was the beginning of History.

In the following passages, we see gossip attacks against Jesus, that's why as a servant of God, if gossips are flying about concerning you, it happened to Jesus, look with me in the Book of **_Mat.9:10-12_**:

> *"And it came to pass, as Jesus sat at meat in the house, behold, many publicans and sinners came and sat down with Him and His disciples;*
> *__vs.11__, and when the Pharisees saw it, they said unto His disciples: Why eateth your master with publican and sinners?*
> *__vs.12__, but when Jesus heard that, He said unto them "They that be whole need not a physician, but they that are sick."*

In other words, Christ came to save sinners, not the righteous: like sick people who think they are well, the Pharisees were sinful but thought they were righteous. Only those who realize they are sinners will respond to Jesus' call! They never understood His reasons for being there, and it was for them, but they used His visit as a topic for gossip.

Mat.11:18-19: Hear what the Lord Jesus said in response to their gossip:

> *"For John came neither eating nor drinking, and they say, he hath a devil: __vs.19__, The Son of man came eating and drinking, and they say, Behold a man gluttonous, and a winebibber, a friend of publicans and sinners. But wisdom is justified of her children."*

Jesus portrayed His unbelieving contemporaries as spoiled children who whined when they did not get their way. In an ancient version of the game *"Simon says, if a designated child played a pretend flute the other children were supposed to dance. If he sang a lament they were supposed to mourn."* However, like unresponsive children. Israel did not pay heed to the ministries of Jesus and John the Baptist. The reference to wisdom's children parallels the reference to the Messiah's works *[vs.2]* and implies that Jesus' claims were vindicated by the acts described in *[verses 4-6].*

Between the time of the Old Testament and the New Testament, Jewish interpreters elaborated on *Prov.8:32-36* and taught that Wisdom was an eternal being who served as God's agent in the creation of the world. By identifying Himself with personified Wisdom. Jesus hinted that He is the eternal One through whom the Father created everything *[John 1:3].*

"John abstained from all social life, John lived a separated life, yet you refused to receive him: I came accepting invitations to eat and you call me a winebibber and a glutton, and you reject me." So, they began their accusations against Him, they set up a trial.

<u>**Mk.14:53-59**</u>: A mockery trial, *[the Sanhedrin, the ruling body of the Jews];* what a time to try any man, at night? Even if He were the worst criminal; this is one of the most impressive acts of the whole story. Showing that this was not a formal judicial trial, but only to get evidence enough to send Him to Pilate.

Listen to <u>vs.56</u>:

> *"For many bare false witnesses against Him." If a man says, "I will destroy this Temple that is built with hand, and within three days, I will build another made without hands."*

Is there a problem in that freedom of speech, what has He said to offend the public or offend the government? Because of their ignorance, they were furious because they didn't know what building He was talking about.

Even some are searching for gossip subjects against Him: <u>**Mk.3:1-6**</u>: *[again here]* meaning another Sabbath …. You know why they watched Him? …. They had no **doubt** of His power to heal, but they were watching to see if He would break the ***Sabbath*** by healing on that day!

They sought occasion to gossip; they sought occasion to accuse Him. The Bible tells us in:

> <u>***Rom.2:1***</u>*, "Therefore thou art inexcusable, O man, whosoever thou art that judgest: for wherein thou judgest another, thou condemnest thyself; for thou that judgest doest the same things."*

Did we hear that, or are we still in doubt that there is no excuse for *gossip, no excuse for slander, no excuse for false witness and all that we do to bring others down that there's no excuse?*

In <u>*I Sam.22*</u>, that we read above; but now from <u>*vs.6*</u>, here we see what tale-bearing can do, we see what gossip can do, we see here in this chapter of the Bible how it exposed the lives of about 85 people to danger that, all 85 priests of the Lord were eventually slaughtered by Saul.

Saul was after David for many years, David fled the king's court and was in hiding; Saul was obsessed with the idea of murdering David, it was all he could think and talk about. 12 whole chapters of 22 in <u>I Samuel</u> which recorded the life of Saul, are devoted mainly to stories relating to this one thing.

Jealousy, hatred, murder, insults, lying, and other major sins were a part of Saul's life, and because of this one obsession, to kill David; so, he spoke his mind and accused all his servants including the priests of conspiring against him in the matter of David: <u>*vs.8*</u>

We can quickly go over it again ourselves, some prophets of the Most High were executed because of the mouth of just one person who was looking for favour: **_vs.9-13,14-16_**, even though he ordered the execution of the priests of the Lord, Saul's soldiers would not kill the priests knowing there was no justification in such execution.

These were priests of Jehovah, but it made no difference to Saul; he would have even sought to destroy Jehovah Himself if such were possible, anything to give vent to his hatred of David; we see here that Saul executed about 85 priests because of on man's mouth, one man's testimony: **_vs.18_**.

Lev.19:16, talks about 'Tale-bearing' means the peddlers those who peddle scandal, obtaining the secret of others and retailing them as gossip wherever they go; this is so serious in itself that singularly it took a whole verse to itself in the lists of rules of Ten Commandments, *[Ex.20:16]*; they do these things to endanger lives, how? It brings out anger and when anger erupts, it becomes dangerous ...... An adage says, *"When you are angry, do nothing because what will spoil will be more than what caused the anger:"*

Deut.19:16-21: Here it is talking about a public execution of the law; *[see church discipline on page in chapter Two of this book]*, a disgrace if you will so that the church will put evil away from among us! The Bible says, in the next verse, *"And those which remain,"* where? In the church, in the family, in the community, the household .... *"Shall hear and fear"* of disgrace and shame and name tagging, *"and shall henceforth commit no more any such evil among you."*

> *"For there is no faithfulness in their mouth; their inward part is very wickedness; their throat is an open sepulcher; they flatter with their tongue." **Ps.5:9**:*

Here it means, for there is no firmness, no steadfastness or stability, no dependence upon what they say; it also speaks of their throat as an open sepulcher.

"They speak vanity everyone with his neighbour: with flattering lips and with a double heart do they speak." Ps.12:2

Throat and *tongue* are metaphors for speech. There is nothing reliable in whatever they say, so all of the enemies' speech is deadly, pictured here as an *open sepulcher*. A similar use of this word picture appears in *Jeremiah 5:16* where **"their quiver is as an open sepulcher,"** meaning their weapons bring death. Since the enemies here were intent on death and destruction, the psalmist asked that God let their own schemes bring about their destruction: ***II Samuel 15:31; Psalms 64:8]***. They are conspirators like Ahithophel, the news that Ahithophel had joined the conspirators with Absalom his son to destroy the king and overthrown him was a blow to David's cause. the king's prayer for God to turn the counsel of Ahithophel to foolishness was a prayer of great faith because his son was involved, his counselor and his priest was also involved in the conspiracy against him and Ahithophel's advice was taken to be like a word from the Lord: but this time, however, his counsel was politically motivated and wise, but immoral since David was still alive and has the right ***ownership to the throne of David! [see Leviticus 20:11]***, this was Absalom's sin against his father and against Israel.

"And the counsel of Ahithophel which he counseled in those days, was as if a man had inquired at the oracle of God: so was all the counsel of Ahithophel both with David and with Absalom."

Now, we're now back home to where we began: ***Ps.15:1-3***: Bravo! We're moving forward!

Vs.1, *"LORD, <u>who shall</u> abide in THY tabernacle? <u>who shall</u> dwell in THY HOLY Hill?*
Vs.2, *<u>He that</u> walketh uprightly, and worketh righteousness, and speaketh the truth in his heart.*

Vs.3, He that *backbiteth not with his tongue, nor doeth evil to his neighbour, nor taketh up a reproach against his neighbour.*

James.1:26, *"If any man among you seem to be religious, and bridleth not his tongue, but deceiveth his own heart, this man's religion is vain.*
vs.27, *Pure religion and undefiled before God and the Father is this, to visit the fatherless and widows in their affliction, and to keep himself unspotted from the world."*

The distinction between the **hearer** who **forgetteth** and the **doer** of the Word who **continueth** is whether he allows **the perfect law of liberty** to shape his life's course. The person who puts faith into action and is **blessed**; his worship influences his life in the same way, the person who refuses to hold his *tongue* is deceived about his faith. He hears and talks, but he does not act on what he has heard. James' **definition of *pure* and *undefiled*** religion is based on action, not heedless hearing and meaningless lip service.

- **Who do no evil to neighbours vs.3 of Ps.15;**

Vs.3, He that *backbiteth not with his tongue, nor doeth evil to his neighbour, nor taketh up a reproach against his neighbour.*

"Thou shalt not raise a false report: put not thine hand with the wicked to be an unrighteous witness." **Exo.23:1**

It is touching on every economic status or personal feeling that might tempt someone to treat another unjustly. Favoritism either to the poor or to the rich is ruled out [Leviticus 19:15].

"Ye shall do no unrighteousness in judgment: thou shalt not respect the person of the poor; nor honour the person of the mighty: but in righteousness shalt thou judge thy neighbour."

The law against unrighteous *judgment* is directed not at judges only *[Deut.1:16; 16:18]*, but at *the people in general*, since any Israelite could be a juror and stand **in judgment of his neighbour *[see Ruth 4]*.** Even in private matters involving the need of an enemy, a believer must not because someone has offended me in the past, now this is my opportunity as a juror to nail him, it is unrighteous **"*[nor doeth evil to his neighbour, or taketh up a reproach against his neighbour]*."**

- **He holds vile people contemned *[to consider and treat as mean and despicable, to neglect as unworthy of regard, to reject with disdain]*;** to disregard the wicked and sinful people, to not party with them, to not dine and wine with them, nor walk in their company in other words be separated, go out from among them: The next one:

    Psalms 15:4: *In whose eyes a vile person is contemned; but he honoureth them that fear the LORD. He that sweareth to his own hurt, and changeth not.*

- They honour them that fear the Lord.

HONOUR:

[Those who honour and respect not just your fellows Christians, not just the members of your church, not just all humanity, but also you honour and respect servants of God of all ages, preachers of the gospel; in other words, you must fear God to be able to give honour].

When you honour man, you honour God, when you dishonour them that the Lord placed over you, you dishonour God; when you honour the anointing of God upon a servant of God, upon a leader, upon a fellow sister/brother you honour God.

Every sin on earth is a sin of dishonour; when you consider the Ten Commandments, the first 4 deal with honoring God, the last 6 deal with honoring people; honour is different from wisdom; wisdom is the recognition of difference, right and wrong .... Righteousness and evil, God and Satan. The Law of honour is the most important law on earth!

Genesis 3, *"And when the woman saw that the tree was good for food:" "**The Lust Of The Flesh**:" "And it was pleasant to the eyes:" "**The Lust Of The Eyes**:" "And a tree to be desired to make one wise:" "**The Pride Of Life**:" "She took of the fruit thereof, and did eat:" "**The Disobedience And Rebellion Of The Heart**:"* We dishonour God in several ways by not listening to Him nor follows His commandments.

Honour is not an Anointing, not a miracle nor an answer to prayer. It is your personal choice to celebrate the distinctive difference in another; honour is the willingness to reward somebody for their difference male or female, young or old. When someone is alive, we don't ever recognize their good works, the difference they're making, we sometimes don't even show love towards that person, we ignore, we neglect them: for some selfish, hatred or race reasons we refuse to commend them or give them credit for their many achievements in the family, in the community, the city, in a nation or the world at large; but when that fellow dies, we make noise of how good he was, how much difference he's made, we give medals in his name. Tell me, do they have any more use for praise nor the medals? In the grave?

How beautiful would that have been had he or she been recognized, had they been honoured, had they received the praises when they were alive to show as a testimony to their children for them also to learn and know that it is good to be good and to strive to make a difference wherever you may be. But we gave the medal to the children who probably didn't listen to this parent's teachings while he was alive, who never wanted to follow his/her footsteps to make a difference himself but are concerned only and waiting for how much in properties and in cash he leaves behind; honour is the seed for access into any environment on earth.

Honour decides who desire you, who accepts you and who rewards you; honour grows in every environment in every single season of your life; honour is the willingness to magnify difference instead of weakness; sow honour as a seed of respect, recognition, honour will compensate and silence all the doubts about every other weakness in your life.

Honour will take you further than genius and all your experiences in life. Jesus judged others by their willingness to show honour; Mary demonstrated Honour when she washed the feet of Jesus *read*: ***[Mat.26:7-13], [read]***.

Honour has a distinctive fragrance; the fragrance of honour is as distinctive as the odor of dishonour; you cannot hide the fragrance of honour; honour has a sound ... a distinctive sound; so, does dishonour.

Listen for the sound of honour; conversations, friendships relationships built on the resumes of people, over an entire life can be deceptive; passions and emotions can be misleading; no one has the greatest resume than Lucifer, he worked next to God for years. He dishonoured God the Father and his position terminated; he was booted out of Heaven:

So never evaluate people by their experience, never evaluate people by their passion; evaluate people by their code of honour; who have they chosen to honour through their words, time and friendship; who have they chosen to dishonour, ignore or trivialize; whose voice have they chosen to trust, what is the character of those they admire?

Do not ridicule nor engage in dragging the name of any servant of God on the ground, or any church, God said you're doing it to Him why? Because they are His servants, they are answerable unto God and not to you, simple; when you trod on other people's anointing or you fail to honour the anointing of others, you cannot be anointed no matter how much you try because what you honour is what increases in your life.

Vessel of Honour and Vessel of Dishonour:

Saul was anointed as the king over Israel when the children of Israel rejected God from being King over them ***I Sam.8:5-7 refers: [read];*** David also was anointed to be king; the problem was, Saul was anointed with the vial of oil, and David was anointed with the horn of oil, what's the difference?

Let me explain. The difference between the two is, one with the *horn* of oil stands for authority, stands for royalty, stands for exaltation and honour; and the other with the *vial* of oil stands for dishonour, 'vial' stands for judgment, if you look at ***Rev.16:2-17. Remember the vessel of honour and vessel of dishonour in your Bible?***

When that vial thing began to haunt Saul he began to dishonour God and disobeyed His laws, when you disobey God's laws, you dishonour Him; well, tests soon came for both of them, Saul's test #1, was that the children of Israel went into hiding in fear of the Philistines after God used Saul's son to stare up the Philistines; if there is sin in your life, fear will take its toll on you, the next thing is to hide, ***I Sam.13*** please read from ***vs.5***:

> *"And the Philistines gathered themselves together to fight with Israel …. To vs.14."*

Saul's self-will against God moved him to disobey the servant of God, he left his own calling and intrudes into the priests' office *[that is making decisions on his own];* he made a sacrifice that was to be offered by the priest and by the priest only; he dishonours God, he dishonour the servant of God, and disrespect his anointing. *[when we begin to make decisions on our own, when the church says, "no for such and such," and we say "yes" this is what I will do, this is what we will do" we are rebellious, we have disobeyed and dishonour God, we are like Achan in the camp of the Israelites!*

For this act of disrespect, the Bible says God rejected Saul as king over His people; *[please note that this rejection took place immediately, but the manifestation was not immediate, but it later came]!* How can one be rejected in just two years into his kingship? Law of Honour!

If you succeed with your life, you will be able to trace your success to those you honour regardless of their age, if you fail with your life, it can be traced to a person you chose to dishonour. He dishonours God because he did not respect the anointing; he left his own calling into someone else's calling.

What has God called you to do, what did God commit into your hand, where has God planted you? God may have called you to be a pastor, a teacher or a prophet, please do not intrude into other people's office, stay in your office and pray for those who are in different offices to succeed in their calling.

If God has called you to be a financier, or a giver; He called and blessed you with what you have, so you in turn can be a blessing to your local assembly and to others, not an oppressor, do not let what you have, or your calling get into your head and disobey or puffed up to dishonour others.

Guess what? We are too small to sponsor the Kingdom, it's an honour given to us; He can raise others that are after His own heart that are far better than me and you, He is God! He ripped off the kingdom from Saul and gave it to his neighbour saying, *"I have found myself a man after mine own heart!"* Someone better than you!!

> *That is why Paul says,*
> *"Now there are diversities of gifts, but the same Spirit: And there are differences of administration, but the same Lord:*

And there are diversities of operations, but it is the same God which worketh in all."

Pray to discover your own calling, obey God and honour Him, that you, your ministry and your household be not rejected for dishonour.

In *vs.11*, *"Samuel said, what has thou done;"* it is an abomination to the Lord when we leave our own office to wade into another people's territory or disobey in the church of Jesus Christ to take our own decision let us please be advised, to not dishonour the anointing and the calling so we don't bring a curse upon ourselves and our household. It is a curse to disobey God, may we not fall into the hand of an angry God. The sin of disobedience is a terrible sin; nothing hinders the children of God from fulfilling their purpose in life like disobedience as we now see in the case of Saul.

Disobedience comes in many shades, it can take the form of refusal to keep to specific instructions, functioning in an office God has not called us into, courting a wrong relationship or operating in a place we are not meant to be in at a particular time. No matter what form it takes, the truth remains that disobedience is a terrible sin in the sight of The Almighty God!

Disobedience compels God to turn blessings into curses, as we see in the account of Adam and Eve *[Genesis 3:17]*. Every act of disobedience erodes your reservoir of God's blessings. Nothing destroys a man faster than the sin of disobedience. That is the reason why we have to check our life today and every day continually to take stock of our soul, so that our sky will not be turned into brass *[Deuteronomy 28:23]*. When this happens, instead of favour, we will experience closed doors.

In *[I Samuel 15:1-23]*, king Saul lost his crown because of partial obedience. God expects full obedience from all His children: He prefers total obedience to partial obedience. This is one of the reasons why many of us are yet to access the blessings of God fully. Abraham was called to leave his father's house behind, but he suffered the consequences of disobedience by taking Lot along with him.

Who are those people the Lord expects you to have dropped but you are still hanging around? What are those things the Lord has warned you about that you are still engaging in? These are the things that will deny you the full blessings of God. *[Numbers 12:8]*, says Moses was so close to God that he conversed with God mouth to mouth, but when he was told to by God to speak to the rock that he did otherwise, he was severely punished, he got the penalty for striking the rock instead of speaking to it: he never got to the Promise Land *[Numbers 20:12]*. Check your life and find out those things that are capable of hindering you from becoming the best that God wants you to be and drop them before they make you drop out of the journey to the Promised Land

When Saul disobeyed and was confronted, what was his answer? He feared man to disobey God, is it man who called you or God called you? He says to not watch the people's countenance when it comes to discharging your duty as an anointed man of God:

[Read to vs.12], "I forced myself therefore and offered a burnt sacrifice."

You are a king, who called you to be a priest? Saul's excuses of self-sufficiency, failure of others, justification of self, and seeming necessity are the pleas of many who force themselves and their efforts into the office of the priest without being divinely called, purged, sanctified and prepared for priesthood. And then they misbehave, and then they do things that are abominable to God: check your life today if you are experiencing perpetual sorrow, suffering, disappointment and unfulfilled desire, check and find out the factors responsible: don't pretend to be okay when you know all is not well with you. If you confess those sins of disobedience, you will surely find mercy, but if you pretend about it, you will be undoing yourself. Some people keep making an effort, yet they never record any success. Several trials and much effort do not guarantee success when disobedience is present.

> *"And Samuel said unto him, The LORD hath rent the kingdom of Israel from thee this day, and hath given it to a neighbour of thine, that is better than thou."*
> *I Samuel 15:28: What is the point here?*

Here is the point I am trying to make! God always has a substitute! If God has honoured you and called you as a servant of God into any office, to raise and oversee a ministry in the church or outside the church; know for sure that God already has a substitute in case the calling gets to your head in so much that you disobey probably for fear of man or otherwise and you misbehaved….

If God has a divine purpose ahead for that ministry, a substitute is waiting around the corner that will carry on the assignment; I don't care if you are the founder of that ministry, a member of the leadership, a musician or a member of the choir ministry, someone is waiting to takeover.

> *"And it came to pass, when men began to multiply on the face of the earth, and daughters were born unto them,*
> *vs.2, That the sons of God saw the daughters of men that they were fair; and they took them wives of all which they choose,*
> *vs.3, And the LORD said, My Spirit shall not always strive with man, for that he also is flesh: yet his days shall be an hundred and twenty years."* **Genesis 6:1-3**

It is so very unfortunate these days that many men of God have become vessels of dishonour a disgrace to the gospel, as they leave their divine estate and purpose to chase after women of all calibers especially young and unmarried women, those whom the Lord put under their care to look after them spiritually.

Those who need spiritual help *[deliverance, healing, assistance in some areas of their lives]*, and those who need our prayers in the area of locating their second half; ministers take advantage of these ones in need to satisfy their insatiable sexual appetite: we see them as fringe benefits, lusting after them with impunity but God requires that which is past!

Please understand this fact, that I am not in any position to judge the behaviours of any man of God who fall into all kinds of sin including the sin of immorality, I'm just saying. Because many have become indifference to sin *"[... such fornication as is not so much as named among the Gentiles ...]"* it is better that we read it in full:

"It is reported commonly that there is fornication among you [ministers of the gospel, teachers and the rest that should have been at the point of no return in Christianity, including members of the house of faith] " ... and such fornication as is not so much as named among the Gentiles, that one should have his father's wife: vs.2, And ye are puffed up, and have not rather mourned, that he that hath done this deed might be taken away: from among you]." I Corinthians 6:1-2

One important thing we need to learn as ministers of God, as leaders in our churches or teachers of the **WORD** is that God always has a substitute. If God says He wants to use you as a vessel of honour, ***"[if God has anointed you to preach good tidings unto the meek, if He has called you to bind up the brokenhearted, to proclaim liberty to the captives and the opening of the prison to them that are bound, to pull down the strongholds of the enemy, to deliver the oppressed]."***

But instead of binding up their wounds or setting them free from being brokenhearted, we put them more in bondage, we take away their freedom; we see them especially the women among the flock as an advantage of a free supply, and we commit immorality with them; especially in the church of Jesus Christ: Breaking News! Even as He is choosing you, He has already prepared a substitute!

I Samuel 2:27-30 tells us about Eli the prophet of God in Israel. God chose Eli and his family to serve Him. God later changed His plans, since Eli honoured his children more than the God who called him and God only honours those who honour Him.

One thing about God's rejection is that the devil takes the place of the resultant vacuum that is created. This is what happened to King Saul. We also have the case of Judas Iscariot in **_John 13:26-27_**. He was a disciple of the Lord Jesus Christ. The moment God rejected him, Satan entered into him, and he ended up hanging himself. Psalm 75:6-7 tells us something interesting:

> *"For promotion cometh neither from the east, nor from the west, nor from the south. But God is the judge: He putteth down one, and setteth up another."*

Whenever God gives us an opportunity to serve Him, please let us humble ourselves in honour of Him who is the caller. It is better for God not to use us at all than to use us and then push us aside. Once He pushes one aside, this then gives room for the devil to come in. My prayer is that God will never substitute us with someone else.

The rejection of King Saul and his replacement by David; no one would have heard of David if King Saul had not lost his crown and position; just as nobody would have heard of Esther if Queen Vashti had not lost her position.

God has given us these examples so that we can learn lessons; God told Samuel to stop mourning over Saul because He had already rejected him. He told Samuel to fill his horn with oil and go anoint one of the sons of Jesse as king. Samuel said, Saul would kill him if he found out about his mission.

This is an interesting statement because it shows clearly that Saul; had degenerated so badly that he could kill a servant of God. It is a terrible thing to backslide. This is why we must never touch sin. We need to study the lives of the people that God rejected in the Bible so that we can learn one or two lessons from their cases.

We have to know what God saw in their lives to make Him reject them so we can run away from their mistakes. Why was Esau rejected? The Bible tells us in **Hebrews 12:15-1** that he was rejected because he could not control his appetite. I pray that our stomachs will not send us to hell. …… *[touch the accursed thing].* Some have never fasted since they became Christians. I pray that your appetite would not put you into trouble to the point where God would reject you in Jesus' name!

People of God, when it comes to the point that we watch the countenance of the congregation as ministers and teachers of the gospel, and we forced ourselves to pervert a message of warning, a message that will deliver, a message that will heal the entire congregation.

Or we fail to take a decisive action in the church and stay on it, lack of knowledge and ignorant of sound doctrine are reasons we are afraid to preach the truth, because we watch the countenance of the people just for one or two people *"who are always rebellious, who are always stiff necked both to God and to man,"* who might be angry and leave the church: We dishonour, and disobeyed God, we entertain fear of what man will do to us rather than how God will feel about our actions. The same reason is why we misbehave on the pulpit when we preach or teach error, we always want to preach what people will be comfortable with.

We are more concerned about some who may disagree and be angry at us and at our sermon, guess what? We neglect God in that instance, and He has no more pleasure in us: we missed it, and we grieved the Holy Spirit, Bible says *"grieve not the Holy Spirit:"* so He does not depart from us!

> *"But in a great house there are not only vessels of gold and of silver, but also of wood and of earth; and some to*

honour, and some to dishonour: <u>vs.21</u>, If a man therefore purge himself from these, he shall be a vessel unto honour, sanctified, and meet for the master's use, and prepared unto every good work." <u>II Timothy 2:20-21</u>

Either for honour or dishonour, everyone is born to fulfill a purpose. We are however responsible for the category of God's purpose we fulfill in His overall operations among men.

A man can also either help or hinder God's purpose for his life. For example, God's purpose for Samson was that he should deliver Israel from their oppressors; but tragically, the completion of his assignment depended on his moral discipline, which he ignored *[Judges 13:5]*.

John the Baptist is an example of a vessel unto honour. God spoke concerning him that he would convert many souls into the Kingdom; for this purpose, he was filled with the Holy Spirit right from his mother's womb: He did not have any opportunity to live a self-seeking life from childhood until his death because of the influence of the Holy Spirit upon him from the womb *[Luke 1:13-17]*.

Judas Iscariot however allowed himself to be used for the other side of the coin of divine purpose; he allowed himself to be used negatively to fulfill a divine purpose; that is, to betray the Saviour of mankind as it was ordained ages before he was born *[John 6:64]*.

In the same spiritual environment where Judas Iscariot was nurtured and turned out to be a thief and a betrayer, John the Beloved also was nurtured and became the most intimate disciple of the Lord *[John 13:23]*. Before you were born, God had a purpose for your life!

<u>Psalms 15:4b</u>, "<u>He that</u> sweareth to his own hurt, and changeth not."

- You keep your word even if it hurts you.

"<u>And Jephthah vowed</u> a vow unto the Lord, and said, If Thou shalt without fail deliver the children of Ammon into mine hands: <u>vs.31,</u> Then it shall be, that whatsoever cometh forth of the doors of my house to meet me, when I return in peace from the children of Ammon, shall surely be the Lord's, and I will offer it up for burnt offerings."

The Lord delivered. Without Him would Jephthah not have been successful? If he didn't make this commitment unto the Lord who knows; so, this will be seen in different areas:

#1. This tells me that God requires a great deal of commitment to Him before satisfying us with whatever we may be asking Him to do for us: it is a good thing to be committed in everything even in our walk with the Lord.

After the vow, the ***Spirit of the LORD*** empowered Jephthah for action. Remember, he committed his ways into the hand of the Most High then he had the confidence that the LORD was with him. He toured **Gilead** and **Manasseh** to muster his troops and headed out against the Ammonites. The Lord in turn gave him victory over the **Ammonites, from** *Aroer* **to** *Minnith* **and** *Abel-keramim "[the plain of the vineyards]"* **three towns that** defined the traditional border between Israel and Ammon. In between the empowerment and victory, though, there was an intervening episode that undermined Jephthah's triumph. Jephthah sought to ensure the Lord's favour by vowing to sacrifice as a whole burnt offering **whatsoever [or whoever]** greeted him after he had won the battle and obtained his victory.

Jephthah smote the Ammonites from a distance of ***30-40 miles; vs.32-33*** confirmed to us that he took ***20 cities***; let us not fool ourselves, it is not really free without your cooperation and commitment to the Lord. That is righteousness!

#2. It seems probable that Jephthah had a human sacrifice in mind, since animals do not normally come out to greet the returning troops. Just as he confused **Chemosh and Molech** in the previous section, so now he confused the Lord with Chemosh and Molech. The gods of the Moabites and Ammonites accepted human burnt offerings as a sign of total dedication *[II Kgs.3]*, but such offerings were an abomination to the Lord. The Lord would have delivered Israel anyway, even without Jephthah's rash vow.

[Verses 36-40]: Jephthah's daughter was very different from her father. She had no recriminations for him, only an exhortation to fulfill his vow, just as the Lord had fulfilled the conditions. Unlike Abraham, whose faithfulness to God's demand resulted in a multitude of descendants, Jephthah's **"faithfulness"** issued in the complete cutting off his line. This is part of what made the fact that she would die a virgin something to be mourned. She died unfulfilled because she would never get married and have children. Such a fate would normally condemn someone to be numbered among the unremembered Israelites. However, though Jephthah's daughter has no name in the text, the ***daughters of Israel*** honoured her memory year after year. The importance of a vow; the Bible says;

> *"When thou vowest a vow unto God, defer not to pay it; for he hath no pleasure in fools: pay that which thou hasth vowed.*
> *vs.5, Better is it that thou shouldest not vow, than that thou shouldest vow and not pay." Ecclesiastes 5:4-5*

> *"And the LORD shall be known to Egypt, and the Egyptians shall know the LORD in that day, and shall do sacrifice and oblation; yea, they shall VOW a vow unto the LORD, and perform it." Isaiah 19:21*

These passages deal with religious behavior, and it warns that we should not try to impress God *[or to say to bribe Him]*. First, positively, come to the ***house of God ready to hear***; negatively, don't try to impress God with big sacrifices and big vows, and then there is a proverb that a big dream and many words come from an overworked fool. Second, positively, fulfill your vow; negatively, don't make a vow you cannot keep; and then a proverb, many *dreams and many words* are futile, so it is better to fear God. The foundation of these teachings is our mortality: **God is in heaven and thou upon earth**. Because we are weak, small and prone to fail, we should give up on trying to impress God with vows, gifts, and promises we cannot keep. We cannot impress Him: our place is to be humble and obedient. These texts call on us to depend on the grace of God and not our religious deeds.

> *"Thus, saith the LORD of hosts, the God of Israel, saying; Ye and your wives have both spoken with your mouths, and fulfilled with your hand, saying, We will surely perform our VOWs that we have VOWed, to burn incense to the queen of heaven, and to pour our drink offerings unto her: ye will surely perform your Vows."* <u>Jeremiah 44:25</u>.

Jeremiah took up a second point in the rebels' argument-that they must be faithful to their vows *[vs.17]*. His response was ironic, if not sarcastic: *"ye will surely accomplish your vows."* Jeremiah must have had in *mind [42:4-6]*, where the people vowed to do whatever the Lord commanded. How could they keep vows to a pagan idol when they could not even keep their vows to the Living God?

We know what I am saying, and we know what prophet Jeremiah is saying here; can we go to **the herbalists, the magicians, the stargazers or the sorcerers**, to give them an assignment of what we want with the promise that we will do this and not perform what we said we would do or pay their charges? With some wicked ones, I don't think we will stay alive to enjoy that thing, but we take God for granted and eat our vows after we received what we asked of the Lord with a vow.

> *"Behold upon the mountains the feet of him that bringeth good tidings, that publisheth peace! O Judah, keep thy solemn feasts, perform thy VOWs: for the wicked shall no more pass through thee; he is utterly cut off."* <u>Nahum 1:15</u>

> *"__He that__ sweareth to his own hurt, and changeth not."*
> __Psalms 15:4b__

- We do the same with people, we take advantage of people in need to increase ourselves both in riches and otherwise what do I mean *'otherwise'* we pull other people down to gain favour, or to promote yourself. That is selfishness, Bible says for us to esteem others than ourselves. We know what will benefit others, but because of envy and jealousy, we withhold such a thing so the person doesn't get richer than us, we say, *"so if I do this, it will be to his credit or advantage, he will now be promoted], what about me?"*

We're not righteous, we're not working the work of righteousness and we're not walking in love. When we have a need when there is *[fire on our roof top or fire on the mountain]* and its more than what we can handle, we begin to look for prayer contractors, we begin to look for firefighters who can pray and get results, even when we don't belong anywhere and *are still shopping for a perfect church;* it is then we will remember the servant of God somewhere or in our local churches, we will charge them with our prayer requests, the man or the woman of God may fast, dedicate themselves, and pray for us but when we get results and the prayers are answered, we don't show up any more, cunningly we will dodge and disappear, we will hide our face so as not to share from what the Lord has allowed into our hands, we will not remember God nor pay tithes to our local assembly; not even to testify so people don't know. We are men-users and God has no respect for users; Bible says, God has no pleasure nor has regard for fools; we are not truthful we have no integrity; we have no honour. But we can change!

> *"[And thou shalt take no gift: for the gift blindeth the wise, and perverteth the words of the righteous." __Exodus 23:8__]*

- You refuse to take bribes. Among many references that speak about gifts and bribes, let's just take this verse of the Book of Samuel and ponder over it, for all it says here concerns, taking of bribes and gifts; Samuel called the people to bring before God and the new king any charges against Samuel's integrity. Samuel wished to settle any wrongs publicly, with God and Saul as his witnesses, before all the people; as we've often seen in the Bible that *"bribes, gifts doth blinded the eyes to pervert justice:"*

"Behold here I am: witness against me before the LORD, and before His anointed: whose ox have I taken? Or whose ass have I taken? or whom have I defrauded? Who have I oppressed? Or of whose hand have I received bribe to blind mine eyes therewith? And I will restore it to you." I Samuel 12:3

- Someone who protects the innocent. Listen to this because they all go together:

"Thou shalt neither vex the stranger, nor oppress him: for ye were strangers in the land of Egypt: vs.22, Ye shall not afflict any widow, or fatherless child: vs.23, If thou afflict them in any wise, and they cry unto me, I will surely hear their cry; vs.24, and my wrath shall wax hot, and I will kill you with the sword; and your wives shall be widows, and your children fatherless." I Samuel 22:21-24

The Israelites *[as well as ourselves, for we are the spiritual Israelites of today]* **were to** remember who they were and their mistreatment in Egypt, and they were to remember that the Lord would take action on behalf of the powerless and vulnerable members of the society. The word translated *'oppress'* in *[verse 21 and 23:9]* is used in *[3:9]* to describe what prompted the Israelites to call out for help. They needed to avoid putting themselves in the position of the Egyptians. The mention of pledge *[collateral]* consisting of a garment needed for warmth at night shows that the loan involved helping a poverty-stricken person survive. No luxury or business venture is in view.

GRACE:

G .... God's
R .... Response
A .... At
C .... Christ's
E .... Expense

Let me tell us in my little knowledge what I think and know that 'grace is all about: *[I say in my little knowledge and judgment, so don't put me on trial here]:* And we are going to use <u>***Ephesians 2***</u> as our text on this most important aspect of our calling because many people, including ministers pastors, teachers, name us all, mislead on grace! So we must first read all of <u>***Ephesians 2:1-22***</u>, but before then, pray and ask the Holy Spirit who is our Best Teacher to reveal to us the secret behind the written Words of God, then READ <u>***Ephesians 2***</u>!

Now I know what you're saying, ***"Pastor, if that is the case, I am human, how can I be perfect, in all of these when God says, His grace is there for us?"*** Well God knows that the *'grace'* is there, like I said that we lie on *'grace'* He also know that we can hide behind this game of *grace* to be so unrighteous, the women married and unmarried can go to their churches half-naked, exposing all the contours of their bodies, too tight for comfort kind of dresses to cause men to fall, they dress like Jezebels with transparent attires to seduce men, to sit in front of the preachers' first pews with short dresses and open their legs, women who can ***spread their legs*** under any tree, men who can go after anything in skirts; many who are ***gold plated*** sinners, they punish the innocent, they pervert justice, knowing all to be sinful and claim a stand on *'grace.'*

This is what <u>***Rom.6:1***</u> is addressing with another serious question that is defining grace which <u>***vs.2***</u>, answers abruptly, <u>***"God forbid."***</u> Then, it continues with another question directed to us in affirmation of the question in <u>***vs.1***</u>, *"How shall we, that <u>are dead</u> to sin, live any longer therein?"* ***"Dead to sin,"*** that's the grace; meaning we're not **_'living therein,'_** we cannot live in sin anymore, that is **_'grace,'_** if we are hiding behind grace and laying claim to the so called 'eternal security:' we shall not be innocent; again, one has to meet the conditions of **_vs.2-5_** of **_Psalms 15_** to go to God's Tabernacle and 'Dwell' and 'Abide' with Him forever!

Ephesians 2, we are going to take **_verses 5-10_**: as our text into this **_'Mystery of Grace'_** as we become partakers of the same!

> *"Even when we are dead in sins, hath quickened us together with Christ, [by grace yea are saved]:*
> *__vs.6__, And hath raised us up together, and made us sit together in heavenly places in Christ Jesus:"*
> *__vs.7__, that in ages to come He might shew the exceeding riches of His grace in His kindness toward us through Christ Jesus:*
> *__vs.8__, For by grace are ye saved through faith; and that not of yourselves: it is the gift of God:*
> *__vs.9__, Not of works, lest any man should boast.*
> *__vs.10__, For we are His workmanship, created in Christ Jesus unto good works, which God hath before ordained that we should walk in them."*

Verses 1-6 *[read from all versions of the Bible you can lay your hands on]*:

Paul drew contrasts between the human condition described in *[verses 1-3 and the new life in verses 4-6]*.

Old Life:	**_New Life_:**
We were dead:	*Now we are alive:*
We were enslaved:	*Now we are enthroned:*
We were objects of wrath:	*Now we are objects of grace:*
We walked among the disobedient:	*Now we fellowship with Christ:*
We were under Satan's dominion:	*Now we are in Union with Christ:*

Trespasses are lapses; *sins* are shortcomings. Apart from Christ, people are without authentic spiritual life. In this state the most vital part of the human personality is *dead*, thus people cannot by their own efforts or ingenuity experience fellowship with God or meet His requirements.

This world is associated with the realm of Satan. the way of life without Christ is in accordance with Satan's ways.

The Greek word translated *conversation* is a different term from the one in *verse 2* translated *"walked,"* though the idea is similar. *"To have conversation"* means to turn to and fro and behave in accordance with certain principles.

Apart from Christ, people are dominated fleshly *lusts*, an orientation away from God toward self-concerns. the plural suggests multiple unredeemed urges in our life apart from Christ. The unredeemed person is completely at the mercy of the tyrannical self and its lustful impulse. The fall into sin described in *[Genesis 3]* was not merely a moral lapse but a deliberate turning away from God in rejection of Him. Sin's entrance brought about a sinful nature in all humanity; men and women are *by nature* hostile to God and estranged from Him. While functioning as free moral agents, sin always negatively influences human decisions and actions. People do not genuinely repent or turn to God apart from divine enablement *[Eph.2:5]*.

Over against the human rejection of God, Paul painted a picture of the new life manifested in God's gracious acceptance of sinners because of Christ. *But God* marks a strong contrast, pointing to God's answer to people's dreadful situation. *Mercy* is God's compassion for the helpless that relieves their situation. While *'grace'* involves God giving believers the blessings *[not to continue sinning]* but blessings they do not deserve. Paul extends his thoughts from *verse 1*, which are viewed in retrospect from the vantage point of redemptive history. Because of God's great love, He made us alive *with Christ*.

God's loving mercy not only makes new life possible, but by it, God has *raised us up* and seated us *in heavenly places*, God's great power has enthroned us with Christ, even as Christ was exalted to God's right hand following the resurrection: here is the implicative question:

[Do we know, after He seated us in heavenly places with Him still commit sin and claim grace? after our enthronement with Christ, can we remain on the throne with Him after sinning presumptuously and now say to Him, "Jesus, I am back after taking a leave from the throne to do my thing to now reclaim my throne?"]

Somebody please explain to ourselves what **Hebrews 10:26-27** underneath is talking about, because to me and to many of us, this looks like *'Punishment For willful Sin:* this I also believe, is talking about sins committed after we are born again and have received the grace to be kings and queens through Christ; or is the grace still standing even when we are unrepented?

> *"For if we sin willfully after that we have received the knowledge of the truth, there remaineth no more sacrifice for sins:*
> *vs.27, But a certain fearful looking for judgment and fiery indignation, which shall devour the adversaries.]"*

<u>Verses 7-10</u>:

The work of reconciliation in these verses is described with four keys terms.
1. **"Kindness"** God's loving action
2. **"Grace"** God's free favour toward ill-deserving people *[a favourite term of the apostles, used over 100 times in his letter]*.
3. **"Saved"** equated with new life, forgiveness of sins, deliverance from the plight described in *verses [1-3]*, liberation, and resurrection:
4. **"Faith"** the instrument that brings us empty handed to God *[see Romans 10:12] read!*

The salvation of men and women is a display of divine *'grace.'* God did all this through Christ with a single goal in view: the exhibition of His divine favour for all of history to see, including angels as well as people *[I Peter 1:10-12]*. The work of salvation is for God's glory and is not accomplished by human works. The whole process of salvation is not a human achievement but is an act of God's goodness. The emphasis is always on Christ, the object of faith, not on the amount of faith. Salvation is by God's completely unmerited favour.

In the Greek text, the grammatical construction of the entire phrase *'by grace ... through faith'* serves as the antecedent of the phrase *'the gift of God.'* We must not portray grace as God's part and faith as our part, for all of salvation is a gift from God and must be referenced, *[respected]!* The work of reconciliation is *'not of ourselves'* and *'not of works.'* This prevents the slightest self-congratulation of boasting in the believer. God alone saves!

The work of salvation is a display of divine *'workmanship'*. **Good works** are the fruit of our salvation, not the cause of it. Also, good works are not incidental to God's plan; they are instead an essential part of His redemption plan for each believer. Good works are demonstrated in gratitude, character and actions.

Verses 11-22: 'Reconciled unto Christ'

This action of Paul's letter touches on three states of being for the recipients.
1. Their former corporate condition apart from Christ: *[vs.11-13]*.
2. Their corporate reconciliation in Christ: *[vs.14-18]*.
3. Their new standing as members of God's new humanity: *[vs.19-22]*.

The theme of this entire section is reconciliation, which involves bringing fallen humanity out of alienation into a state of peace and harmony with God, Jesus, as Reconciler, heals the separation and brokenness created by sin and restores communion between

God and people. Reconciliation is not a process by which people gradually become more acceptable to God but a decisive act *[like a legal verdict]* by which believers are delivered from estrangement to fellowship with God.

Verses 11-12:
Not only were the **'Gentiles'** morally separated from God *[vs.1-3]*, but they were also separated from God's covenant people. They were **without** any knowledge of Christ. They had no rights in God's family and were not recipients of God's **covenant**. They were without hope and ultimately **'without God.'** Paul did not reproach the Gentiles for their plight; he merely recorded the sad truth of the matter.

Verse 13:
Paul used the strong transitional phrase **but now** to point to the Gentiles' new relationship to God. The Gentile believers no longer were in their alienated state. They knew Christ, took part in God's covenant blessings, and hope and fellowship with God. This remarkable turnaround took place **in Christ Jesus**. Those who trust in Him have a present salvation and a future hope.

Verses 14-16: **'Christ Our Peace'**

This passage emphasizes the centrality of Jesus Christ in bringing Gentiles and Jews together, not only with one another but also with God. Christ is both our peace and **our** Peacemaker. His reconciling death on the cross has made the two-Jews and Gentiles-into **one**. Gentiles do not become Jews, but the two groups become one at a deeper level than ethnicity, forming Christ's church. God has torn down **the middle wall of partition** and removed the hatred forever. By **"wall"** Paul likely had in mind the area in the Jerusalem temple that separated the court of the Gentiles from the temple.

The temple was constructed on an elevated platform. Around it was the court of priests. East of this was the court of Israel. Farther east was the court of women. These three courts were all on the same elevation as the temple. From here a walled platform was five steps away. Fourteen steps away was another wall, which was the outer court of the Gentiles. There was an inscription on this wall warning Gentiles of their ensuing death if they entered the enclosure around the temple. In Christ this dividing wall was broken down, thus banishing the specific *commandments* that separated Jews from Gentiles.

The burden of the commandments was taken away at the cross in our Lord's crucified body. The goal was not merely to reconcile two groups but to reconcile *them unto God*. The *one body* is the church, the new humanity, the place of peace. At the cross, everything that caused the *enmity* was destroyed.

Verses 17-22: 'Christ Our Cornerstone:'

The Gentiles are afar off *[vs.12]* and the Jews *that were nigh* both were reconciled to God in Christ.
The imagery is of a court official who conducts visitors into the king's presence. Through Christ's reconciling work, *both* Jews and Gentiles *have access* to God's Presence.

Verse 19:
Strangers means short-term transients nonresidents with no rights. *Foreigners* is similar word, pointing to resident aliens who had settled permanently in the country of their choice but who nevertheless had only limited rights. These terms described the Gentiles' position. Now they enjoy all privileges of God's *household*, implying togetherness and inclusion. Believers are adopted into God's family and are united with the saints of every era-past, present and future.

Verse 20:
God's new family is not only a new nation, but also a new building. *The apostles and prophets* in their unique relationship to Christ, exemplified by the authoritative teachings they communicated to the church, are the *foundation*. Paul proclaimed Christ Jesus as the *'Chief Cornerstone'* of the foundation, a capstone that holds and entire structure together. In ancient structures it had the royal name

inscribed on it to signify the ruler who took credit for the building's construction.

Verses 21-22:

The description conveys the idea of a dynamic church in the process of growing. The major theme of union with Christ reappears: God's **habitation** is not the Jerusalem temple but, in the Church, which is accomplished by the work of the *'Holy Spirit'* who indwells the new believing community.

Having been reconciled to the Father through the Lord Jesus Christ our Saviour should we now and again put ourselves back into slavery becoming slaves to sin by going back to our vomit, did we ever see it in the Bible that Jesus Christ has to die the second time and go through all of the above glorious work again in order to bring back the backsliders that are astray who backslides into sin? He did the great work for us to remain within and not without *"How can we who are dead to sin thereby live in it?"*

> *Vs.1, "LORD, who shall abide in THY tabernacle? Who shall dwell in THY HOLY Hill?*
> *Vs.2, He that walketh uprightly, and worketh righteousness, and speaketh the truth in his heart.*
> *Vs.3, He that backbiteth not with his tongue, nor doeth evil to his neighbour, nor taketh up a reproach against his neighbour.*
> *Vs.4, In whose eyes a vile person is contemned; but he honoureth them that fear the LORD. He that sweareth to his own hurt, and changeth not."*

God is asking for perfection of man, because of what we stand to enjoy and gain from Him, because of the blessings of His hands, because of the Abrahamic covenant. He knows we can do it; we can be perfect before Him and in Him in everything even when it comes to pleasing Him, we can if, and when we want. May the Good Lord help and perfect us in Jesus Mighty Name. Amen!

CHAPTER FIVE

THE ADONAI - *The LORD My Great GOD:*
The Master and majestic LORD. GOD, our Total Authority!

PSALMS 15:5

Vs.5, "He that putteth not out his money to usury, nor taketh reward against the innocent. He that doeth these things shall never be moved."

4 commands to Be Perfect:

First to Abraham in ***Gen.17:1***: God appeared unto Abraham when he was ninety-nine years old! What does God want from a ninety-nine-year-old man almost 100 years old? Yet God told him He said:

"I am the almighty God, walk before me and be thou perfect!"

It was the 5th of God's appearance to Abraham, but this time He has a purpose in mind, God wants to bless Abraham, God wants to establish the Abrahamic covenants with Abraham which was why He re-affirmed to Abraham as saying, *"I am the Almighty God:"* meaning, *'El Shaddai,' El, signifies 'The Strong One.' and Shaddai, 'The Breasted One.'*

This pictures God, as the *'Strong-Nourisher,' 'The Strength Giver,' 'The Satisfier,' and All Bountiful, The Supplier of the needs of His people!* Its first occurrence here reveals God as *'The Fruitful-One'* Who was to multiply Abraham abundantly!

'The Life-Giver' Who was to restore life to Abraham and Sarah who were as good as dead, as far as off-spring was concerned. Through Him, they were to have future off-spring as the dust: that was God's Promise to Abraham in **Gen.13:16**, and in **Gen.22:17**: because of all Abraham stands to gain if he obeys the LORD or lose if he refuses to hearken to the Lord, same is us.

> *He says, "And I will make thy seed as the dust of the earth: so that if a man can number the dust of the earth, then shall thy seed also be numbered!"*

That is after we pleased God with perfection, that is the condition for us to come into this inheritance; and so, if we're asking God for blessing or for the desires of our heart to be met, He also requires something, please note, it is our inheritance, it is what He wants for us, but we have to please Him!

> *In <u>Gen.22:17</u>, He says, "That in Blessing I will bless thee," "but you must satisfy Me in perfection;" "and in multiplying, I will multiply thy seed as the stars of the heaven, and as the sand which is upon the sea shore; and thy seed shall possess the gates of their enemies:" "but fulfill My requirements!"*

Brief note on *'<u>Genesis 22:15-18</u>:'* [read the reference], As the angel [meaning the "messenger"] of the LORD who had the Lord's authority, the divine emissary delivered a second message *[vs.12]*, this one in the first person. Because Abraham had passed the "priorities test" by obeying God and not withholding his *'only son'*, the LORD would indeed *bless him* with offspring, victory, land, and goodwill. Since there is nothing greater, God swears by Himself **[Exo.32:13; Isa.45:23; Jer.22:5;9:13]**. Ironically, since Abraham was willing to accept the loss of his covenant offspring. God would make those offspring as numerous *"as the stars of the heaven, and as the sand which is upon the seashore."*

They would ***possess*** each fortified city ***gate*** and thus the cities of their ***enemies***, a promise of both military victory and expanded territory. But more than being feared as conquerors. Abraham's offspring would be recognized as a fountainhead of blessing for ***all the nations of the earth.***

And so, in order for you Abraham to be qualified for all of the mentioned blessings and promises, you must walk in righteousness, you must be ***"perfect before 'Me:"*** these are the qualifications and the requirements for Abraham; it's the same thing that God wants from us as His children to be able to come into the Abrahamic covenant; well, you say, how can I, seeing that I am human.

Well, God would not have required your perfection if it were not possible for man to walk perfectly before Him, God would not have charged Abraham to appear as such if it isn't impossible. The standard of Holiness and perfection was no higher under the Abrahamic covenant than it is under the new covenant. If God could help Abraham to be perfect, could He not also help believers in Christ today to be the same?

<u>Second command to be perfect</u>: To Israel it says in **<u>Deut.18:13</u>**:

"Thou shalt be perfect with the Lord thy God:" perfection here to Israel simply means to refrain from all these pagan practices of **<u>vs.9-14</u>**:

> ***"When thou art come into the land which the LORD thy God giveth thee, thou shalt not learn to do after the abominations of those nations:***
> **<u>vs.10</u>**, ***There shall not be found among you anyone that maketh his son or his daughter to pass through fire, or that useth divination, or an observer of times, or an enchanter, or a witch:***
> **<u>vs.11</u>**, ***Or a charmer, or a consulter with familiar spirits, or a wizard, or a necromancer.***

> ***vs.12,*** *For all that do these things are an abomination unto the LORD: and because of these abominations the LORD thy God doth drive them out from before thee:*
> ***vs.13,*** *Thou shalt be perfect with the LORD thy God.*
> ***vs.14,*** *For these nations, which thou shalt possess, hearkened unto observers of times, and unto diviners: but as for thee, the LORD thy God hath not suffered thee so to do."*

Abominations refers to anything, especially of a religious nature, that is offensive to the Lord We as the children of God must not imitate these practices that were characteristic of paganism because we have been chosen from among the nations to show a better way *[Exo.19:5-6; Lev.18:1-5; Deut.7:6]*. To pass through the fire was to offer human sacrifice. *[you say, "but that was in the old times,]"* No, it still happens in our days, even in Christendom, we see people *'sneak'* out of the church to consult with pagan gods, politicians in the third world who claim to be Christians but have no knowledge of the Word, no sound doctrine, they engage in fetish things and commit all kinds of abominations because of power.

Divination, the consulting of natural phenomena such as animal entrails, smoke formations, oil slicks, and the like, was undertaken to determine the plans and purposes of the gods before they happened. ***Familiar spirits*** were another way of referring to necromancy, the *"science"* of inquiring of the dead *[I Samuel 28:3,9; Isaiah 8:19]*. All such things are essential to religious systems that have no concept of divine revelation. Having no other means of knowing the future, they attempt to elicit this knowledge by forbidden means. A major reason for the expulsion and destruction of the Canaanites nations is that they practiced ***these abominations*** and were therefore likely to infect God's people with their detestable customs *[7:14]*.
In the context of this verses to be perfect with the LORD was to avoid all the pagan practices outlined in *[verses '10 and 11]*. "Perfect" refers not to sinless perfection but to the avoidance of all that the Lord detests.

Third Command from Solomon:

> In <u>*I Kgs.8:61*</u>, *"Let your heart therefore be perfect with the Lord our God, to walk in His statutes, and to keep His commandments, as at this day."*

The result of this faithfulness brings us again to the major theme of the Old Testament's missions-that all the people of the earth may know that the LORD is God. With these words, Solomon made a worldwide mission proclamation: Our hearts must be undivided with the Lord our God; not divided between Jehovah and other gods, but wholly devoted to God, but too bad Solomon himself made this proclamation to the Israelites, had he himself not failed in doing this, his kingdom would have been established forever.

"Who Shall Abide, Who shall Dwell:" when we're **'Abiding' and Dwelling,"** means, it will make a whole lot of difference in our lives; it reestablished us in the Abrahamic Covenant, we enjoy the heaven on earth; everything we ever wanted will be at our disposal because we are 'Abiding' and 'Dwelling' with the Father in His tabernacle.

In <u>*Ps.24:3-4*</u>, **it says:**

> *"Who shall ascend into the Hill of the Lord? or who shall stand in His Holy Place?" This Holy Place refers to the Capital Building of Christ: <u>vs.4</u> says, "He that hath clean hands, and a pure heart: who hath not lifted his soul unto vanity, nor sworn deceitfully."*

The use of rhetorical questions about those who are worthy to enter into Jehovah's Presence: it says here:

> *"[.... he that hath clean hands and a pure heart]"*

To be honest in our hearts, can we seriously say that we have clean hands, and our hearts are pure in all of what we've discussed from *'Chapter One'* of this book, it is the same thing we are looking into in *Psalms 15*; can we say that we are innocent and that our integrity is impeccable? Like it says in *[Psalms 73:13, "Verily I have cleansed my heart in vain, and washed my hands in innocency]"* because washing hands was part of an oath of innocency: are we clean both in our hearts and in our deeds; how do we react when other people step on our toes, how do we handle things that have to do with another person; do we speak truthfully when we're in a spot? Speaking truthfully also means that we don't back out of something that we know we're involved in and quickly push it on someone else because we are smart, and the other fellow is gentle.

> <u>*Psalms 15:2,*</u> *<u>He that</u> walketh uprightly, and worketh righteousness, and speaketh the truth in his heart.*
> <u>*Vs.3,*</u> *<u>He that</u> backbiteth not with his tongue, nor doeth evil to his neighbour, nor taketh up a reproach against his neighbour"*

[Meaning we don't use the name of the Lord to endorse our insincerity] that is what it meant by 'sworn deceitfully:' when we have issues with another person or at our place of work, even in the house of God, when we are in a situation and in order to get out of whatever it is, we tell lies, not only that, we swear deceitfully and we use God's name when we know we're lying, it is an abomination unto the Lord!

Fourth Command to Be Perfect:

> *"Finally, brethren, farewell: Be perfect, be of good comfort, be of one mind, live in peace; and the God of love and peace shall be with you."* <u>*II Cor.13:11*</u>

To all Christians, to you and I; this is a *'six-fold parting admonition'* to the Corinthians from Paul, for the Corinthians to remain perfect with the lord and with each other in Christ: to be of good comfort sharing with one another, fellowshipping with one another: to deal with one another with one mind and not with deceit: *"and the God of love and of peace shall be with you:"* Listen, this is not an after death encounter, it applies to the quality of life we live here on earth; there are enough of problems on planet earth that we need to be abiding and dwelling in His pavilion to be able to live a victorious life.

David was asking God a question, he addressed God by His first name **'JEHOVAH'** before throwing the question at Him:

"Who shall abide in Thy Tabernacle?"

Here, David is asking for trouble because God has to tell David as well as telling us the conditions to be met before one can 'dwell and abide' with Him. ***"Okay, David, you want to know, you really, really want to know David?"*** But first let's ask us a question:

What kind of tabernacle or which of the tabernacles are we talking about here? Because we haven't really seen or heard about this Tabernacle in question; there are many kinds of tabernacles which we will see in this study.

The tabernacle referred to here surely "The Tabernacle and Holy Hill no doubt refers to the Heavenly Mt. Zion and the City of God, the New Jerusalem where God lives! *Liars cannot dwell there, Adulterers and adulteresses cannot dwell there, fornicators cannot dwell there, deceivers cannot dwell there, gossips and those who give false witness cannot dwell there, angry people cannot dwell there!*

["Sing A Worship Song Here:"] Are You Ready?

> <u>Heb.12:22-24</u> says, "<u>But ye are come unto Mount Sion</u>, and unto the City of The Living God, The heavenly Jerusalem, and to an innumerable company of Angels."
> <u>Vs.23</u>, "To the General assembly and Church of the Firstborn, which are written in Heaven, and to God The Judge of all, and to The Spirits of 'just men' <u>made perfect</u>!"

***Vs.24**, "<u>And to</u> Jesus The Mediator of the new covenant, and to The Blood of sprinkling, that speaketh <u>better things</u> than that of Abel."*

People of God, have we read about the Place we're talking about, or should we be looking for another? This is the place all Christians desires, this should be a place of our focus as children of God doing everything, we can with God the Father helping us and perfecting us.

Now, giving the explanation and the account of where David was asking about as said, should we be any different from being perfect? Should we be deep in sin hiding behind and, misquoting the meaning of grace and then expect to go to this place, should we not be walking in love, should we be filthy at all and expect to dwell and abide in this Holy Place, The Habitation of The Almighty? Absolutely not! So, think again!

The Bible did mention here *and in all of our study from the start of this book* the kind of perfection that is perfected by grace when He says, *"and to The Spirits of 'just men' made perfect!"* because we will be mocking God hiding behind grace to perpetuate evil, meaning to continue in sin indefinitely.

> ***<u>Rev.14:1</u>**, "And I looked, and, lo, <u>A Lamb</u> stood on the <u>Mount Sion</u>, and <u>with Him</u> an hundred forty and four thousand <u>having</u> His Father's name written <u>in</u> their foreheads:" The abiding, the dwellers!*

If you notice at the end of this verse what it says, *"having the Father's name written '<u>in</u>' their foreheads:"* the same are those who belong to the devil, Satan, the beast will receive his mark or have the mark of the beast *written '<u>in</u>' their foreheads*: same pattern as you see in this verse below:

> *"And he causeth all, both small and great, rich and poor, free and bond, to receive the mark in their right hand, or in their foreheads." <u>Rev.13:16</u>*

Who Is A Perfect Man? Who Is A Perfect Woman?

[Read all references]:
Please note: this Mount Sion is the heavenly one, that is why it is spelled differently starts with 'S' while the other Mount starts with 'Z.'

The scene described here from ***vs.1-5*** is heavenly; the ***144.000*** mentioned here are the *'man-child'* referred to in ***Rev.12:5; Rev.7&14***.

Also, for our information, the Earthly Mt. Zion which starts with a **'Z'** is not mentioned in all of the Book of Revelation, everything here is heavenly!

There are several kinds of tabernacles, and in probably some of these 7 tabernacles, we can apply grace to dwell there but honestly, not the kind of Tabernacle the Book of ***Hebrew 12:22-24*** describes no, definitely not the same; for us to be able to dwell and abide in this Holy Tabernacle, demands for perfection, righteousness and purity.

Here in ***Mat.17:4***; and ***Mk.9:5***, there is this kind of a temporary dwellings which is the preview of the coming Kingdom 'The Mount of Transfiguration;'

> ***"Then answered Peter and said unto Jesus, <u>Lord</u>, it is good for us to be here: if Thou wilt, let us make here three tabernacles; one for Thee, and one for Moses, and one for Elias."***

Supposing this is the end of the journey, the much talked about Kingdom as thought by Peter: but this is just the beginning, because Jesus knew where He is taking all believers, so He couldn't settle for less, the goal is the Presence of God the Father who sent Him to the earth to Rapture His people ....

- Second is 'the tabernacle of Moloch,' Israel's rejection of God because of continued rebellion as in ***Jgs.2:11-14*** and in ***Amos 5:25-27*** and God gave them to their reprobate minds, they turned away from God to make a calf to represent their god.

Bible says in <u>Acts 7:42-44</u>, "Then God turned, and gave them up to worship the host of heaven as it is written in the book of the prophets, 'O ye house of Israel, have ye offered to me slain beasts and sacrifices by the space of forty years in the wilderness?"

"Yea, ye took up the tabernacle of Moloch, and the star of your god Remphan, figures which ye made to worship them: and I will carry you away beyond Babylon:" "Our fathers had the tabernacle of witness in the wilderness, as had appointed, speaking unto Moses, that he should make it according to the fashion that he had seen."

- Third, the Bible talks about another tabernacle in the Book of **_Acts 15:16_**, which is like what is described to us in Hebrews; this also is talking about after the completion of the church age and after the rapture of the church.

God will begin to rebuild the nation of Israel getting it ready for the eternal reign of the Messiah and setting up the kingdom of David again when Christ returns. ***Hosea 3:4-5, Isa.9:6-7;***

"For unto us a Child is born, unto us a Son is given."

Not a daughter, for man and not woman was given the responsibility of headship and source of the race; so, it took a man to fulfill the responsibility of the redemption of the race-a-man born of a woman and called the seed of the woman. *[Gen.3:14]:* Thus, man and woman played a part in redemption; but the Redeemer Himself, had to be a man born of a woman to fulfill prophesy and meet God's demand. What is God's demand .... for us to be able to answer the great question of man "Who shall dwell, who shall abide:" that again is what we're looking at.

JESUS AND ATONEMENT IN THE OLD TESTAMENT:
[Please read all references in this Colum:]

The word *"atonement"* occurs frequently in the Old Testament and represents a key concept of Old Testament theology. Christians maintain that Jesus is the fulfillment of the Old Testament, especially the human need for atonement for sin. But what is atonement, and what does Jesus have to do with it?

Many Christians think atonement in the Old Testament originated with the Mosaic law, but in reality, humans recognized their need for atonement long before the time of Moses. When Adam and Eve committed the first sin, they hid themselves from God because they were ashamed *[Genesis 3:8]*. Rather than giving them up as hopeless, God initiated a plan of atonement whereby the ruptured fellowship between Himself and humanity could be restored. Our English word *"atonement" [at-one-ment]* explains well the theology behind such restoration, for it suggests that God and humanity can relationally be *"at one"* again.

How does atonement work? The first *[indirect]* Old Testament reference to atonement occurs when God provided animal skins to cover Adam and Eve's nakedness, and act necessitating the death of a sinless animal and hence the shedding of its blood on their behalf *[Genesis 3:21]*. This introduces a theme that runs throughout the Bible: atonement involves an innocent party taking the punishment that was due to a guilty party.

The Hebrew word translated *"atonement"* is *kaphar*, **meaning *"to cover."*** This suggests that through the act of atonement sin is covered so that God no longer sees it. Throughout the Old Testament the covering is achieved, ostensibly at least, with the blood of an innocent animal whose innocence renders the repentant sinner innocent as well *[Leviticus 1:4-5; 17:11]*. The New Testament term *hilasterion, "propitiation,"* continues this Old Testament concept, again in contexts of blood sacrifice *[Romans 3:25]*.

What does any of these have to do with Jesus? While animals served as provisional sacrifice for human sins during the Old Testament era, they could not ultimately atone for humans *[Hebrews 10:4]*. Humanity needed one of their own, one who knew no sin, to stand in and take the punishment that is due to all sinners. **Genesis 3:15** gives the first prophetic glimpse at God's final solution to this need and hints at the central role Jesus plays in that solution. speaking ultimately of Jesus and His role in redemption, it asserts that the seed of the woman would be bruised, but that He would in turn bruise the head of the serpent *[the devil]*, achieving victory over sin and death. The bruising mentioned here is reminiscent of the bruising experienced by the Suffering Servant in *Isaiah 52:13-53:12*, a passage that has atonement as its central theme.

Jesus Christ is both the subject and fulfillment of Isaiah's prophecy. In the events that unfolded during His trial, crucifixion, and resurrection, Jesus was the Suffering Servant on our behalf. Though innocent of all sin, Jesus stood in our place to take our punishment, shedding His Blood to atone for us. *"Neither by the blood of goats and calves, but by His own Blood He entered in once into the Holy place, having obtained eternal redemption for us [Hebrews 9:12]. "By the sacrifice of Himself" [Hebrews 9:26]* Jesus satisfied God's wrath against sin. That Old Testament atonement finds its culmination in Jesus Christ is put beyond question by John the Baptist who, seeing Jesus, proclaimed, *"Behold the Lamb of God, which taketh away the sin of the world" [John 1:29]*.

Jesus Christ is the Redeemer, Jesus Christ is the Reconciler who has come to reconcile us back to God, because the Bible says in *Psalms 51:5:*

> *"Behold, I was shapen in iniquity; and in sin did my mother conceived me]."*

We have the nature of sin, and sin cannot 'Dwell and Abide' with the Father of Spirits, Jesus Christ's role in our redemption is what we should be clinging to and trusting in, that is the grace He has brought to us, to remain in Him is to *'flee'* according to God's laws, deliberate and premeditated sins of all kinds such as adultery and murder, these were referred to as sins of *"the high hand" "[presumptuously" in Numbers 15:30-31]. Their punishment was being "cut off"* from the community, which in many cases meant death. Jesus came and dominion was given unto Him, and glory, and a kingdom that all people, nations and languages, should serve Him, know His doctrines, understand the rules, let Him be the ruler in all of our lives, by these, as we have Him in us and we in Him, He will perfect us to be able to 'Dwell and Abide with the Father; it can never be by our works no matter how much we try we can only be perfect in Him!

> *"I saw in the night visions, and behold, One like the Son of Man came with the clouds of heaven, and came to the Ancient of Days, and they brought Him near Him:*
> *<u>vs.14</u>, And there was given Him dominion, and glory, and a kingdom, that all people, nations, and languages, should serve Him: His dominion is an everlasting dominion, which shall not pass away, and His kingdom that which shall not be destroyed."* <u>Dan. 7:13-14</u>

Although some have maintained that the Son of Man is the archangel Michael or a collective personification of the "saints of the Most High" [vs.18], this ONE is none other than the Divine Messiah Himself, who will fulfill the destiny of humanity [Psalms 8; Hebrews 2:5-18]. Jesus understood it to be a messianic title [Mark 14:61-62], and He used it to speak of Himself. Later rabbis saw it as one of the names of the Messiah.

<u>ONE</u>, the Son of Man referred to in the above ***verses 13-14***, is the Lord Jesus Christ, not The Ancient of Days of <u>***vs.9 & 10***</u>:

> *"I beheld till the thrones were cast down, and The Ancient of Days did sit, whose garment was white as snow, and the hair of His Head like the pure wool: His throne was like the fiery flame, and His wheels as burning fire:*

vs.10, A fiery stream issued and came forth from before Him: thousand thousands ministered unto Him, and ten thousand times ten thousand stood before Him: the judgment was set, and the books were opened." <u>Daniel 7:9-10</u>

The Ancient of Days refers to God's eternal nature!

<u>*Lk.1:32-33*</u>*, "He shall be Great, and shall be called The Son of The Highest and The Lord God shall give unto Him The Throne of His father David: And He shall reign over the house of Jacob 'for ever' and of His Kingdom, there shall be no end!"* <u>*Rev.11:15*</u>*;* <u>*Rev.20:1-10*</u> *and* <u>*Rev.22:4-5*</u>*.*

Let us go back to perfection:

<u>Ten Things We Can Be Perfect In</u>:

<u>Our Walk</u>: <u>Gen.17:1</u>, "And when Abram was ninety years old and nine, the LORD appeared to Abram, and said unto him, I am the Almighty God; walk before me, and <u>Gal.5:16</u>, "This I say then, <u>Walk in the spirit</u>, and <u>ye shall not</u> fulfill the lust of the flesh."

1. "Be thou perfect."

That is, to keep us from devouring, harming, hating, insulting and angry at each other, to keep us from offending each other, to keep us from calling of names, from storing in and keeping in, the offenses of one another, we must live the Christian life.

It is the lust of the flesh, it is the root of hatred, it is also pride for us to engage in keeping and storing of offenses of others, documenting in whatever form what ills done to us by others.

It is more dangerous and cancerous if we keep those offenses against us in mind. The implications are:

- We're not able to flow, we may try to flow but we cannot; we're not free with whoever we remember has offended us in the past: we will be bitter at just about anything: full of self-pity! We're far from worship; therefore, it becomes a wounded worship.
- We cannot render any help to such a one whenever his or her offense crept to mind, and as we remember, a kind of hatred will erupt on the inside and we may suffer a little if not more set back in our health.
- We will always be angry, and once we remember any of those offenses just because we cannot let go, we will misbehave to anyone around us, and an angry man cannot please God:
- Believe this or not, we will begin to develop in our body some kind of illnesses and diseases that doctors may not be able to diagnose, they sometimes can't find what actually is wrong with us, therefore medication for an ailment that is not found nor diagnose will be difficult: We then may be surprised that as soon as we let go, healings begin to take place:
- More implication we may notice, our body or our system may become a poisonous container of acidic fluids that can explode any time under pressure at the slightest of provocation if care is not taken:
- No matter how you cut it or slice it to convince ourselves that we're okay, we may be fooling ourselves, our health is not perfect, we're not happy on the inside simply because you refuse to forgive and forget; people of God, this is dangerous:
- Anger is a small madness, therefore, when you are angry, do nothing otherwise, what will spoil and damage to an irreparable stage will be more than what caused the anger!

Vs.17, "For the flesh lusteth against the spirit, and the spirit against the flesh: and these are contrary the one to the other: so that ye cannot do the things that ye would."

This verse is much misunderstood as referring to constant warfare between the flesh and spirit, making one a victim of the flesh and helpless to live right: this is not the thought at all, it does describe the condition of Galatians or anyone else fallen from grace and seeking perfection through the flesh and self-efforts:

> ***"I marvel that ye are soon removed from Him that called you into the grace of Christ unto another gospel: vs.7, Which is not another; but there be some that trouble you, and would pervert the Gospel of Christ: vs.8, But though we, or an angel from heaven, preach any other gospel unto you than that which we have preached unto you, let him be accursed!" Gal.1:6-8***

The message and purpose of the Book of Galatians was to clarify and defend *"the truth of the Gospel" [Galatians 2:5]* in the face of a false gospel. This was done by:

[1]. Defending Paul's message and authority as an apostle:
[2]. Considering the Old Testament basis of the *Gospel* message and
[3]. Demonstrating how the *Gospel* message Paul preached worked practically in daily Christian living.

Paul chose this approach to correct those in the Galatians churches in regard to both their faith and their practice related to the *Gospel*. Most ancient letters, and all but one of Paul's other letters, contain a thanksgiving section at this point. This letter abruptly begins with a reprimand. Paul marveled at the *Galatians'* quick apostasy. To reject the *Gospel* message is the same as rejecting God. After Paul left Galatia, the Galatians thought they had heard and responded to *another gospel* that was better, but it was actually no true gospel. The purity of the *Gospel* is so important that even the apostles *or an angel* should be put under a curse eternally *[Greek - anathema]* if they tampered with it. So, if we believe in the true *Gospel* and *doctrine* of our Lord Jesus Christ let us follow what the next verse is saying:

2. Holiness: II cor.7:1:

"Having therefore these promises, dearly beloved, <u>let us cleanse ourselves from all filthiness of the flesh and spirit, perfecting holiness</u> in the fear of God:" which promises?

The promises of the Bible that only holiness can bring, same as giving Abraham the conditions for the Abrahamic covenant.

3. <u>**Our Ways**</u>: *"God is my strength and power: and maketh my way perfect:"* **<u>Ps.18:32</u>**, *"It is God that <u>girdeth me</u> with strength, and maketh my way perfect:"* perfection in our ways is what will bring the same testimony of blessings as in **<u>II Sam.22:33-51</u>** upon us to live a victorious life.

4. **<u>Peace</u>**: **<u>Isa.26:3</u>**, *"Thou wilt keep him in perfect peace, whose mind is stayed on Thee: because he trusteth in Thee:"* we can be at peace with others without strive, anger or jealousy, that is what qualify us to be perfectly kept in peace by Him.

5. **<u>Unity</u>:** **<u>Jn.17:23</u>**, *"I in them, and thou in me, that they may be made perfect in one; and that the world may know that Thou hast sent me, and hast loved them as Thou hast loved me."*

This is one of the prayers of our Lord Jesus Christ on our behalf, and He is praying to the Father for the oneness of all believers as God and Christ are One: 'Unity!'

6. **<u>Good Works</u>**: You see, we can be perfect in good works:'

<u>Heb.13:21</u>, "<u>Make you</u> perfect in every good work to do His will, <u>working in you</u> that which is well pleasing in His sight, <u>through</u> Jesus Christ; to Whom be glory forever and ever, Amen!"

II Tim.3:16-17, *read and meditate in this:*

> *"**All** *** Scripture is **given** *** **by inspiration** of God, and **is profitable for** doctrine, for reproof, for correction, for instruction in righteousness: That the man of God may be perfect, thoroughly furnished unto all good works."*

It is lack of knowledge of the Word that is making us to misbehave, making us to look like we've never heard the gospel, making us to behave like unbelievers: lack of knowledge!

Look with me in to <u>vs.15</u> of the same,

> *"And that from a child thou hast known the holy Scriptures, **which are able** to make thee wise unto salvation through faith which is in Christ Jesus:" lack of knowledge, lack of wisdom!*

Many times, we lack what is called *"Soft Answer"* we don't know how to respond to issues as they arise in many cases; we just open our mouths and let out anything like I said earlier on, we don't care if we're hurting someone else as long as we are okay there is no humility in us. We are like the people of *'[Ephraim' we can curse, we can strive, we can look for trouble in peaceful waters we can throw our salvation to the winds and confront no matter what and we argue its right to confront]:* Let us use here below an illustration of the people of *Ephraim*:

A SOFT ANSWER

> *"A soft answer turneth away wrath: but grievous words stir up anger."* **Proverbs 15:1**

> *"Death and Life are in the Power of the Tongue."* **Proverbs.18:12**

Who Is A Perfect Man? Who Is A Perfect Woman?

It is amazing what great blessing and what great damage can be done by the words we speak. It is always good looking into the Book of Proverbs to get wisdom from God's heart about the way we speak and respond to people, there are certain kinds of words that foolish people will speak; so, the book of **Proverbs** is going to guide us and give us an insight to how we should learn how to speak wisely. It is the difference between soft words and rough or hash words.

There are many different words in Proverbs that talk about soft words—gentle words, pleasant words, sweet words. And the contrast is words that are harsh or rough. We are all familiar with the verse in **_Proverbs.15:1_** and it says, *"A soft answer turneth away wrath: but grievous words stir up anger."*

There is a powerful illustration of the contrast between these two kinds of words that I will like us to look at in the Book of Judges if I can just ask us to pick up our Bibles and turn in to **_Judges.8_**, you may want to put your finger there and then we are going to turn over to **_Judges.12_**.

In both cases, the men of Ephraim, which is one of the tribes of Israel, were involved; then you are going to see in both of these instances, that the men of Ephraim were an angry, easily-offended people; many of us are like these men of Ephraim, we are easily offended, we are angry people even though we are Christians; the old self, the old nature is still in us, we love to fight we like wars like these men of Ephraim and we don't want to care to what extent.

We are easily offended in our homes, we are easily offended at our jobs, and surprisingly we are easily offended in the house of God can you imagine; we are so selfish people we want to be pleased and worshipped; we want to be pampered; we are so arrogant the pastor or the leaders of the church cannot advise or chastise us.

We scrutinize all messages in the church of Jesus Christ, we want to see where the preacher has offended us and instead of us to repent we want to take a pound of flesh from whosoever crosses our way; whatever we hear we misinterpret and exaggerate and add salt and pepper to, we change it here and there so we can be pitied and jointly pitch a tent against the preacher; we are like the people of Ephraim.

> ***"And the men of Ephraim said unto him, [to Gideon] why hast thou served us thus, that thou calledst us not, when thou wentest to fight with the Midianites? And they did chide with him sharply." Chapter 8:1***

Now Gideon had just won a great battle in the power of the Lord against the Midianites. The men of Ephraim called him to task, when they should have been cheering him on for what he had done to help the nation of Israel. But instead, they had a beef with him. And they said, *'Why did you do this to us by not calling us when you went to fight with the Midianites?'*

And they reprimanded him sharply; please note, those were the people who had been tormenting them for God knows how long, they had no guts to face them, now God raised a man from among them, empowered him to liberate them from the Midianites, but instead of cheering and praising him, they reprimanded him so sharply they wanted to take a revenge against him for not calling them to war.

These were fighting words. They were incensed, they were offended, they were chastising, and they were rebuking him. And Gideon says in **vs.3** **"God hath delivered into your hands"** note the word here, **'into your hands not the word of pride, 'I have;' not delivered into 'my hand;' but into 'your hands;'**

> ***"The princes of Midian ... and what was I able to do in comparison of you;"***

"Who am I compared with you?" [You see the Word of the Bible here, esteem others better than yourself].

Even though he was the one whom the Lord used single handedly to win that battle, he took the pathway of humility. He gives a soft answer; he diffuses their wrath with a humble word. And the Scripture says in the end of **vs.3**

> *"Then their anger was abated toward him, when he had said that."*

Another version says **'Subsided;'** soft word, humble response, he humbled himself before the angry and violent people. Oh God, I earnestly pray that we your people all over the world, in nations, all cities, villages and towns be this humble in Jesus' name! Amen!

Now we can turn over to **_Judges.12_** now, I hope you are enjoying this as I am? You see the men of Ephraim once again are upset. To me, it looks like these men of Ephraim are arrogant, they are people who love to fight; they like wars like many of us, they're not peaceful people, they love confrontations:

Many Christians today are like those people, we don't want to take <u>no</u> for an answer, we are quick in getting angry at issues that are simple, we want to confront, we want to fight, we want to demonstrate, we want to show we are tough, we want to be critical, we want to show our anger that we are no nonsense people, some of us will say *"well, I cannot pretend;"* well okay, but aren't we doing it to want to prove some point. But God said for us to be meek, in our way of approach, how we deal with other people, in all that we do, we must try to be meek!

Some will say *"he/she can't try that with me, I will give it back to him in full force; [even a hundred-fold]."* What did Jesus tell us in **_Mat.11:29_**?

"Take My yoke upon you, and learn of Me:" are we seriously taking His yoke upon ourselves the way we behave as Christians secretly or publicly, and are we learning of Him.

"For I am meek and '<u>lowly</u>' in heart: and ye shall find <u>rest unto your souls</u>, for my yoke is <u>easy</u> and My burden is <u>light</u>."

Food for thought people of God, food for thought!

The man involved here is another one of the judges of Israel. His name is Jephthah; we know from another passage that Jephthah was a man who was too quick to speak, that he spoke rashly with his words; he made a rash vow that ultimately cost the life of his daughter, we just read about him a little while ago in this same book. That is the Jephthah who is involved here again with the men of Ephraim.

> *<u>Vs.1</u> of chapter <u>12</u>, "And the men of Ephraim gathered themselves together, and went northward, and said unto Jephthah, wherefore passedst thou over to fight against the children of Ammon, and didst not call us to go with thee? We will burn thine house upon thee with fire!"*

Now, watch how Jephthah responds, in verses *<u>2 & 3</u> "Hey! You want war? Congratulations, I got war, and I got plenty of it, I will give you war. Remember? I just won one that cost me the life of my daughter of which I've not yet recovered, I'll give you more war than you can ever imagine!"*

> *"And Jephthah said unto them, I and my people were at great strife with the children of Ammon: and when I called you, ye delivered me not out of their hands."*

Which indicates that he actually asked them for help, but didn't get one, so he took the responsibility upon himself to go fight his own war with his own enemy; so, the accusation of *Ephraim* is groundless, but they accused him though.

Do you see the difference in his approach? He was attached as Gideon was. But he comes back in attach mode, now when you have two people in attach mode the outcome is inevitable. There's going to be a battle. And sure enough, there was a battle.

In vs.4, "Then Jephthah gathered together all men of Gilead, and fought with Ephraim."

And there was now an enormous loss of life. You can read the rest in your own time. Did you see the contrast here? In both cases Gideon and Jephthah both were faced with hash words. The difference was in how they responded to those hash words. In Gideon's case it diffused an angry situation. In Jephthah's case it led to a more serious war.

The question is, are we more often like Gideon or like Jephthah when we respond to cross words, to hurtful words, to words that are said that are unkind or that attack you? The way you respond can make a huge difference in the outcome, it could lead to war, and it could also lead to peace.

All through Proverbs we see this emphasis on having words that are gentle, pleasant and sweet and I think this is one theme that women today particularly need to hear; it is not also only to hear, but to be the doer of what we are talking about today both men and women who are called by His name.

If you watch any amount of television one of the things that kind of just seeps into your system is the way that women talk, women talking roughly and harshly and garbage-talk, trash-talk, some end it up with a slap on the face of their opponent especially if that opponent is a man knowing he dare not respond.

Are we any different because it is even true that Christian women today are also doing the same; and is it any wonder that we are raising a teenage generation that is rough and ugly and unkind in many cases in their talk. ***Pro.16:21*** tells us that:

"The wise in heart will be called prudent, and sweetness of the lips increases learning."

Do we ever have the feeling that if we don't yell, our children aren't going to get it? Well, that is the way it may seem in the short term. But in the long run 'sweetness of the lips increases learning.'

Some of us are home schooling our children and if we are a mother, we are teaching our children-no matter where they go to school, we are teaching our children. And it should be encouraging to us to realize that we can motivate our children to learn by speaking words that are sweet.

We can create a climate in our home that is conducive to growth; **Pro.18:23** is a verse we should allow God to use in all of our lives, it says, *"The poor useth entreaties; but the rich answereth roughly."* He pleads, he appeals because he knows that if he doesn't, he is probably not going to get what he needs. But the rich answer roughly; this can be interpreted in terms of material poverty and wealth.

And we will find it is true that often those who have the greatest material wealth are the most damaging at times with their tongues, they can speak roughly and feel they can get away with it. Many do that because of their position. We've just seen it in **Mat.11:29** that Christ wants us to have a humble spirit.

The humble person will use appeals; will use entreaties, whereas the person who is arrogant in his spirit will speak roughly to others. And then this verse in **Pro.25:15** that would be hard to believe if it weren't in the Word of God. But it is in the Word of God, and it is an incredible promise. It says,

> *"By long forbearance a ruler is persuaded, and a gentle tongue breaks a bone."*

What Proverb is saying here is that *'by long forbearance, by long putting up with the other person,* the person in authority can be persuaded.

You think of that authority at work or that authority in your home who just isn't seeing things right. How do you come up against that person? Do you push, do you demand, do you insist, or do you wait?

Do you forbear or do you speak gentle words? In time, patience and humility and gentleness can accomplish more than anger or force. So, the Scripture tells us that if we are wise, we will speak words that are soft, words that are gentle, words that are pleasant and sweet.

What are some of those words? Words like *"I love you; I am praying for you."* Those are sweet words. Words like, *"Is there anything I can do for you?* **Try saying that at home. Words like** *"please and thank you."* Those are not just old-fashioned courtesies; those are expressions of a sweet spirit.

Words like *"please forgive me, I am so sorry."* When you tell your children or your grandchildren *"I am so glad God gave you to us."* Those are sweet words, those are pleasant words, and those are words that minister grace to the ear. People of God, I know, and I believe we can change. May the Lord renew and perfect us in Jesus' name!

What about road courtesy when we're driving on the streets, I like to use myself as an example of what we call or what we can term to be road rage; many, many years ago, majority of the time I think it will be in the 70s, I knew not the difference between a church goer and been born again I just then thought we are Christians as long as we go to church on Sunday I never knew that Christianity is as this deep and must affect every area of our lives.

I thought I had what we call road courtesy in me though but just to a point, and so when you drive rough and you cut in front of me in whichever way, I will make sure you don't get far before you pay, you may even pay because I will make you hit the curb and God help you if there's a ditch nearby, my friends always call me by a name only on the road when someone drives rough in my way. But I soon realize it's a bad habit of youthful behaviour by not letting go of whatever wrong done to me anywhere; and then I realized it was wrong and I desist from doing all that and learned road courtesy in the real sense, I now became so gentle on the road far to the extent that if I missed giving a right of way to another driver male or female in difficulty or probably to enter the intercession or come in front of me, maybe I didn't see him or her coming from side streets, I always feel bad that it wasn't me who is letting that fellow come into the major road.

Another way of showing courtesy and love to others begins from when we leave our room in the morning, we can assist someone in the elevator, we must care for the elderly people knowing that we will one day be in their situation, in short, we must try to be our brother's keeper. We must learn of Him, He says His yoke is easy, we must learn to be gentle not like *"you're not giving me a full cup and I'm not taking a half, not like the chicken ran into my stuff and messed it up, I must break her eggs, not I will show you who I am kind of a thing"* Old things must pass away all things in our lives must become new!

Things The Word of God Is Able To Do in our lives: *[read all references]*:

1. Make us wise unto salvation: *[Rom.1:16; Jas.1:21]*
2. Produces faith in us: *[Rom.10:17]*
3. Makes Jesus Christ known to us: *[Jn.5:39; I Cor.15:1-8]*
4. Build us up: *[Acts 20:32]*
5. Give inheritance: *[Acts 20:32]*
6. Produce profit in doctrine, reproof, correction and instruction in righteousness if you read *vs.16* again to understand.
7. Is able to persuade that God Is Able to keep until that day, [which day]? until the appearing of Christ! *[II Tim.4:8; I Tim.6:14*

Now back to 10 things we can be perfect in:

7. God's Will: Rom.12:1-2,

> "*I BESEECH you therefore, brethren, <u>by the mercies of God</u>, that <u>ye present your bodies</u> a living <u>sacrifice</u>, <u>holy acceptable unto God</u>, which is your <u>reasonable</u> service: and <u>be not conformed</u> to this world: but <u>be ye transformed</u> by the renewing of your <u>mind</u>, that ye may prove what is that <u>good</u>, and <u>acceptable</u>, and <u>perfect</u> will of God.*"

8. **Patience:** *<u>James.1:4</u>,* "*But let patience have her perfect work, that ye may be perfect and entire, wanting nothing.*"

6 Perfect Things in James
1. Perfect work of patience: **<u>vs.4</u>**
2. Perfect knowledge **<u>Phil.3:15</u>**
3. Perfect gifts: **<u>vs.17</u>**
4. Perfect law of liberty: **<u>vs.25</u>**
5. Perfect faith by works: **<u>vs.2:22</u>**
6. Perfect man by restraint: **<u>vs. 3:2</u>**

9. **Faith**: *<u>Jas.2:22</u>,* "*Seest thou faith wrought in his works, and by works was faith made perfect?* Whose faith is the Bible talking about?" **<u>vs.20-21</u>**

"*AGAPE LOVE*" 'GOD IS LOVE'

Agape love is an unconditional love, you see this demonstrated through the people in Emergency Rooms, the teachers, musicians, drivers who want to stick their necks out for you on the streets; when you see some who cares enough to stop to render help you are amazed because it's pretty negative to find things like that happening; but believe me, they are out there as well as the mean ones; we don't have to know anyone to be able to render help even on the streets, ***love is within*** if we care to stir it up; no human being give us a perfect love as God did and demonstrated it through His creative actions.

10. **Love:** *I John 2:5,* *"But whoso keepeth his word, in him verily is the love of God perfected: hereby know we that we are in Him."*

I Jn.4:17-18, *"Herein is our love made perfect, that we may have boldness in the day of judgment because as he is, so are we in this world."*

By God dwelling in us, by us dwelling in Him, by having the fullness of love in our lives, and by the perfection of that love in daily manifestation, we may have boldness in the day of judgment because we have become like Him!

Vs.18 **says:**

"There is no fear in love; but perfect love casteth out fear: because fear hath torment. He that feareth is not made perfect in love."

"And now, Israel, what doth the LORD thy God require of thee, but to fear the LORD they God, to walk in all His ways, and to love Him, and to serve the LORD they God with all thy heart and with all thy soul." Deuteronomy 10:12:

"Therefore, thou shalt love the LORD thy God, and keep his charge, and His statutes, and His judgments, and His commandments, always." Deuteronomy 11:1

"If thou shalt keep all these commandments to do them, which I command thee this day, to love the LORD thy God, and to walk ever in His ways; then shalt thou add three cities more for thee, beside these three." Deuteronomy 19:9

"In that I command thee this day to love the LORD thy God, to walk in HIs ways, and to keep His commandments

and His statutes and His judgments, that thou mayest live and multiply: and the LORD thy God shall bless thee in the land whither thou goest to possess it." Deuteronomy 30:16

"That thou mayest love the LORD thy God, and that thou mayest obey His voice, and that thou mayest cleave unto Him: for He is thy life, and the length of thy days: that thou mayest dwell in the land which the LORD sware unto thy fathers, to Abraham, to Isaac, and to Jacob, to give them." Deuteronomy 30:20

"Honour thy father and thy mother: and thou shalt love thy neighbour as thyself." Matthew 19:19

"And the second is like unto it, thou shalt love thy neighbour as thyself." Matthew 22:39

"And the second is like, namely this, thou shalt love thy neighbour as thyself: there is none other commandment greater than these." Mark 12:31

It's all over the place in the Bible, to love the LORD, to obey His commandments and to love your neighbour as thyself as, *"there is none other commandment greater than this."*

CHARITY *['LOVE']* NEVER FAILS:

"But the fruit of the Spirit is love, joy, peace, longsuffering, gentleness, goodness, faith, Vs.23, meekness temperance: against such there is no law." Galatians 5:22

[Please read all references below]:

The fruit illustration calls to mind the vine and the branches that produce **fruit *[John 15:1-5]*.** The mention of *'love'* **first in the list looks back to *[Galatians 5:6, 13-14]*.** Such loving behaviour comes through the power of the Holy Spirit by faith. *'Temperance' [Greek: egkrateia; "holding in passions and appetites"]* is place last in the list for emphasis, because all the works of the flesh reflect lack of self-control.

This brings us to the issue of *"AGAPE LOVE;"* there are three kinds of love. We can see the ingredients of love in *I Cor.13*: the one who dreads judgment has a reason to fear, his love is not perfect, he must therefore purify himself. Love is the most powerful force on earth: what this power is I cannot say; all I know is that it exists: *'Love'* is an element which, though physically unseen is as real as air or water. It is an acting, living moving force .... it moves in waves and currents like those of the ocean: *"Take away love and our earth is a tomb! Love is the force that moves you:"*

Every Scripture we have gone through in this book, every warning and chastisement *[chastening]* we have received in this book, all our sins and iniquity that have been exposed to us in this book, the instructions, all what and what not and God's commandments, now bottled down into these few verses of the Bible, it is all about love; think along as you read about all that are said here as written below, let us put ourselves on the scale and see how we measure up.

> *"Though I speak with the tongue of men and of angels, and have no charity, I am become as sounding brass, or a tinkling cymbal:*
> *vs.2, And though I have the gift of prophecy, and understand all mysteries, and all knowledge; and though I have all faith, so that I could remove mountains, and have not charity, I am nothing:*
> *vs.3, And though I bestow all my goods to feed the poor, and though I give my body to be burned, and have not charity, it profiteth me nothing:*
> *vs.4, Charity suffereth long, and is kind; charity envieth not; charity vaunteth not itself, is not puffed up:*
> *vs.5, Doth not behave itself unseemly, seeketh not her own, is not easily provoked, thinketh no evil:*
> *vs.6, Rejoiceth not in iniquity, but rejoiceth in the truth:*
> *vs.7, Beareth all things, believeth all things, hopeth all things, endureth all things." I Corinthians 13:1-7*

If not accompanied by love, the ability to *'speak'* all earthly and even celestial languages would be unbearable to others, like misused musical instruments. Supreme spirituality that is not motivated and directed by charity is useless. *[Vs.3]*, Sacrifice of one's life can be the ultimate act of love *[John 15:13; Romans 5:6-8] but* is also possible to make such sacrifice with wrong motives. Paul personifies love in order to show his daily character and choices; The **Corinthians** would have recognized these faults as taking place among them. Contrary to common perception, love is not marked by tolerance from error.

Generally speaking, love is a deep affection for or attachment or devotion to someone. It could also be described as a strong, usually passionate, affection of one person for another, or goodwill towards one another or others. Love **endureth** in this age with a sure expectation of better things to come in the next. Many aspects of church life will cease at the end of this current age but love never ends. This permanence signals love's priority within the church.

Kinds of Love

There are three kinds of love: **(1) Agape (2) Filio (3) Eros**

- *Agape* is unconditional love of God.
- *Filio* is brotherly love that is based on one form of relationship or the other. It could be blood, social or business. Emotion plays a principal part in this type of love.
- *Eros* is the type of love that has to do with sexual relationship or desire. It could be said of lusting after someone.

It is important to note that in this study we are concerned with the Agape love which is God's kind of love that is not based on any condition. *[Filio and Eros are conditional].* Agape is the kind of love that is expected of Born Again Children of God an-un-conditional love, especially your gifts and your love mostly to those who cannot and have nothing to give back is more appreciated by God!

How did God express His Love?
By sending His only begotten son Jesus to come and die for our sin to reconcile us back to Himself; we who are nothing without Him and have nothing to give back. *[John 3:16, John 15:13 and Rom. 5:7-8]*

What benefits do we derive from expression of God's love? *[read references]*.
- Salvation – *John 3:16-17, Rom. 5:8-9 and Rev. 1:5.*
- Peace – *John15:10, John 16:33*
- Faith – *[fear is driven away] 1 John 4:18.*
- Hope that does not disappoint – *Rom. 5:5*
- Victory in all situations – *Rom. 8:37.*
- Regeneration and Renewing of our minds by the Holy Spirit – *Titus 3:4-7.*

The bottom line is, when you love you will *give! When we give something to others, we end up getting so much back; whatever is not given is lost!* When we don't give it is because we don't have love! The Bible says, *[For God so loved the world, that He gave:"* It is love that makes us give *[you so much loved that fiancé of yours that you bought her a diamond ring costing thousands of dollars]*. That is the *"POWER of love."* Love is the most powerful weapon on earth, and it is an eternal gift: and believe me, there are a whole lot of people out there who are filled with love willing to help anyone in trouble: *Love is the most powerful and still most unknown energy in the world*: Love says:

> *"Give and it shall be giving unto you; good measure, pressed down, and shaken together, and running over, shall men give into your bosom. For with the same measure that ye mete withal it shall be measured to you again."* <u>Luke 6:38</u>

What you give you receive either to God or to man: One word frees us of all the weight and pain of life. That word is *'Love:'* Love is the fulfilling of the law:

- *Love is not weak, feeble, or soft, 'Love' is the positive force of life.*
- *The positive force of love can create anything good, increase the good things and change anything negative in your life.*
- *The measure of love is love without measure.*
- *Everything you want to be, do, or have comes from love.*
- *The law of attraction is the law of love, and it is the law that is operating in your life.*
- *Whatever you give out in life is what you receive back in life: Give positivity: you receive back positivity; give negativity, you receive back negativity.*
- *A change of feeling is a change of destiny.*
- *Love, because when you love you are using the greatest power in the universe.*

II Chronicles 16:9 It says *"the eyes of the Lord goes through and fro looking for a man whose heart is perfect toward Him:"* God checks your heart before He measures your act **Jeremiah 17:10**; so your heart is the foundation for God's reaction towards you, if you are going to fly high here on planet earth, you need a heart for God, and a heart for God will always translate a heart for men: he said *"to love the Lord your God first and then love your neighbour as you love yourself."*

Have we seen what **Dr. Phil does?** Have we seen this great man of love and the great work he's doing reshaping families and lives of individuals all over America? What he's doing, helping mankind to regain themselves? He certainly is a man of faith, a man of integrity, a man of wisdom, a man full of love! He is a man ordained of God who has found his calling and manifesting in his calling. **Dr. Phil** certainly is a man called doing the work of good apostles, a work that ministers of the gospel should be doing alongside with ministrations. **Dr. Phil** is preaching good tidings to the meek, only a meek man can do the same. He has been sent to bind up the brokenhearted; he has been sent to proclaim liberty to the captives; many families, homes, children individuals are seriously in captivity and captivity within. And, spiritually, **Dr. Phil** is opening the door of the prison to them that are bound because many are bound within themselves like they are in the prison of life.

If **Dr. Phil** is reading this book, **"A Big Kudos to You thou great man of God"** may you continually be blessed from above and may the Lord endow more upon your life the wisdom with which you need to continue the good job. My advice to ministers is to emulate this good work to help humanity with what we have received from above so it will last. My regards to Ministers of the Most High God like **Bishop T. D. Jakes, Pastor Benny Hinn** and many other men of God that are using their resources in rural areas of Asia and Africa helping those children across the globe setting up schools in places where they have no hope of ever going to schools putting smiles on the faces of the hopeless also like **Jeff Bezos of Amazon, Bill Gates of Microsoft and his dear wife, Oprah Winfrey,** this is love unconditional, that is what wealth is given for. So, tell me how God will overlook this expression of love? May you all live to the fulfillment of your days as you keep building the kingdom for God here on earth your mansion in heaven is undoubted!

Men of God are not called to be celebrities, we are not called to abandon our first estate, we are not called to neglect and operate within me, myself and I; we are called to pray .... we are called to preach the gospel, we are called to touch lives so that lives can be transformed...... we are not called to add to the problems, we are called to be a solution to the problems, we are called to positively affect lives!

Our love for our neighbour, for our brothers and sisters, being our brother's keeper *[what Bishop T. D. Jakes, Pastor Benny Hinn, Dr. Phil, Oprah Winfrey, Jeff Bezos of Amazon, Bill Gates of Microsoft and his dear wife, and a few others are doing],* is what gives the validation that we have love for God. If we claim to love God, we must love our neighbour and if we love our neighbour we must also love everything ... about our neighbour, *'who he/she is, who they serve, where they worship, their interest whether or not we like it, whether they have or not, where they live does not matter, in America, Asia, Africa, Europe wherever because we are ONE people;'* and if so, why do we have to kill or tear each other apart? Is it a must that we must belong to the same faith? What happens to ***freedom of expression, freedom of speech, or freedom of religion?*** Freedom or no freedom, religion or no religion, the Bibles says, ***"Thou shalt not kill!"*** We cannot give life, why do we take lives? Taking of lives is hate religion and God forbids it because ***"God Is Love!"***

When our love for God is translated to our love for men, God lifts us up with ease *I John 4:21, ... **"And this commandment have we from Him, that he who loveth God love his brother also:"*** followers of Christ love God and love others-or they are not true disciples of Christ!
In *Acts 10*, the man Cornelius, the Angel said to him, ***"God has heard your prayers and your alms,"*** in other words, God has heard your prayers and He has seen your love. Love touches the heart of God when extended to man and that love that Cornelius extended to man answered for him.

Love does something in every life, that is, love enthrones among other things by empowering us for wealth, it empowers us for wealth because we cannot be a lover without being a giver and if we're not givers, we're not permitted to prosper. ***"And Solomon loved the Lord:"*** *[I Kings 3:3]* **and in <u>verse 4</u>,** ***"a thousand burnt offerings did he offer!"*** Every lover result in giving and every giver creates a platform for prosperity, the bedrock of prosperity is liberality and when liberality is in place, you are empowered for wealth.

God wanted to harvest the whole world, He needed to give something *John 3:16* He so much ***"loved the world that He gave His only begotten Son,"*** and as One gift was given, God harvested all of us, so God prospered by His given, His given to mankind!

<u>MANIFESTATION OF LOVE</u>: *[Read all references]*.

If God is love and He has expressed His love towards us by sending His only begotten son Jesus to die for our sins, we who are created in

His image and born of His spirit must manifest and express the love of God towards God Himself and towards one another.

Now, how do we manifest and express this love?

LOVE TOWARDS GOD – *Matthew 22:37*
- By keeping His commandments – *John 14:15*
- By upholding the integrity of the gospel both in public and in private, we must note that our love towards God must be undivided. *Luke 16:13*.

BUT WHY MUST WE LOVE GOD?
- Because He is love – *1 John 4:8*
- Because He first loved us – *1 John 4:9*
- The plans of God for those who love Him are unimaginably great *1 Cor. 2:9*
- It is a command to love God – *Matt. 22:37*
- Loving God enables us to hate evil – *Psalm 97:10*
- So that we can inherit eternal life which He has promised those that love Him – *James 1:12, James 2:5*
- All things work together for good to them that love Him – *Rom. 8:28*
- So that God will preserve us – *Psalm 145:20*

LOVE TOWARDS ONE ANOTHER – *Matthew 19:19*

In what way can we express the love of God towards one another?

Please be encouraged and give at least five examples, Note, however, that the operation principle in manifesting and expressing God's love is *GIVING* and *CARING*. Also look at the following scriptures. *Mk. 12:31; Rom. 13:8; Rom. 12:10; I Thess. 3:12*

Expression of love must not be only in the words of our mouth. It must have a proof – *II Cor. 8:24*

Who Is A Perfect Man? Who Is A Perfect Woman?
WHY MUST WE SHOW LOVE TO ANOTHER?

- So that God will dwell in us: *No man hath seen God* the Father in His Heavenly splendor, but God the Son makes the Invisible Father clearly known: *[John 1:18]*; – *I John 4:12*

"No man hath seen God at any time. If we love one another, God dweleth in us, and His love is perfected in us:"

- It is a command – *John 13:34*

"A new commandment I give unto you, that ye love one another; as I have loved you, that ye also love one another:"

- So that men and women will know that we are the disciples of Jesus – *John 13:35*
- Because our labor of love will be remembered by God *[this is a great and enduring promise]*

Majority of Christians worldwide politicians and individuals openly manifest their true leaf *[because the opposite of love is hated]* when they always condemn a man whom the majority of the people and the world see as an embodiment of love, humility and peace: a patient man! A President who not only love the people and his country The United States of American but love all other countries of the world and humanity as the Lord Jesus commands that we love even our enemies. Everything this man has done, everything this man has said or everything this man does he did out of love, his love for America and all other nations of the world is great, his love for mankind is unimaginable alongside his vice President Joe Biden.

He is a man who will not neglect the poor nor see them suffer, a man who would not dance to the tunes of evil, a man who believes in dialogue instead of arms, a man who shares the feeling of the people in distress, a man chosen by God, a man full of love. *That man is the United States President Barak Obama and Vice President Joe Biden!*

How did I know this? He is the **President of the most powerful nation on earth** which makes him the **most powerful man** in the world, yet he chose to listen to people before he acts on any issue affecting the people or any nation of the world; he yet endures all darts of arrows fired at him in hatred without retaliation, a complete gentleman, a family man, a very decent man of God! We may agree together or not but when we look closely while closing our physical eyes to re-count and then see him with the eyes of the spirit, we will all see him as a man worthy of emulation: in spite of hatred from all quarters he kept taking them in calmly with good spirit and coming back with love without fighting back in words and deeds. *A global Model!* We also have another *global Model* in the person of **Pope Francis [Jorge Mario Bergolo] a philosopher, a Theologian** who is always advocating for **global peace**, a man of love and integrity, always happy at the success of others, he is worthy of emulation.

We can hide the truth about **Barak Obama and Joe Biden** in this area of love and other areas as we have always done but the truth about these men remains, and it remains unedited! To me and to millions of people, he is a man of God and a man after God's own heart. A man chosen by God for such a time as this! A man that has given all and most unappreciated. **Barak Obama and Joe Biden** are not about politics. **Barak Obama and Joe Biden** are about the people if we have watched and studied both of them closely. I am not talking about their presidency; I am talking about their people. Figuratively speaking, when the people of the middle-class sneezes, **Barak Obama and Joe Biden** are two people that will catch cold; when the poor cries **Barak Obama and Joe Biden** bleed on the inside!

Please do not misunderstand me, I am not saying **Barak Obama and Joe Biden** are perfect, no one is, I am not, you are not, we are not but they one of the most beautiful people I have ever seen, most open, most calculated men who has the love of the people. Nobody can become a king or a president of any nation unless that person is ordained of God, God chooses who becomes who or what; and once the he or she is sworn in, we immediately begin to accord him or her honour and respect due because it is of God knowing that as we do that and obey the law of the land honouring our leaders, we are honouring God and if it is of God, no amount of pressure, no amount of opposition, the chosen one must prevail because of the assignment God wants to use him or her for at that particular time in history.

The Bible says, *"All have sinned"* but if we claim to be followers of Jesus Christ shouldn't we love all? But we go against everything he does for the people and for the nation and in our cruelty of hearts we refuse to give him credits on his achievements, the question is, are we Christians or a people of love? When we secretly or openly show hatred and criticism against our brothers whom JESUS said to love unconditionally, should we not be asking ourselves some questions as to how serious and genuine our Christianity is, one more thing, what would Jesus do or how will JESUS feel? The Bible says:

> *"Shall the throne of iniquity have fellowship with Thee, which frameth mischief by a law." Psalms 94:20*

Let me explain the above reference, it simply means that corrupt, godless, wicked rulers or politicians always enact legislations that will favour or allow them to remain in power or grab power, legislations that persecutes the righteous, legislations that oppresses the poor more and more and enables wickedness, which is clearly contrary to God's will; and anything that is contrary to God's will puts the enactors in perpetual bondage and in God's judgment to their generations as the law of sowing and reaping is still very much alive!

Are we Christians at all? Can we *"Dwell"* and *"Abide"* with the Father? Do we read the same Bible or haters have a different Bible that preaches a different thing? How can we be good Christians and we try to suppress the basic human rights of other people and we do it in everything with all manner of gimmicks because of power, isn't that a *power-grab* are we not ashamed? If we're sure of what we preach or what we're selling to the people, shouldn't we allow the people to have their choice of who or what they want; must we impose ourselves or impose our religion on everyone or must it be like a matter of do-or-die? Sincerely speaking, we have all drifted away from the Lord chasing the wind and He drifts away from us as we of Him, but except we repent and return unto Him we will all perish! *[Please See eternal judgment in chapter seven with all the Bible references]* The Bible is not lying, and our God is not a liar either! All must give account!

Love must be unconditional; love must be the distinguishing mark of Jesus' disciples. ***Jesus' new commandment*** closely resembled the Mosaic commands to love the Lord *[Deuteronomy 6:5]* and one's neighbour as oneself *[Leviticus 19:18; Mark 12:28-33]*. Elsewhere Jesus said we must love even our enemies *[Matthew 5:43-48]*. While the command to love God and one's neighbour was thus not new, Jesus' example *"[as I have loved you]"* was unparalleled.

> *"By this shall all men know that ye are my disciples, if ye have love one to another!"*

So, what are we doing preaching when we cannot love one another? What are we preaching or what God are we preaching to other people when we have no love but hate? Are we justified to preach against hate crime? It is an abomination unto the Lord when we stand on the pulpit to talk about God of love with hatred for the masses or of another human being in our hearts; then, do we really believe Him to be a God of Love? We need repentance and deliverance from the demon spirit of hatred!

> *"Remembering without ceasing your work of faith, and labour of love, and patience of hope in our Lord Jesus Christ, in the sight of God and our Father." <u>I Thess.1:3</u>*

Permit me to say this, **President Barak Obama** is not the pastor of United State of America *[as in the case of Pope Francis]* and was not sworn in as such. **Barak Obama** took the oath of office to protect the constitution of the United States of America, to protect the interests of all Americans within and without to also protect their interests regardless of their race, color, orientation sexually and otherwise, your height, who you serve, or worship makes no difference. He is not called to preach the gospel to the people. **Barak Obama** was not sworn in to choose for anyone who to love and who not to worship: *"don't sleep here, don't sleep there, don't love this don't love that, drink that water don't drink this"* well, that is not his job. So what **Barak Obama** is teaching and telling us even though he is not a pastor in essence is to welcome and love all as God loved us, gay or straight, lesbian or otherwise, we are to manifest His love to everyone as we love ourselves, embrace all, show that you care, no separation, no segregation, no hatred of any kind; he is teaching us including Christians that are not practicing love, to love all regardless of race, color, religion, orientation sexually and otherwise, regardless of your height, who you serve or worship, politically, what or who you believe makes no difference, this is the teaching of our Lord Jesus Christ. How many of us critics and haters don't even have our names in the Bible? *[laugh]*.

Well, **'Barak'** is in the Bible. **'Barak'** in the Bible is a **'Warrior!'** a warrior who never lose any battle *[read your Bible]*: the meaning of *'Barak'* is *"lightning,"* can anyone fight against lightning? *[See the Book of Judges 4:6-22] where after twenty years of oppression in Israel, Deborah the prophetess called on Barak to champion and take the lead in the fighting, gave Barak the Lord's plan of battle, deploying 10,000 men of Naphtali and Zebulun on mount Tabor, a strategic location at the north-east corner of the Jezreel Valley. Further she assured Barak of the Lord's victory over Israel's enemy verses 14-17, Barak destroys Sisera's army and in Judges 5:1-13, Prophetess Deborah and Barak sang songs of victory to the Lord as Israel became victorious!"*

Reading further we will see where the Lord had gone in front of Barak just as the Lord did with the Egyptian forces at the time of the exodus *[Exodus 14:24]*. All that was left for **Barak** was mopping-up operation. No matter whom you are, when you possess everything in your name and you have love, God always go ahead of you and fight for you, your love also will speak for you. We saw this happen in the life of *"Barak Obama," [lessons we must learn when we do evil to others];* everything that was used against him backfired, the most powerful of the land rose against him with all kinds of weapon, amidst the most expensive election ever with over a billion dollar to drown him, he emerged with a landslide victory both of the times. That is what love can do; with love you can conquer your enemies, in any and every situation your love for all people will always stand for you!

<u>*II Chronicles 16:9*</u> **It says *"the eyes of the Lord goes through and fro looking for a man whose heart is perfect toward Him:"*** God checks your heart before He measures your act <u>*Jeremiah 17:10*</u>; so your heart is the foundation for God's reaction towards you, if you are going to fly high here on planet earth, you need a heart for God, and a heart for God will always translate a heart for men: he said *"to love the Lord your God first and then love your neighbour as you love yourself."*

> *"And what shall I more say? for the time would fail me to tell of Gedeon and of Barak, and of Samson, and of Jephthae; of David also, and Samuel and of the prophets:*
> <u>*vs.33*</u>*, Who through faith subdued kingdoms, wrought righteousness, obtained promises, stopped the mouths of lions:*
> <u>*vs.34*</u>*, Quenched the violence of fire, escaped the edge of the sword, out of weakness were made strong, waxed valiant in fight, turned to flight the armies of the aliens."*
> <u>*Hebrews 11:32-34*</u>

If God appoints you, no one can defeat you! Your righteousness must stand for you, your love must speak for you, you will always be victorious. Because Jesus Christ is the *"Author and Finisher"* of the Christian faith, the author of Hebrews called on Christians to keep their focus on Jesus. The Christian who has faith, *[who has love]* will *lay aside* every sinful encumbrance and *run* toward Christ in the face of adversity. Just as Jesus **endures the Cross, despising**

the shame in order to attain the joy of rejoining the Father on His Throne, so should Christians run their race with ***patience***.

A guy named **'*James*'** sat in front of our office one day for hours, I was so curious as to what might he be doing sitting there for hours or what might be troubling him; as I opened the door and invited him in, he looked so lonely but with much persuasion he came in, and as we were talking he asked what my feelings would be if I knew he was gay! I looked at him and I said, "what do you mean my feelings, it makes no difference to me what matters to me is that you are a human being, you are a person!" Then he said, like maybe I would not welcome him; and I said why not, that I love him as a human being not because of who he think he is ***[because that is not who he is, that is what he does or like to do, there's a difference between his person and what he does]:*** but because of who Jesus called him, ***"A Child of God, God's creation,"*** he was so perplexed and he began to pour out his mind with tears in his eyes, He said, and I quote, ***"where are we supposed to go to serve God, I love God and love Jesus but everywhere we went we were rejected, we were pushed out, nobody wanted to be seen with us, I like to go to church but which of the churches; I am a member of ...... church]*** *[I will not mention the name of the church]* so very gentle looking of a man. I brew coffee for him asked him to feel relaxed and at home, preached to him, prayed for him and because of his response to my prayers, I lead him to Christ and invited him to our church with his partner, in the end, I gave him a gift of The Holy Bible, white, brand new unopened ***[he said, 'I have a Bible and you're given me a new Bible?]'*** and I told him **'*yes*'** that I love him regardless, that the Bible is the prove of the love of Jesus for him. He was so surprised that he was weeping, grabbed me and gave me a hug! ***James*** if you are reading this book wherever you are, please come back you are loved with the love of the Lord!

- We cannot be talking about love without mentioning an important case of religion, the religion of Islam which to others is a controversial religion, why should there be any controversy about the religion of Islam? Why should we classify the act of terrorism as representing the whole of Islam? If we do, we have no love for others, we are creating more hatred and we're looking for more enemies as we will not like ours to be branded with evil. Do we not we have superficial ***Christians*** who are only ***"Christians"*** by the word of mouth and their deeds are evil? Don't we have murderers, robbers, rapists, violent children from Christian homes who also are ***"Christians as they claim?"*** The ***GUYANA TRAGEDY [Jonestown Massacre by Reverend Jim Jones]*** is an example of one of the evils of men. Reverend Jim Jones was an American cult leader and community organizer. Jones was the founder and the leader of The People's Temple, he was best known for the mass murder-suicide in November 18 1978 where 900 members *[nine hundred]* of his church died in that massacre tragedy, the religious leader who mislead his people in the name of *"God"*; he was a man who served as student pastor in the Methodist Church in 1952 in Indianapolis who later started his church of misery.

Reverend Warren Jeff (born December 3, 1955) is a former president of (FLDS Church) and ... **_Fundamentalist Church of - Rulon Jeffs_** - **_YFZ Ranch_** Warren Jeffs' Followers Are Fleeing The Fundamentalist Church of Jesus Christ of Latter-Day Saints In Droves Prior to his father's death, Jeffs held the position of counselor to the church leader. When Rulon Jeffs died in 2002, Warren Jeffs became his successor with his official title in the FLDS Church becoming "President and Prophet, Seer and Revelator" as well as **_"President of the Priesthood"_**. The latter concerned being head of the organization of all adult male church members that were deemed worthy to hold the **_priesthood_**, a tradition carried over from the LDS Church.

Following his father's death, Jeffs told the high-ranking FLDS officials, "I won't say much, but I will say this—hands off my father's wives." When addressing his father's widows he said, ***"You women will live as if Father is still alive and in the next room."*** Within a week, Jeffs had married all but two of his father's wives; one fled the compound, the other refused to marry Jeffs and was subsequently prohibited from ever marrying again. _Rebecca Wall_, sister of Elissa Wall who was instrumental in Warren's incarceration, left the sect and married Jeffs' nephew. Naomi Jessop was one of the first to marry Jeffs subsequently becoming his favorite wife and confidant. Jessop was with Jeffs at the time of his arrest.

As the sole individual in the church with the authority to perform marriages, Jeffs was responsible for assigning wives to husbands. He also had the authority to discipline male church members by "reassigning their wives, children and homes to another man." Are all these in the name of God?

Until courts in Utah intervened, Jeffs controlled almost all of the land in **_Colorado City, Arizona_**, **and _Hildale, Utah_**, which was part of a church trust, the United Effort Plan (UEP). The land has been estimated to be worth over $100 million. Currently, all UEP assets are in the custody of the Utah court system pending further litigation. As the result of a November 2012 court decision, much of the UEP land is to be sold to those who live on it.

In January 2004, Jeffs expelled a group of 20 men from Colorado City, including the mayor, and reassigned their wives and children to other men in the community. Jeffs, like his predecessors, continued the standard FLDS and **_Mormon fundamentalist_** tenet that faithful men must follow what is known as the doctrine of "celestial" or **_plural marriage_** in order to attain **_exaltation_** in the afterlife. Jeffs specifically taught that a devoted church member is expected to have at least three wives in order to get into heaven, and the more wives a man has, the closer he is to heaven.

In July 2004, Jeffs' nephew, Brent Jeffs, filed a lawsuit against him alleging that in the late 1980s his uncle **_sodomized_** him in the Salt Lake Valley compound then owned by the FLDS Church. Brent Jeffs said he was five or six years old at the time, and that Jeffs' brothers, also named in the lawsuit, watched and participated in the abuse. Two of Jeffs' other nephews also made similar abuse claims against him. One of the alleged victims, Clayne Jeffs, committed suicide with a firearm after accusing Jeffs of **<u>sexually assaulting</u>** him as a child. There were other *Sex crime allegations*, and he became the FBI's Most Wanted: a servant of "God?" How can that be?

Sexual immorality is unique among sins insomuch as it is sin against the *body*, thus assaulting the sanctity of a believer's sacred oneness with Christ [sealed by *the Holy Ghost which is in you]* and the oneness of holy matrimony *[I Corinthians 7:2].* The point is that the believer's body is a sacred vessel, *bought with a price* by the *Son of God*. Believers thus have no business doing anything with the Lord's body that does not glorify Him as well as using His name to endorse our insincerity. All of the above confirms what I earlier said in *Chapter Three* that there are so many gospels that are not the Gospel of the Bible. When you read the Bible, God of the Bible will speak to you: you cannot find truth anywhere in the world neither can you find where truth is spoken except in the Bible. Also there are many professed Christians who don't know who the real God is even though there has been miracles and testimonies in their lives yet they are confused as to who is behind it all; the reason is we have too many objects of worship before us: to many of them, whoever says *"god,"* they don't want to check to know which of the gods, they just run after them when the Bible says to *"[... test all spirits whether they be of God ..]"* and so they are confused and are deceived as to who the real god is which made it easy for some false prophets and false teachers to manipulate and deceive the people!

Don't be deceived, the false prophets and teachers even false Christians are all over the place around the globe who are culturally or *"traditionally Christians"* so called Christians who are married to culture and traditions of men; those who are sons and daughters or related to priests, whose parents are ministers and they are not practicing Christians, many of them are *'gold plated sinners'* while hanging crucifix pendants on their necks even in their sinful acts. Tell me what does Christianity have to do with culture and traditions, they are two opposites, you cannot be associated with culture and tradition and be a good Christian, when God is calling, your culture or tradition is also calling, who do you follow or answer first? God, your culture, or your tradition? *No man can serve two masters,"* the Bible says, *"you either love one and despise the other"* you can't love both. So, we do have in all religions and until we realize that Christianity is not a religion, we will continue to line it up with the religion of the world! Christianity instead, is a relationship, a relationship with the Heavenly Father, a relationship with the Lord Jesus who came to reconcile us with the Father by translating us from our old ways of life into a life of meaning with Christ.

If therefore we are in relationship with the Father, the Father and the God of love: If we truly believe in freedom, we should be embracing our brothers and sisters who are Muslims as well as in other religion; we are not in competition with each other and we cannot fight for God, only God has the right to judge, we are too close to the conflict too close to the situation, we are in no position to judge anyone or any religion. God only is the Master Corona! There are millions of Muslims with good spirit who are living an exemplary life, who can stick their necks out to help mankind, there are Muslim doctors, nurses, lawyers, teachers, individuals who are doing great jobs out there and can do anything to help humanity the only difference is their inability to believe in Christ just like you also do not believe in who they serve.

We are talking about freedom of speech, freedom of expression, freedom of religion, freedom of worship, freedom of movement, freedom in everything which shouldn't take anyone to the gas-chamber! Why can we not practice our faith without extremes? There should be what we call religious liberty whereby everyone is free to worship who or what you believe in without being crucified by anyone because only God is the judge. No one should be forcing anybody into his or her religion. But with our love and prayer the vacuum of the lives of unbelievers can be filled, we can win anyone over for the Lord and they can become good Christians!

Cornelius in the Book of Acts of the Apostles chapter 10 *[please read from verse 1 through to verse 48].* .... There we will see the account from *verse 1-8]*, Cornelius' vision: from *[verses 9-22]*, Peter's Trance and vision: from *[verses 23-33]*, the visitation of Peter to Cornelius: *verses 34-43]*, Peter's preaching to Cornelius: and *[verses 454-48]*, As Gentiles Received The Holy Spirit: When our love for God is translated to our love for men, God lifts us up with ease *[I John 4:21, ... "And these commandments have we from Him, that he who loveth God love his brother also:]"* followers of Christ love God and love others-or they are not true disciples of Christ!

- In *Acts 10*, the man Cornelius, the Angel said to him, *"God has heard your prayers and your alms,"* in other words, God has heard your prayers and He has seen your love. Love touches the heart of God when extended to man and that love that Cornelius extended to man answered for him; and so, his love for man in giving alms and helping the poor stood for him, that love that Cornelius had, made a way for him, he received a divine visitation, and Angelic Being from God The Father and his life was perfected. Whatever you give out in life is what you receive back in life: Give positivity, you receive back positivity; give negativity, you receive back negativity:

Love is the most powerful weapon on planet earth. With love, we can win anyone, even the most adamant souls can be won to the Lord: with love, we can subdue kings, with love we can subdue kingdoms, try it, it works!

In *I Thessalonians 1:3*, Paul commended the Thessalonians for their *faith ... love ... and hope*. He later singled out these three virtues as having special prominence for the Christian community *[I Corinthians 13:13]*. Their *work* and *labour* were evident in that the gospel had gone through not only their province of Macedonia but into the neighbouring province of Achaia *[vs. 7-8]*. Patience would have been especially needed in the midst of persecution.

"Owe no man anything, but to love one another: for he that loveth another hath fulfilled the law:

vs.9, For this, Thou shalt not commit adultery, Thou shalt not kill, Thou shalt not steel, Thou shalt not bear false witness, Thou shalt not cover; and if there be any other commandment, it is briefly comprehended in this saying, namely, You shalt love thy neighbour as thyself:
vs.10, Love worketh no ill to his neighbour: therefore love is the fulfilling of the law." Romans 13:8-10

The Christian is to pay all his obligations, but there is one debt we can never repay. This is the debt of *"AGAPE LOVE."* Some have misinterpreted this verse as prohibiting all monetary debt, including having a mortgage on a house or buying a car on an installment plan. It may be wise never to go into monetary debt *"[the borrower is servant to the lender: Proverbs 22:7]"* but this verse has little to do with modern method of finance. It is about fulfilling obligations of all kinds. We can never stop *"loving" [Agape Love] as long as we live. Love fulfills the law* because we fulfill the first four commands by loving the Lord and the rest of the law as we love our *neighbour*.

THINGS WE SHOULD NOT LOVE:

As we manifest and express love there are things that God has specifically warned us, by His word not to love.

What are those things? *[Class should be allowed to identify some of them]*
IT IS IMPORTANT to explain love and emphasize the explanation within the operational Biblical context so that people won't ignorantly abandon their physical needs.

- **WE MUST NOT LOVE THE WORLD** *[Col. 3:2, Matt. 6:19-21]*
- **WE MUST NOT LOVE MONEY** *[I Tim. 6:10]*
- **WE MUST NOT LOVE SLEEP** *[Prov. 20:13]*

In furtherance to this teaching on love, it is important we look at the relevance of love to the exercise of faith which is central in our relationship with God.

[a] Without FAITH it is impossible to please God *[Heb. 11:6]*, and God is Love *[I John 4:8]* It follows logically that without faith, it would be impossible to express God's kind of love. Expression of love is, therefore, not a function of feeling or mood but a conscious deliberate decision based on the principle of faith. **Gal. 5:6**

[b] We do not see God; we believe Him by faith. So, the command to love because God is Love can only be obeyed by faith – *I John 4:12, I John 4:20*

[c] The miracle and blessings of God are received by FAITH and LOVE is the key to the miraculous – *Matt. 14:14*. Expression of love produces faith to reside in the recipient.

Ponder On....
GOD's Love and The Authority We Have in CHRIST JESUS......
[Read all references here:] John 3:16-18,27 John 6:35-40 Luke 10:19-22 Psalm 24:1-5, 1 Chronicles 29:10-13, James 1:17, John 3:27, Matthew 28:9-10, Philippians 2:11, Colossians 2:15, Proverbs 20:24, Jeremiah 10:23, Galatians 6:6-20, John 14:21-23 ,26.

The Bible says that God is Love. His Love is made real to us in Christ Jesus. He is the perfection of *'Agape Love.'* It is only as we can trust God and bask in Christly love that we can function in trustful loving-kindness. With His perfect love, our fears are cast off, then we can truly love other people. Without this grace at work in our lives, we manipulate others but label it as **'love'**. It is Christ-like unique selfless love that energizes and makes this world livable. Only His love makes our world go round. Human love is hypocrisy. This is a sad truth.

The Bible says that *"One day the Spirit of Love will be taken away from this world."* Then those who remain will know what a precious gift the Presence of the Holy Spirit has availed us. It is of God's love and compassion that He lifts us up from the traits of common animals. The power of the Spirit and our instinct to receive and give His love makes Christians unique. His love when fully operational in our lives avails us the power of self-constraint. We are empowered to lay down our lives for others. ***Acts 7:55-60. John 15:10-16.*** Yes, if we abide in Christ, and He abides in us, we can function in His power to love the un-lovable in our paths. This is impossible for most. Many are called. But few pay the costly price. Seek to be among the faithful few. Ponder on this. ***See 1 Corinthians 13***.

God sits in heaven. He watches and seeks those who will stoop to receive His love and be granted His power to reign in life as kings. This is a divine paradox. Both the Old and New Testament unfold this truth to the diligent disciple and student. The Bible says, *'God's* Spirit goes all over the world seeking those whose hearts are perfect towards Him. He then, makes such strong on His behalf'. This is stated in ***2 Chronicles 16:9***. And in our text: ***Psalm 15***.

Reading from ***1 Corinthians 13:10-13***, refers here: The ***perfect*** refers to the next age, the eternal age when the Messiah reigns: Paul uses the analogy of infancy versus adulthood to explain the contrast between our present understanding and the understanding we will have in the next age. Believers are granted to know truth in this age, but only partially so. Our imprecise perception of Christ will be made perfect in eternity. Love is the greatest virtue because it continues into the next age. Both faith and hope will be fulfilled in eternity, and so will not remain:

The fact still remains that no one is empowered and should kill in the name of God if we really believe as we always claim that *'God Is Love,'* and if we understand this concept of love and God's intention, we will realize the concept of creation and then understand the **"Book of Revelation in chapter 4:11; as it reads:**

"THOU ART WORTHY, O LORD, TO RECEIVE GLORY AND HONOUR AND POWER: FOR THOU HAST

CREATED ALL THINGS, AND FOR THY PLEASURE THY ARE AND WERE CREATED."

The beginning point of worship is to recognize that God is completely **'WORTHY'** to be recognized for His unrivaled Glory and Honour and Power, and His work as Creator and Sustainer of All Things!

Therefore, we are created for His Glory and Honour and Power, to give Him and only Him pleasure, what does the Bible mean here when it says giving Him pleasure? *[see The Creation next page].* Then we will have to understand the creation and we have a lot of question to ask ourselves and to answer: If God is thus powerful as to the History of Creation how can we justify ourselves avenging God, is God not strong and powerful enough to avenge Himself, how can we justify the killings and slaughtering of other human beings, does God need human avengers, can God not avenge Himself and do we need to help Him? Bible says, **"He that sitteth in the Heaven shall laugh:"** shall laugh at our ignorance, shall laugh at our lack of knowledge **"for which we perish" as the Bible puts it:"** He shall laugh at our foolishness! Because He did not create us for destruction, He created us for love and to give Him pleasure as we make Him happy!

In what way is the church manifesting this love because it looks like **'the world at large is sick'** and we need an antidote, we need the Lord. The last time I checked incidentally, the only antidote I know of, that is so sure, that is so perfect for our world right now, that we need, that can only be offered by the church and **'It Is Prayer!'** Bible commands that we pray for our nations and pray for the people in authority for God's wisdom, so they can make the right decisions, this is an assignment for the church, in His wisdom: if we have love the way God loves us, if we have the love for the nation we live in and if we love our neighbours we will not relent in our prayers.

You say, **"but we're praying," O yes, we are!** But for prosperity, for my family, praying for my peace, for my convenience, for my joy, my, my, my, but we forget that if the nation is not at peace, if the world at large is not at peace the inhabitants will not be at peace, the experience, the confirmation of what we are witnessing right now in the middle east.

"Yes pastor, we are praying," **O yes, we're praying**, but there is hunger everywhere; *"O yes, we're praying,* but there is rape, incest, murder; teens running away from Christians homes to marry in foreign lands to join the jihadists, enlisting themselves in the army of murderers in tens and thousands, are we pleased with that? *"O yes pastor, we're praying,"* Women, mothers living their family homes, wrapping themselves up in explosive vests and becoming suicide bombers, blowing people up in public places. Have we been bewitched?

The church is relaxing when the whole world is adrift and are perishing; another of the primary assignment of the church is evangelism, to evangelize the world beginning from our immediate family *"our children in particular"*, our neighbours, our community, *".... and then to the uttermost parts of the world"* that is what the Bible says.

Don't get me wrong, there is nothing wrong with a servant of God, ministers of the gospel or Christians being rich in fact, wealth is for the children of God as well as His servants and ministers *[Ecclesiastes 7:12b says, ".... money is a defense .... and 10:19 says, ... money answereth all things.]"* but to set our mind at it, that riches now become a defining factor in our lives or lifestyles is evil. It is one of the gimmicks of the devil for the church to forget our assignments and chase after mundane things, or peg ourselves to preaching prosperity; then we get prosperity, who do we remember? Me, myself and I, we then want to prove that we have arrived; we create *TV shows*, we show our mansions that are ostentatiously furnished, we parade our fleet of *exotic cars* and *SUVs* at the expense of the church, we *buy limousines*, we buy the best *private jets*, we don't want to walk on the earth, *we want to fly on wings and compete with angels and birds in the sky in our airplanes at the expense of the gospel and at the expense of the souls that are perishing;* we established great universities, but for the children of the rich; we neglect the poor, if it were possible, we would want to sleep one hour in each room of our mansions before the day breaks.

We have been given so much, but we have delivered so little. Selfishness has eaten deep into our spirit that we only think about ourselves, we are consumed with our comfort, we are consumed with our convenience, we are concerned with our promotion, we are mindful of our breakthrough, we only take and take and take and we close our eyes to what is going on around us and the world at large. Are we shepherds or wolves?

> *"How is the gold become dim! How is the most fine gold changed! The stones of the sanctuary are poured out in the top of every street:*
> *vs.2, The precious sons of Zion, comparable to fine gold, how are they esteemed as earthen pitchers, the work of the hands of the potter!*
> *vs.3, Even the sea monsters draw out the breast, they give suck to their young ones: the daughter of my people is become cruel, like the ostriches in the wilderness:*
> *vs.4, The tongue of the suckling child cleaveth to the roof of his mouth for thirst: the young children ask bread, and no man breaketh it unto them:*
> *vs.5, They that did feed delicately are desolate in the streets: they that were brought up in scarlet embrace dunghills."*
> **Lamentations 4:1-5**

Prophet Jeremiah in Lamentations is concerned about both the spiritual and physical state of affairs of the people of God of his time. This state of affairs sadly reflects the current state of affairs of the ministers and that of God's people today. The Bibles say that these were written as examples for those upon whom the end of the world is come *[I Corinthians 10:11]*. This state of affairs is therefore indicative of the times we live in; these are the end times. Many pastors and preachers are no longer building with precious stones on the Sure-Foundation Jesus Christ. Rather, they are building with rubble, i.e., the philosophy of men and modern ideologies in order to make Christianity "intelligible" to a 21st century audience. ***"[Even the sea monsters draw out breasts and give suck to their young ones]"*** but the teachers of God's people have become cruel denying the flock the sincere milk of the Word, not even when sincere seekers of truth demand for it.

In ***Lamentations*** as quoted above, the holy nation had been like gold or even *fine gold* before God, but now, smeared with sin, they were regarded as *earthen pitchers* or *scattered rubble.* Even the most fearsome creatures are nurturing parents, but the ministers of God neglected their young during the crisis *[we refuse to pray for nations and people, which is our primary assignment].* We have become like *ostriches*, which are legendary for their habit of laying eggs and then leaving those eggs *[Job 39:13-18].*

We pursue prosperity instead of pursuing discipleship, we are so sold out and so sensitive to money that we lost all sense of spirituality, we stop raising disciples, we focus on raising millions. What led to the collapse of Christianity in Turkey? Selfishness, tribalism and racism! Many, many years ago, Turkey was 100% Christians. Today in Turkey, Christianity is only 0.21%; Turkey today is 96.04 Islam. We cannot underestimate Islam; I lived in a predominant Islam territory for 18 years and I know what they are capable of doing because I once witnessed a massacre! If they can uproot Christianity that was for over 1, 123 years in a nation [Turkey] they can repeat it again.

1. The seven churches that Jesus Christ wrote letters to in Revelation 2&3 are located in Turkey.
2. Apostle Paul the champion of the church was a citizen of Turkey.
3. The Macedonia vision that Paul saw "come over to Macedonia and help us" Paul received it in Turkey!
4. Turkey had solid Christian foundation, yet Islam uprooted everything!

The story is almost the same all over Europe and Africa because the ministers, the Christians are asleep, we chase after mundane things while Satan is sowing tares; we are so selfish to allow the growth of Christianity, we cannot seek the face of God for redemption from the Ishmaelite's. The canker worm is eating deep, and people are dying. Are we shepherds or wolves?

Because our selfishness and wickedness, racism, tribalism, sectionalism are weakening the church of Jesus Christ every church is on its own; amongst the group of believers there is no togetherness in Christianity even amongst the ministers of the Gospel. Let us learn one or two lessons from all of the above and more lessons from this lamentation to deliver our soul from impending doom. God will hold the church responsible! Not everyone who is called a pastor has been called to set up a church, many will be far more better assisting the existing ministries than setting up a church. Many modern-day pastors and ministers of the gospel of all categories are failing to live by the injunction of the dying Apostle Paul to Timothy, his son in the Lord, and by extension, to all ministers of the gospel in *[II Timothy 4:2&5]*:

> *"Preach the Word; be instant in season, out of season; reprove, rebuke, exhort with all longsuffering and doctrine. But watch thou in all things, endure afflictions, do the work of an evangelist, make full proof of thy ministry."*

The Bible warns ministers of the gospel against negligence or dereliction of duty in ***Ezekiel 3:18-21***. Ezekiel was also told not to consider the unfriendly countenance of his audience but rather to deliver the word as he was asked to *[Ezekiel 2:6-7]*. The reason we have worship centers all over the place without godly impact is because God's watchmen are not doing their duty right. Some pastors don't consider if members of their congregation are heaven-bound or not in as much as they keep on bringing their offerings, "all is well." The church is not united, the ministers are not united, many of the members of the congregation cannot get along together and we claim to be Christians serving One God, but we are not one!

> *"And Jesus knew their thoughts, and said unto them, Every kingdom divided against itself is brought to desolation; and every city or house divided against itself shall not stand." Matthew 12:25: the same statement in Mark 3:25; Luke 11:17*

Do we seriously think if we continue at the rate Christianity is going right now without seriousness and unity in Christendom, we are going to hand-over Christianity to our children in **30 - 40 years** from now amidst the ongoing war, provocation, persecution and killing of Christians in thousands worldwide, with the promise and vow by the other group to eradicate Christianity and Islamize the whole world and instill *"the Sharia Law"* while we look on? I don't think so!

There are many in our churches today that are miracle seekers, even many ministers have their own agenda. They want God's miracles but want to have nothing to do with the God of miracles, no relationship because they are not disciples. Christians in the third-world countries are being bought over and they use their **thumb to dig the grave of the church** because of money *[voting for money]*; and whether we care about the disintegration of the church or not, we will all stand before Christ who paid the price with His blood to give account!

> *"The priests said not, Where is the Lord? And they that handle the law knew me not: the pastors also transgressed against me, and the prophets prophesied by Baal and walked after things that do not profit." Jeremiah 2:8*

> *"The prophets prophesy falsely, and the priests bear rule by their means; and my people love to have it so: and what will you do in the end there of?" Jeremiah 5:31*

It is disgraceful for we make merchandise of the anointing, we become popular, and the real *gospel* becomes a thing of show and a thing of the past; because we handle the Word of God **without knowing Him without asking where the Lord is!** We become celebrities like movie stars, because *the Word of God is not in us!* We flaunt our wealth all over the place because *we bear rule by means*, what in the name of God do ministers have anything to do with creating *TV shows*; while brilliant, intelligent, talented good children that may become scientists tomorrow, computer programmers tomorrow, great physicians and great presidents tomorrow are wasting away; they cannot go to our universities even Christian universities because they are all built for the rich. This is not our calling, we are called to minister to the meek and set the captives free, but the reverse is the case, and the Bible says, *"... he that sitteth in the heavens shall laugh ...."* At our ignorance, at our lack of knowledge and at our failure when we shall say, *".... Lord when did we see You and not feed You, and not cloth You, and not care for You ...?"* and His reply shall be, *".... in as much as you did not feed these ones that you see, in as much as you did not cloth these ones, in as much as you did not care for these ones that you see; you did not do it for Me!"* Please read *Jeremiah 23:1-2*.

> *"For who maketh thee to differ from another? and what hast thou that thou didst not receive? now if thou didst receive it, why dost thou glory, as if thou hadst not received it?* <u>*I Corinthians 4:7*</u>

Paul offered a rhetorical response to those who were claiming superiority in the **Corinthian** church and were not sharing their wealth. He who receives a gift by grace has no grounds for boasting. When we struggle and work hard enough to get to the top of the ladder, we don't slam the door shut behind us leaving others below the ladder, we need to reach back with the hands of fellowship and hands of faith and of love to pull others along; we must be willing to help others:

> *"But thou shalt remember the LORD thy God: for it is He that giveth thee power to get wealth, that he may establish His covenant which He sware unto thy fathers, as it is this day."* <u>*Deuteronomy 8:18*</u>

No matter how clever, intelligent, or hard-working a person might be, success flows only from the gracious hand of the Lord *[James 4:13-16]*.

Just what was the sins of Sodom and Gomorrah? Does God not owe Sodom and Gomorrah and apology? Just this once let me ask the rich a question with an apology! Who and what is our wealth for, is it only for me, myself, and I? Is it only for my family? Yes, your family needs it but not only for them. That God giving wealth is not for the angels nor for the dead? Well guess what? The dead or the angels don't need our wealth!

That talented boy, that brilliant girl next door whom the parents cannot afford to send to schools, the woman with four children or more who lives in shelter, the man scavenging the dumpster looking for your leftovers so he can eat something, those sleeping under the bridge because they cannot afford to pay high or low rents, I mean, it goes on and on; these are those who need our help and our wealth if we can only remember them: remember businesses are going bankrupt, banks may go bankrupt, things may happen not only that, natural happenings may occur even in the area of health and you lose everything but what we do for others stands for a very long time even after our tenor here on planet earth. We can say, *"I'll do it tomorrow,"* well, if tomorrow comes!

I pray, may the Lord help, keep and protect us and not allow the enemy to buffet us, may we not lose in our lives in Jesus' name. Amen! The church, the ministers, the congregations, Christians all over the world must return to the Cross, we mut return to repentance, we must return to discipleship, we must return to holiness, we must re-assess our Christian life that we perish not!

THE CREATION:

"In the beginning God created the heaven and the earth.

vs.2**, And the earth was without form, and void: and darkness was upon the face of the deep. And the Spirit of God moved upon the face of the waters." **Genesis 1:1-2

This opening verse of the Bible, seven words in the Hebrew, establishes seven key truths upon which the rest of the Bible is based.

First, God exists. The essential first step in pleasing God is recognizing He existence *[Hebrews 11:6]*.

Second, God existed before there was a universe and will exist after the universe perishes *[Hebrews 1:10-12]*.

Third, God is the main character in the Bible. He is the subject of the first verb in the Bible *[in fact, He is the subject of more verbs than any other character]* and performs a wider variety of activities than any other being in the Bible.

Fourth, as Creator God has done what no human being could ever do; in its active form the Hebrew verb *'bara,'* meaning to create, never has a human subject. Thus *'bara'* signifies a work that is uniquely God's.

Fifth, God is mysterious; though the Hebrew word for God is plural, the verb form of which *"God"* is the subject is singular. This is perhaps an allusion to God's Trinitarian nature: He is three ***Divine*** Persons in one ***Divine*** essence.

Sixth, God is the Creator of Heaven and Earth. He doesn't just modify pre-existing matter but calls matter into being out of nothing *[Psalms 33:6,9; Hebrews 11:3]*.

Seventh, God is not dependent on the universe, but the universe is totally dependent on God [Hebrews 1:3].

Verse 2: Bible translations since the time of the Septuagint, the translation of the Old Testament into *[Greek-- 175 BC]*, have *rendered the first Hebrew verb in this verse as 'was.'* However, in an effort to explain the origins of evil and/or find biblical evidence for an old earth, some Bible scholars have suggested that this verb should be translated as *"became."* Citing evidence in ***Isaiah 14:12-21 and Ezekiel 28:12-19,* they believe a time gap, possibly a vast one, exists between the first two verses of the Bible, during**

which Satan led a rebellion in heaven against God. This allows interpreters to suggest that the early earth was *"without form, and void"* because Satan's rebellion marred God's good creation. However, the construction of this sentence in the original Hebrew favours the traditional translation *"[was" rather than "became]."*

The sense of ***verse 2*** is that God created the earth *"without form, and void"* as an unfinished and unfulfilled state. Working through an orderly process over a period of six days. God formed *[days 1-3]* and filled *[days 4-6]* His created handiwork. **The** *"forming"* was accomplished by means of three acts of separating or sorting various elements of creation from one another. The *"filling"* was carried out through five acts of populating the newly created door mains. *"The Deep,"* a single word in Hebrew, suggests and original state of creation that was shapeless as liquid water. The Hebrew verb translated *"moved"* translated *"fluttereth"* in *[Deuteronomy 32:11].* suggests that the Spirit of God was watching over His creation just as a bird watch over its young. God's sovereignty is worthy of praise and worship: *"Book of Revelation in chapter 4:11;* as it reads:

> *"Thou art worthy, O Lord, to receive glory and power: for thou hast created all things, and for thy pleasure they are and were created."*

His creations, The Ocean and all that are therein, The Trees, The Plants of the fields, The Birds of the air, The Animals of all species in their kinds, among His creations even The Angels; all are created *"for His glory and to give Him pleasure:"* We need to give Him our time, our treasures, our spirit soul and body belongs to Him, ***can we hide from Him?*** He owns it all He is the giver, nothing we own or have that cannot be traced to Him! Let Him manage you and your time:

IMPORTANCE OF TIME MANAGEMENT OF BELIEVERS

The world is moving faster than the speed of social media, and time is flying through our fingers; for many of us, the word "chockablock" can describe our lives, we're jammed full of things to do, places to go, tasks to tackle, and obligations to meet; we have forgotten our purpose of creation, we have forgotten what God has in mind before He created us, we have no time for Him. What God gave to us all is time, but we find out that even 24 hours of everyday is not enough for quite a number of human beings, like every other thing in life we always want more time wishing one day will be a stretch of three days; trust human beings, it can never be long enough! What can we do about it?

Let me suggest a good dose of **Psalm 90**, which is one of the greatest treatises ever penned on the subject of time, eternity, and the span of our lives.

THE ETERNITY OF GOD:

<u>**Psalms 90**</u> was written by Moses, making it the oldest datable Psalm. It begins with a mind-boggling affirmation:

> ***"Lord, thou hast been our dwelling place in all generations: Before the mountains were brought forth, or ever thou hadst formed the earth and the world, even from everlasting to everlasting, Thou Art God!" <u>vs. 1-2</u>***

The Bible tells us God existed before the mountains were made or the world was formed. He is The Creator of time, above time, unaffected by the passing of time. He inhabits eternity.
We cannot explain that. It's a truth beyond our finite minds to grasp. The Bible tells us that from God's perspective, a day is like a thousand years, and a thousand years are like a day. In other words, each year before us is like 365,000 years to God. How do we explain that?

THE BREVITY OF LIFE:

Moses went on in <u>**Ps. 90**</u> to contrast God's eternal nature with the brevity of our lives. He compares us to grass, which springs up in the morning and is mowed down in the evening *[vs. 6]*. Other biblical passages reinforce this. ***Job 7:6***, says, *"our days are swifter than a weaver's shuttle." **I Chronicles 29:15**,* compares them to a shadow. **According to *Psalm 78:39*,** our lives are like a wind that passes and doesn't return. James compares them to a mist or vapor that appears for a moment and then vanishes, and Isaiah says, we're like daylilies that bloom in the morning and fade in the evening ***[James 4:14; Isaiah 40:6]***.

This is extremely depressing for those without Christ. It is so depressing that Jesus Christ came to do something about it. the whole purpose of birth, death, and resurrection of Christ was to provide hope to the world and everlasting life to all who receive Him by faith. *Peter said to Him, Lord, to whom shall we go? You have the Words of eternal life" [John 6:68]. Jesus Himself promised, "My sheep hear my voice, and I know them, and they follow Me. and I give them eternal life, and they shall never perish; neither shall anyone snatch them out of my hand" [John 10:27-28].*

THE GRAVITY OF TIME:

That leads us to consider the gravity of time and the urgency of claiming our moments and using our minutes wisely. In ***Psalm 90***, Moses went on to say, in effect, that since God is eternal and our earthly lives so brief, we're to count our days and present God with a heart of wisdom *[vs.12]*. We're to make each day count for eternity.

How do we do that when our lives are chockablock with obligations? How do we manage our time so we're accomplishing what God intends? time is a gift that comes to us from a royal source each day, bright and sparkling, absolutely untouched and unspoiled. Each day we receive a fresh new supply: 24 hours; 1,440 minutes; 86,400 seconds. How well did we invest our time last year? What can we do better this year?

First, remember that God has places us on planet earth with a set of assigned tasks, and our time doesn't belong to us--it belongs to Him.

Ephesians 2:10 says, *"We are God's handiwork, created in Christ Jesus to do good works, which God prepared in advance for us to do" [NIV]* ***Psalm 139:16*** says, *"In Your book they all were written, the days fashioned for me,"* God has planned our work and the days required to accomplish it. Our times are in His hands, and so are our tasks. This mindset is the core of our stewardship of time.

Second, we must de-clutter our schedules. If your life is jammed with activities, there's a good chance you're doing some things God really hasn't assigned. Those who have grown rose bushes or fruit trees know a little pruning is needed from time to time. The same is true for our calendars. Look at your obligations for this year. What can you delete in order to make time to the Study of the Word of God, in order to make time to attend church services, in order to make time for the owner and the giver of time? Is there something good you can leave out, allowing more time for the best?

Third, take advantage of small segments of time. Sometimes it's hard to devote a whole week to a project, or even a day. But it's amazing what we can do with fifteen minutes here and an extra moment there. It's not that we're to become those who never rest or relax. But just as we don't want to throw away our spare change, we want to make the most of the loose coinage of time.
Henry Ford said, *"It has been my observation that most people get ahead during the time that others waste."*

Fourth, make sure that you take time for the most important things. Many of us are a little skittish about New Year's resolutions, for they are easier to make than to keep. But sometimes we do need to take stock of our lives and make some changes to our priorities and agendas. When God manages our calendars, He always leaves room for Himself. Make sure you order and arrange your days, so you'll have time for Bible Study, prayer meetings, and a regular appointment with Him. When we seek Him first--even the first thing each morning--everything else will fall into place and be added to us, *[Matthew 6:33]*.

There is nothing greater than accomplishing even the smallest duty that Christ assigns, it is also greater in God's eyes than building the pyramids or acquiring a vast domain. As we undertake each day's work for Jesus, we can lay our heads on our pillows night after night knowing we've been about our Father's business. the next morning, we arise to a new God-planned day; and we find joy in the journey. the child of God never awakens to a day unplanned by heaven or unattended by the Lord.

When the alarm goes off each morning, we roll out of bed knowing we have a divine purpose, plan, and Presence. There are no blackout dates on the calendars God keeps for our lives. There are no mistakes in His almanac. There is always enough work for the days He has given us; and exactly enough days for the work He has assigned. Those words hold the secret to managing our schedules. I hope this season, this year, you will move from chockablock to counting your days and claiming the time. If so, you will live life to its fullest. instead of being a slave to the clock, you can gain mastery over hours. You can seize the wisdom to serve the Master with all your moments and all your days.

> ***Psalms 15:5**: **He that** putteth not out his money to usury, nor taketh reward against the innocent. **He that** doeth these things shall never be moved."*

USURY:

> *"Take thou no usury of him, or increase: but fear thy God; that thy brother may live with thee." **Leviticus 25:36***
>
> *"Thou shalt not lend upon usury to thy brother; usury of money, usury of victuals, usury of any thing that is lent upon usury:" **Deuteronomy 23:19**:*
>
> *"He that by usury and unjust gain increaseth his substance, he shall gather it for him that will pity the poor:" **Proverbs 28:8**:*

The above references are talking about **"Redemption of The Poor,"** in the first reference *[Leviticus 25:36],* A poor Christian was supposed to be relieved, *[strengthened if you will]* by fellow Christians not to be extorted, we are not allowed to profit from the needs of the poor. The text implies that if a person took advantage of his impoverished brother, he did not *fear.... God.* **While *[Proverbs 28:8]*** is saying in this life or eternity, God will punish those who exploit the poor and reward those who help the poor which in which case means as we gather such increase, we may not enjoy it because it will be transferred to the just.

When it comes to the issue of money we must fear God, many Christians don't fear God, many men don't respect their wives and the majority of wives don't respect their husbands; when it comes to the issue of money; especially the women both married and unmarried, we will hate, we will curse, we will disrespect and call ourselves names, the woman can trash out anything against the husband to any degree when the issue of money arises; to the husband, it is, *"our money,"* to the wife, it is, *"my money,"* but when we understand the concept of *[Genesis 2:24-25]* which says:

"Therefore shall a man leave his father and his mother, and shall cleave unto his wife: and they shall be one flesh. vs.25, And they were both naked, the man and his wife, and were not ashamed."

God's timeless design for marriage is declared here. The **one flesh** represents many things and means a lot! The *one flesh* certainly involves sexual union, but also includes a husband and wife coming together in spiritual, mental and emotional harmony. To realize this is to realize that in marriage, there can never be or must ever be any separation of anything; it must always be **"one body, one family, on bank account, one bed, one relationship one of everything one marriage:"** when it comes to the issue of money, the wives respects only one person, *"me, myself and I,"* I don't blame them though if we look at what women need money for *[especially for their up-keep and security]* but why must we be so angry and aggressive about money to utter angry words and curse each other even to our parents; why should the issue of money be anything if there is genuine love in between the one who have become one-body.

Many will throw their salvation to the winds and lash out at the husbands, lash out at their parents just because money is involved, we are always very, very bitter when it comes to money issue; don't we realize that from these, all kinds of machinations will begin to brew? We've seen children that are waiting to come into their parent's inheritance and are in so much a hurry that they arrange murder for hire and eliminate both parents, husbands and wives killing each other by murder for hire just to claim the insurance benefits on the diseased. *"The love of money, the root of all evil,"* lives of innocent people are in danger every day because of money; men and women even children go into the business of selling drugs because of money; the Bible says! Can anyone involved in this evil escape the judgment? Think about it! in Jeremiah God says, *"Shall I not judge for this, or shall I not visit their iniquities? [See "Eternal Judgment" Chapter Seven].*

CHAPTER SIX

"THOU SHALL BE A GOOD MINISTER!"

JEHOVAH ROHI - THE LORD IS MY SHEPHERD:
The Lord protects, provides, directs, leads, and cares for His people, God tenderly takes care of us as a strong and patient shepherd!

THE 15 VITAL TRAITS FOR LEADERS:

1. *Secure In Self*: Leaders are marked by confidence in themselves. Being secure in yourself builds confidence for others to follow you.
2. *In Control of Attitude*: If you lose control, you lose. Period! Leaders control their attitude, because people read the leader all the time.
3. *Tenacious*: Keep going until something stops you, then keep going. Leaders are persistent and determined. Nothing ever happens in one day, one request or one prayer. Keep going.
4. *Continuously Improving*: Leaders can't go along day to day without growth and improvement. They want to be better. They talk to people, learn from mistakes, learn from others' experiences and learn something new each day.
5. *Honest And Ethical*: Honesty builds trust and confidence. People want to follow a leader they can trust. Duplicity always catches up with the individual.
6. *Think Before Talking*: A leader is responsible for his words and their results. Most people don't stop, pre-think their comment and then speak. Leaders do.
7. *Original*: Leaders are visionaries and are always looking at doing things differently.
8. *Publicly Modest*: Secure people are modest. Being modest doesn't mean being shy or undervaluing yourself. But neither does it mean being pretentious or being a braggart.

9. **Risk Takers**: A person is as good as his courage. Risk takers are able to face obstacles with a resolve despite criticism and attacks.
10. **Detail Oriented**: The small things will always make the big difference. Paying attention to detail saves you time that would be lost in going down the wrong path.
11. **Willing To Lead**: Leaders lead! They set expectations for people, communicate the vision and are willing to set the direction for the group.
12. **Fighters For Their People**: If you want people to back you, back them! Be loyal, spread the credit, share the spirit and share the lead.
13. **Willing To Admit Mistakes**: Leaders admit mistakes. What separates effective people is their ability to handle the inevitable mistakes in life. The leader acknowledges it, corrects it and goes on.
14. **Straightforward**: Leaders have to be clear in their communication. Although wisdom and tact are always called for, so is clear communication. People have to know what you're saying.
15. **Nice**: "Do unto others as you would have them, do unto you." You make yourself a better leader if you're nice first. Being coarse, unpleasant or rude will not get you far.

LEADERSHIP:

God is looking for men to elevate to position of leadership! *[Has He found you?]* Every fresh move of the Spirit has been marked by God raising up new leadership, prepared and chosen for the task. Another such fresh outpouring of the Spirit is at the door. A major change in human events signals this is taking place now.

God needs men who will *"stand in the gap"* for Him and *"make up the hedge" [Ezekiel 22:30]*, men who will know the ways and WORD of the LORD and say, *"this is the way .... walk ye in it" [Isaiah 30:21]*. There is a need for every leader to wait on the Lord *[Isaiah 43:31]*. This is the first priority of every spiritual leader and as we wait, the Lord takes away our strength and replaces it with

His own; an exchange takes place. There is necessity of learning to hear God's voice and a vital principle to a successful ministry is that man lives by *"every word that proceedeth out of* [and continues to be spoken by] *the mouth of God."*

As leaders or want to be a leader, our heart must be pure and yield to the Lord before we can hear Him. Then as we hear and obey Him in every area of our lives, our faith will begin to grow, and as our faith grows, we will hear Him talking to us of great things He wants to do through us. God uses the troubles we experience to prove and refine His words of instruction and direction to us. Through the furnace of affliction, we advance from being *"called,"* to being *"chosen."* Such refinement is necessary, because through it, He prepares us to face the intense spiritual warfare we will know in spiritual leadership. Joseph provides the prime example of this: God has permitted circumstances to bring him into Pharaoh's dungeon to build his character. Then he was released from prison, had an audience with Pharaoh and was made Prime Minister of Egypt.

This change from the hardships of prison to his place of responsibility could have easily given Joseph a false sense of his importance and prominence. But God had worked humility into him in that dungeon and this saved him from the snare of pride.

1. We may be asking, "Just how long will it take for God to prepare me as a leader?"

There is no set length of time: Moses was in preparation for forty years on the back side of the desert tending his father-in-law Jethro's sheep. Only fourteen years after his conversion, Paul was released and sent out as a leader *[Acts 13:1-3].* However, in his case there were many years of training in the Scriptures, before his conversion.

From the time of his dreams until he became Prime Minister of Egypt spanned thirteen years of Joseph's life. Two things determine how long it will take God to make you a leader.

- The magnitude and nature of the ministry God has prepared for you, and
- The way you respond to His dealings as He prepares you.

a. **Mechanic or Doctor?** How much God wants to accomplish through you and how much you want to accomplish for God determine the intensity of His dealings. The same thing is true in the world: a person can be a good auto mechanic with only a few years of training, but you can't be a surgeon without many years of intense, hard preparation and schooling. If you want God to use you in a prominent and powerful ministry with lots of miracles and authority, the time of your preparation will be long and painful. The greater your responsibility will be, the more severe your preparation. It takes a lot more heat to refine a vessel made of gold for God's honour than it does to make an earthen vessel, for common use.

b. **Stubborn or Obedient?** The second factor is your response to God's dealings as He prepares you. If you are slow to learn what God teaches you, this will lengthen the time and severity of preparation. The blacksmith must apply a heavy hammer and a lot of heat to shape the hard inflexible iron. The jeweler need only apply modest amounts of pressure to shape the pliable gold.

The secret is to be responsive, pliable and obedient to the Lord. When He brings a lesson into your life, learn it quickly. Don't talk or be stubborn. If you do, God will have to use much *"heat and hammer"* on you to shape you for leadership.

2. Causalities Abound:

It is folly to suppose that once you become a leader you have no further need for spiritual growth. Thinking such has led to the downfall of many. The Apostle Paul knew this. ***"I fear that after having preached to others, I myself might be declared unfit and asked to stand aside:"*** <u>I Corinthians 9:27</u>:

Many who aspire to leadership think, ***"Once I make it to a position of leadership, I'll be home free!"*** Not true! As a leader, a man is much more vulnerable to spiritual attack and failure because of his prominence and visibility.

3. The Price Is High:

Preparation for leadership involves a lot of weeping and painful testing *[see Hebrews 5:7,8]*. This is because you are being trained to stand the fierce pressures that befall a leader. Christian leadership isn't glamorous; it is warfare. You are at war with Satan and the world. You are misunderstood by family members, friends and fellow-Christians. Along with this, you are often times criticized by people motivated by jealousy or fear.

The Bible account of Moses in the Book of Numbers is an accurate picture of what is involved in leadership. ***Moses was responsible for about two million five hundred thousand people [2,500,000].*** They were a bunch of grumbling complaining, back-biting rebels. They would see a miracle and then gripe about something right afterwards. They fomented one rebellion right after another.

Even Moses' own brother and sister were critical of him and challenged his leadership *[and were judged for it]*. It's a little wonder that God prepared Moses for over forty years before he came to his place of leadership. If Moses hadn't spent those forty years on the back side of the desert with his father-in-law's problem sheep, he would never have been the great leader he turned out to be.

Moses and Elijah were the two who appeared on the Mount of Transfiguration with Jesus. From this *[and other Scriptures]* we assume they were the two greatest and most important leaders of the Old Testament. A measure of stress that a man of God suffers in leadership is illustrated in the lives of both Moses and Elijah.

a. ***Moses.*** Even though Moses had all those years of preparation, the pressures became so great that ***Moses asked God to kill him.*** A man is not praying this way unless his life is very miserable.

> *"Moses said to the Lord, 'Why pick on me, to give me the burden of a people like this? Are they my children? Am I their father? Is that why you have given me the job of nursing them along like babies, until we get to the land you promised their ancestors?*
>
> *"Where am I supposed to get meat for all these people? For they weep to me saying, "Give us meat!" I can't carry this nation by myself! The load is far too heavy! If you are going to treat me like this, please kill me right now; it will be a kindness! Let me out of this impossible situation!"* [Numbers 11:11-15, TLB]

Only those who have been there, know. Leadership has some very heavy burdens that go with it. Moses was so discouraged and depressed with the situation, he wanted to die.

b. **Elijah.** Elijah also had a low point in his ministry. It came after his greatest triumph, when he had called down fire from Heaven and killed the four hundred prophets of Baal. Unfortunately, valleys of despair often follow mountain-top experiences of great victories.

> *"When Ahab told Queen Jezebel what Elijah had done, and that he slaughtered the prophets of Baal, she sent this message to Elijah: 'You killed my prophets, and now I swear by the gods that I am going to kill you by this time tomorrow night.' "So, Elijah fled for his life; he went to Beersheba, a city of Judah, and left his servant there. Then he went on alone into the wilderness, travelling all day, and sat down under a broom bush and prayed that he might die. "I've had enough, 'he told the Lord, "Take away my life. I've got to die sometime, and it might as well be now"'* [I Kings 19:1-4 TLB].

The Lord answered Elijah's prayer and released him. He was taken up to Heaven in a chariot some weeks after praying this prayer. It is a great statement of the Lord's love and understanding of His leaders, that He honoured Moses and Elijah by allowing them there at His transfiguration *[see Matthew 17]*.

Yes, there is a price to pay to be a leader. If the preparation seems hard, just remember: the pressures that go with prominent leadership will be much harder than the training that got you there.

DISTRACTION:

> **Is.43:18 says, "Remember <u>Not</u> the former things, neither consider the things of old."**

Why is this important for you and I *Not* to remember those things of old the things we're used to doing? They are distractions, we can be distracted through many things amongst which are what we used to have or enjoy and are no longer there.

One Book said, *'remember not'* the other Book said for you to remember; remember what? ***Lk.17:32 "Remember Lot's wife;"*** who because of the affairs of this world lost her glory, who because of the entanglement of this world lost the Kingdom; she remembers her friends, her jewelries, her parties, she looked back, and the Bible says, *"she became a pillar of salt."*

> *"In the year that king Uzziah died I <u>SAW</u> also the Lord sitting upon a throne, high and lifted up, and his train filled the temple."*
> <u>vs.2</u>, *"Above it stood the seraphim's: each one had six wings; with twain he covered his face, and with twain he covered his feet, and with twain he did fly:"*
> <u>vs.3</u>, *"And one cried unto another, and said, Holy, holy, holy, is the LORD of hosts: the whole earth is full of his glory."*
> <u>vs.4</u>, *"And the posts of the door moved at the voice of him that cried, and the house was filled with smoke."*
> <u>Vs.5</u>, *"Then said I, Woe is me! for I am undone; because I am a man of unclean lips, and I dwell in the midst of a*

people of unclean lips: for mine eyes have seen the King, the LORD of hosts."

vs.6, *"Then flew one of the seraphims unto me, having a live coal in his hand, which he had taken with the tongs from off the altar."*

vs.7, *"And he laid it upon my mouth, and said, Lo, this hath touched thy lips; and thine iniquity is taken away, and thy sin purged."*

vs.8, *"Also I heard the voice of the Lord, saying, Whom shall I send, and who will go for us? Then said I, Here am I; send me."* Isaiah 6:1-10

King Uzziah had become a distraction to Isaiah, the Bible says it was only when that king died; what is your own distraction, what is that thing that is representing king Uzziah in your life that is making you to drift away, distracting you from being your best for the Lord, is it one of the blessings that God gave to you, your wife/husband, your child or your job or your position. Many of us, it is the blessings of God in our lives, God's gifts that are distraction to us.

Or is it that you have become too comfortable to serve the Lord or to be the best for him; listen to this maybe you will learn wisdom; Isaiah did not see the Lord until that king who became a distraction to him died.

Ex.20:5 said, *"God is a jealous God."* People of God, please do not wait for whatever is distracting you from serving God to be withdraw before you see the Lord! God wants you to see Him now that …. You still have that wife, job, son.

Isaiah learned that position was not what he should be seeking! Recognition was not what he should be seeking; Uzziah gave him a position, and when he got his position, he lost sight of God! I want you to notice Isaiah's 3-fold vision.

When the man who had taken care of him died, Isaiah turned again to the Lord, and it was then that he received his vision! In the year that king Uzziah died I <u>SAW</u> also the Lord sitting upon a throne, high and lifted up, and his train filled the temple.

Isaiah said, when my distractions were eliminated, then I saw the Lord! First, he saw himself as undone and unclean. The greatest miracle in our lives starts from the moment God reveals yourself to you.

When I stopped looking at the arm of the flesh, I saw the Lord! When I stopped self-recognition; when I stopped looking to see who will approve of me, I saw the Lord, when I got my focus right and off of the things that man could do for me and to me, I saw the Lord!

After Isaiah saw the Lord, he saw himself! Without first seeing the Lord, you cannot see yourself which is the beginning of great miracles in your life.

Then said I, Woe is me! For I am undone; because I *am* a man of unclean lips, and I dwell in the midst of a people of unclean lips: for mine eyes have seen the King, the LORD of hosts.

Isaiah saw the Beauty, the Majesty, the Glory of a Pure Mighty God and realized how far he had drifted away when he finally saw God again! He realized how unclean he was after he got a vision of God! And immediately he began to repent!

And, finally, after he saw God and himself, he got a vision of the world that he was sent to witness to. **"Also, I heard the voice of the Lord, saying, whom shall I send,"** [please note this, he was in his own world until he saw the *Majesty, the Glory, the Beauty, the Purity of God,* and then realized himself before he heard the voice of God, seeking] "who will go for us?"

4. *"Then said I, "Here am I; send me."* This account is a message in itself for leaders. The call had always being there, the position has remained open.

> *"Then saith he unto his disciples, The harvest truly is plenteous, but the labourers are few: Pray ye therefore the Lord of the harvest, that he will send forth labourers into his harvest." Mat. 9:37-38*

I am saying this to the church and leaders today, God has a job for someone to do! There are works to be done, and the positions are open, who will fill it; the advert has gone forth? Who will go, who will do the work of God in this generation?

> *"Go ye therefore, and teach all nations, baptizing them in the name of the Father, and of the Son, and of the Holy Ghost." Mat. 28:19*
>
> *"And he said unto them, Go ye into all the world, and preach the gospel to every creature: He that believeth and is baptized shall be saved; but he that believeth not shall be damned." Mk. 16:15-16*
>
> *Acts 1:8, "But ye shall receive power, after that the Holy Ghost is come upon you: and ye shall be witnesses unto me both in Jerusalem."*

What is the implication here, or what is the Bible saying? It is an assignment for us to first win the lost members of our household, those who belong nowhere and hate to serve the Lord; then we can now graduate into moving out *"and in all Judaea, and in Samaria, and unto the uttermost part of the earth:"* then with the anointing and unction of power we have receiving winning at home we can now win those who are far off.

The job? Reach the lost at any cost! The Pay?

> *Mat. 16:26-27, "For what is a man profited, if he shall gain the whole world, and lose his own soul? or what shall a man give in exchange for his soul?*
> *vs. 27, For the Son of man shall come in the glory of his Father with his angels; and then he shall reward every man according to his works.*

The benefits? **Rom.14:17** *"**For the kingdom of God is not meat and drink; but righteousness, and peace, and joy in the Holy Ghost.**"* And a life insurance policy that is out of this world!

But, I would say to you today, that, it is not the most qualified, not the most well-dressed, not the first on the scene, and not the ones with the most ability that will get the job, but the ones that will get the nod from the *Lord* of the Harvest are those who will hear *His still, small, voice* and understand what the purpose of the church is in this day!

Those whose attention is not diverted by the other sounds that clamor all around, those who don't think that they have already arrived and deserve the job because of their superior qualifications, but those who are listening and understanding the voice of God!

We can argue all day long amongst ourselves, and use scripture to back up why we are right, and everyone else is wrong, but while we are crossing theological swords, people are dying and going to hell!

The problem now is, it depends on what your priorities are, who your master is, who you listen to, because the ones whom God will work through in this generation are the ones who have eliminated the distraction in their lives, the ones who will look away from the entanglements of life.

Far too many Uzziahs have become kings in many lives that they cannot remain focused;

> *Jesus said, "And if thy right eye offend thee, pluck it out and cast it from thee: for it is profitable for thee that one of thy members should perish, and not thy whole body should be cast into hell."*

That is one of the reasons many left Him and said His teachings are too hard; they soon realized that their threat of leaving would not make Him rule out some of the laws and lower the standard of making heaven.

Not the most educated: Not the best dressed: Not the ones with the most impressive pedigree or heritage: But those who have eliminated distractions!

> **<u>Ps.24:3-6</u>**, *"Who shall ascend into the hill of the LORD? or who shall stand in his holy place? He that hath clean hands, and a pure heart; who hath not lifted up his soul unto vanity, nor sworn deceitfully: He shall receive the blessing from the LORD, and righteousness from the God of his salvation. This is the generation of them that seek Him, that seek thy face, O Jacob. Selah."*

It's interesting to note that one of the meanings of both of the words used here, **CLEAN** and **PURE**, is **CLEAR!** Not muddled or double-minded, but a clear, unhindered direction. **<u>Mat.6:22</u>**, *"The light of the body is the eye: if therefore thine eye be single, thy whole body shall be full of light."*

I truly believe that what God is looking for in this generation is not talent, ability, pedigree, heritage, etc.

I BELIEVE THAT GOD IS SIMPLY LOOKING FOR PEOPLE WHO WILL ELIMINATE DISTRACTIONS!

PEOPLE WHO WILL KEEP THEIR PURPOSE CLEAR AND PURE, THEIR LIVES UNCLUTTERED, AND FREE FROM THE THINGS OF THE WORLD THAT WILL DIVERT OUR ATTENTION AWAY FROM THE STILL, SMALL VOICE OF GOD! People that will not only hear, but understand what God is saying.

B. Our Own Worst Enemy: The church leader's most dangerous enemy is himself. His own flesh and indwelling sin nature constitute a vicious and deceptive foe. Compared to this, his external foes are easy to combat.

1. ***The Three Prime Pitfalls of Leadership***: The three areas of sin which are at the root of the downfall of any Christian leader are the love of women *[illicit sexual immorality]*, the love of money *[the desire to become rich]*, and the love of position and prominence *[pride]*.

Experience only confirms the testimony of Scripture: *"Love not the world, neither the things that are in the world. If anyone loves the world, the love of the Father is not in him. For all that is in the world, the lust of the flesh, the lust of the eyes, and the boastful pride of life, is not from the Father, but is from the world!"* <u>I John 2:15-16</u>

No one is immune to these things. I don't consider myself immune to them nor have I ever met anyone who did. There is a high rate of failure among Christian leaders because of them. Every wise leader knows that if he doesn't exercise self-control, he can fall into either one, two or all three of these snares. These are no doubt, some of the besetting sins mentioned in Hebrews 12:1.

According to *John 2:15*, a lack of love for the Father leaves room for a love for the world to develop. This makes you especially vulnerable to these areas of attack if you are in leadership.

Proper training and preparation for leadership involves developing an absolute trust in God and His Word. If you walk in faith, you will not be insecure. You will be able to avoid the snares of sexual sin, covetousness and pride. These three areas of sin proceed out of insecurity *[a lack of faith and trust in the Lord]*.

a. **Immorality**. Immorality generally results from an insecure marriage that may be failing because of poor self-esteem. This makes you self-conscious, self-centered, and selfish. The unhappy spouse fights back and the leader feels driven out of her affection into the arms of someone who seems more understanding and loving.

1. ***Family: A High Priority***: The leader must fight for time to spend with his wife and children. He must take an active interest in the

members of his family. The intense pressures and busy schedule created by church responsibilities and problems will infringe on this very high priority.

2. ***A Word to The Wife:*** The wife must also bring concern, sensitivity and support to her husband. He will constantly be battered with the pressures of an ever-expanding job. He may feel inadequate to handle all that it demands of him and get frustrated and frightened, isolated and lonely. At such times, kind words and tender touch can make all the difference in the world to the harassed church leader. Understanding and support from the wife might save him and his ministry.

3. ***A Lasting Scar***: Moral failure is especially dangerous. Solomon says of someone who falls into fornication, ***"a wound and dishonour shall he get, and his reproach shall not be wiped away" [Proverbs 6:33]***. It will impede your ministry for the rest of your life.

God's forgiveness and restoring grace never fail to be available, but the *"wound and reproach"* continue to have an effect. Through moral failure you will lose all you could have gained by the years of preparation in becoming a leader.

b. ***Covetousness***: Covetousness *[the love of money]* comes from insecurity about God' provision. As a spiritual leader you must ***".... seek first the kingdom of God and His righteousness ...."*** If you do, Jesus said, ***"all these things will be added unto you." [Matthew 6:33]***

He will add to you the food, clothing, health, housing and transportation you need if you faithfully practice the principle of prosperity found in the Bible. This principle is as follows: ***"Give and it shall be given unto you." Luke 6:38***

1. ***Learn To Give:*** Until you learn to consistently give a tithe *[10 %]* of your income to the Lord you will never know God's provision for your needs. You will break the curse of poverty by giving a tithe *[tenth]* of all God blesses you with.

Give to your mission outreach, to help widows, orphans, the poor around you, and God promises *"I will ... open ... the windows of heaven, and pour you out a blessing, that there shall not be room enough to receive it." [Malachi 3:7-11]*

2. **Teach Others to Give**: Once you have started practicing this, start teaching all the brothers and sisters to do the same. As they learn to bring their tithes to the church, the curse of poverty will be broken from them also. Giving to the Lord's work breaks the hold of sin of *"the love of money."* Practice it regularly and save yourself a lot of heartbreak. Save yourself from poverty. Save your church from poverty by teaching them to give, too.

c. **Pride**. Pride is the result of insecurity about your call and your own sense of self-worth. Pride is the easiest of failures for others to see. It is also the hardest one for us to see in ourselves. It shows itself by a boastful attitude. Boasting broadcasts insecurity. A person who has an effective ministry doesn't have to boast about it. *"Let another praise thee, and not thine own lips" [Proverbs 27:2]*. If someone feels he needs to advertise he is an apostle, for example, it means that he doubts it himself and doubts others will think so unless he says something about it. Boasting is clear evidence that a person is full of pride and insecurity.

1] A Servant Not a Lord: "*The elders* [leaders] *who are among you I exhort... do not act as lords over God's heritage but be examples to the flock" [I Peter 5:1,2]*. True leaders are not lords. They function as servants of God's people. Church leadership isn't a place of lordship, but it is a place of lowly servants. God's preparations are to teach us to have the attitude of a servant.

Jesus was the most humble and lowly of all men. Like Jesus, a true leader won't avoid certain jobs because he feels they a below his dignity as a leader. A secure leader is not threatened by menial tasks or humble responsibilities. Paul wrote of Jesus, *".... although He existed in the form of God,* [He] *did not regard equality with God a thing to be grasped after, but emptied Himself, taking the form of a bondservant and was made in the likeness of men. And being found in the appearance as a man, He humbled Himself by becoming obedient to the point of death, even death on a cross:"* **"Philippians 2:6-8.** Jesus was so secure in who He was, He didn't need to exalt Himself.

John 13 makes this even clearer: *"Jesus, knowing that the Father had given all things into His hands, and that He had come forth from God, and was going back to God, rose from supper, and laid aside His garments: and taking a towel, girded Himself about. Then He poured water into a basin and began to wash the disciples' feet, and to wipe them with the towel with which He was girded." [John 13:3-5]*

Notice the word *"knowing."* Because Jesus knew who He was, He could take the lowliest place of service and not have His *"image as a great Leader"* threatened. Contrast this with present-day church pontiff's regal robes and sometimes ostentatious ways. Washing feet was one of the basest tasks in the culture of Jesus' day. It was a job usually done by a house slave. Just as we offer a visitor hospitality, so in Jesus' time the house servant customarily washed a visitor's feet.

Washing feet was an undesirable responsibility. The roads were dusty, but the filth of the road was more than dust. The transportation of that day was the camel, the donkey, the horse and the mule. It takes a little imagination to understand that the streets and roads were littered with manure. The traveler's feet would be covered with this dung as well as being caked with dust. The washing of feet was assigned to the lowliest slave because it meant handling the filth of the streets. This job was thought to be below the dignity of the *"good man of the house."*

Yet it was this task to which our Lord of Glory stooped. The violent protests of the disciples are quite easy to understand. How could Jesus do this? How could He their Master and King wash dung from His follower's feet? He could do it because He was secure in Who

He was. He knew the Father had put all things into His hands. He knew He had come from the Father and that He was the Son of God and promised Messiah.

He knew He was going back to the Father after He defeated sin, death, hell and the grave. He didn't have to prove anything to Himself or others. His life had already proven who He was to see who had spiritual perception to see.

3] Reach for Responsibility: **someone well said,** ***"If you see a man reaching for authority, watch him-he will cause trouble. If you see a man reaching for responsibility, promote him-he will be a blessing:"*** We must reach for responsibility, not authority. In church leadership, the love for position destroys many ministers. Paul says, ***"He who desires the office of an overseer desires a good work."*** However, if your desire is for position and authority and not for responsibility, your downfall will be as certain as Satan's was.

The church leader overcomes this because he remains aware of the pride that dwells in him *[Romans 7:14-24]*. He walks in a repentant attitude of heart, seeking to excel in service, and he avoids those things which will tend to make him think more highly of himself than he ought to think.

C. PRIDE: THE ESSENCE OF SIN

Uzziah — a contracted form of Azariah the Lord is my strength. [1.] One of Amaziah's sons, whom the people made king of Judah in his father's stead *[II Kings 14:21; II Chr.26:1]*. His long reign of about fifty-two years was "the most prosperous except that of Jehoshaphat since the time of Solomon."

He was a vigorous and able ruler, and "his name spread abroad, even to the entering in of Egypt" *[II Chr.26:8, 14]*. In the earlier part of his reign, under the influence of Zechariah, he was faithful to Jehovah, and "did that which was right in the sight of the Lord" *[II Kings 15:3; II Chr.26:4, 5]*; but what killed Uzziah; ***pride***.

Because toward the close of his long life "his heart was lifted up to his destruction," and he wantonly invaded the priest's office *[IIChr.26:16]*, and entering the sanctuary proceeded to offer incense on the golden altar.

Azariah the high priest saw the tendency of such a daring act on the part of the king, and with a band of eighty priests he withstood him *[II Chr.26:17]*, saying, "It appertaineth not unto thee, Uzziah, to burn incense."

Without considering his faithfulness and good work, Uzziah was suddenly struck with leprosy while in the act of offering incense *[26:19–21]*, and he was driven from the temple and compelled to reside in "a several house" to the day of his
death *[II Kings 15:5, 27; II Chr.26:3]*. He was buried in a separate grave "in the field of the burial which belonged to the kings" *[II Kings 15:7; II Chr.26:16-23]*.
To some it is their *pride*, sometimes, *spiritual pride*, lack of honour, giving honour to whom it is due; "I know it more than the pastor, I know it more than the elder; Holy Spirit or not, instruction or not pastor or not, I want it done my own way, do what I want, timing or no timing, take it or leave it, that was what killed Uzziah.

1. **Symptoms of Pride:** The subtle symptoms of pride are quite easy to spot once you know what they are. Here are two or three indicators:

a. *"I am More Important."* Thinking certain people are or jobs are *"beneath your dignity"* or thinking you are more important than others because you have a place of leadership.

b. *"I Want to Be Served:"* Accepting special honour as a leader and being served by others rather than devoting yourself to serving them.

c. *"I am The Best:"* Paul warns us against *"thinking more highly of ourselves than we ought to think" [Romans 12:3].* Pride is beginning to dominate us if we esteem ourselves more than we ought. These and other similar traits warn us that we have been poisoned by that subtle sin, pride.

God hates pride because it is the essence of sin. Satan fell because of pride. *"Your heart was filled with pride because of all your beauty .... Therefore, I have cast you down ...." [Ezekiel 28:17].* Eve fell because of Satan's appeal to her pride, *".... ye shall be like Elohim [God] ..." [Genesis 3:5].* Pride brings our certain downfall. *"Pride goes before destruction and a haughty spirit before a fall" [Proverbs 16:18].*

2. **Pride Is Dangerous:** Pride is dangerous because it is subtle. Pride is like a weed among the crops: It will grow and take over if we don't take positive action to prevent it.

You may begin as a humble leader and presume that you have mastered humility. When you are *"proud of"* your humility, you do not have any humility.

Pride is a destroyer: This is why it is God's will for a novice to take on responsibility a little bit at a time so he can grow into an enlarged responsibility without the danger of being destroyed by pride. *"An overseer must not be one who is newly saved [a novice], lest he become conceited and fall into the same condemnation incurred by the devil" [I Timothy 3:2,6].*

3. *Avoid the Pitfall of Pride*: If pride is so hard to detect and so insidious an enemy, how can we guard against it? How can we protect ourselves from this serpentine sin? Here are some steps we must take to avoid being trapped by this prime pitfall for leaders:

a. *Stay close to God:* Maintain close contact with the Lord Jesus through disciplined daily prayer, diligent study of Bible and determined meditation of His Word to you. This will keep you focused on His Glory and thus help you maintain a sober view of your real importance.

b. *Fast and Pray:* If there is pride in your life, deal with it. David said, "I humbled my soul with fasting..." [Psalms 35:13].

c. *Stay Close to Others:* **Leadership isolates you from people. The Bible says we are to** *"continue in fellowship" [Acts 2:42].* Always maintain some close relationships with those you will allow to speak into your life--correctively if need be.

The leader who doesn't receive consistent, honest input from trusted friends may lose his perspective and give way to pride. Since as Jeremiah affirms, *"The heart is deceitful above all things, and desperately wicked" [Jeremiah 17:9],* we are sure to stray because of pride if we don't have protection.

d. ***Don't Strive for Position:*** **Psalm 75:6 tells us** *"Promotion comes from the Lord."* God will promote you to the place of leadership He has for you no matter what your circumstances are. He knows who you are, and He will exalt you at the proper time *[I Peter 5:1-6].*

e. ***Seek to Excel as A Servant of Others:*** A good servant strives to make those he serves successful. If they succeed, you have already succeeded. If you focus on your own success, pride will easily infect you *[see Philippians 2:4].*

f. ***Have A Foot-Washing Service:*** Whenever a man is licensed or ordained to the ministry, one of his first responsibilities ought to be to wash the feet of those he is going to serve. If it is a large meeting point, then a leadership group should represent the brothers and sisters, and the one being put into a leadership role washes their feet. Whenever strife breaks out in a church, foot-washing serves as the best antidote we've seen, as it breaks the pride which is behind contention. Have the women wash the women's feet-and the men, the men's feet.

g. ***CONCLUSION***: To be saved from failing because of pride pray this prayer out loud to the Lord right now:

"Dear Lord Jesus, You promised that You would lead me in a straight path and protect me from all evil. Make me the servant You want me to be. Keep me from presumptuous sins of immorality, covetousness and pride.

Search out my heart and reveal any of these sins to me that I am not aware of. Keep me open to any correction others would bring me.

Give me grace to accept Your chastisement. Thank You for making me a humble servant like You. AMEN!

AS A LEADER HOW DO I INFLUENCE OTHERS?

1. You can impress people from afar, but you impact them from up close:

Leaders get involved in the lives of the people they lead with an intentional focus on those who are in the process of becoming a leader. You can't model from the pulpit. Modeling is life on life. Modeling says, *"come do this with me."* Modeling lets people see your mistakes and how you handle pressure. Because this is true, we can discern that we don't truly model for large numbers. Your church may be large, but you model for just a few. Know who they are and be intentional about it. be real and be yourself while also being the best of Christianity that you can.

2. You Reproduce Who You Are:

The principle of mirror leadership is very sobering. Mirror leadership means that after about 36 months of leadership, the people around you reflect very closely who you are.

Look closely and learn from who you attract, and the people who stay with you under your modelling, equipping and developing. When good people leave you, find out why. Your skills and personality may determine who you attract, but your character, integrity, and lifestyle will determine who you keep over the long haul.

3. Out Lifestyle Influences Others:

In many arenas of life, it is your skill that earns you the right to influence others, but for us as Christian leaders it is first our character- our lifestyle that earns us the right. What we do when no one is looking is as important as our level of competency. Competency is critical, but it's not the whole picture.

Modelling integrity is what makes the difference between a shallow short-term project and meaningful ministry that lasts. We are about changed lives, changed by the power of God. Although this can happen in a moment, for most it's a process, and a slow one at that. People aren't projects and they don't fit into formulas or timetables. Meaning is feud over the course of a journey. Anyone can behave for a short period of time. What counts is your ability to live well over the long haul.

Bring Order to Your Private World:

When we talk of modeling, it seems like an external display because we talk in terms of what others observe about your life. The truth is that modeling is an inside job. How you live the life that others see is determined completely by the life you live that no one sees. How you handle your thought life, your motives, and your temptations has everything to do with how well you model life for others.

Determine A Distinctive Set of Values and Demonstrate Them In Daily Life:

There is no such thing as default value. Either you choose your own values and live by them or someone else will choose them for you. There are plenty of people who are happy to do so. Know what you believe, why you believe it, and live it out in an intentional way.

Live By the Same Set Of Rules:

As leaders, one of the most dangerous things we can do is to live above the law. By that I mean that you have one set of rules and standards for others but don't follow them yourself.

Roll Up Your Sleeves, Get Involved and Show the Way:

You can either lead or model from an ivory tower. You may not do all the tasks that those you lead must perform, but they must see you "in the game."

How about you? Will you take a moment and reflect on the kind of model you are? For what do you have to be thankful? and what might you need to improve upon?

12 Killers of Good Leadership:
I know numerous leaders with great potential...
They have all the appearance of being a good leader...
But they lack one thing...or two...
There are a few killers of good leadership...

Any one of these can squelch good leadership…
It's like a wrecking ball of potential…
It's not that they can't lead, but to continue to grow as a leader… to be successful at a higher level or for the long-term…they must address these issues.

Here are 12 killers of good leadership:
Defensiveness – Good leaders don't wear their feelings on their shoulders. They know other's opinions matter and aren't afraid to be challenged.

Jealousy – A good leader enjoys watching others on the team excel.

Revenge – The leader that succeeds for the long term must be forgiving and knows that "getting even" only comes back to harm them and the organization.

Fearfulness – The good leader remains committed when no one else is and must take risks no one else will. Others will follow. That's what leaders do.

Favoritism – Good leaders don't have favorites on the team. They reward results not partiality.

Ungratefulness – Good leaders value people, knowing they cannot attain success without others.

Small-mindedness – Good leaders think bigger than today. They are dreamers and idea people.

Pridefulness – Pride comes before the fall. Good leaders remain humbled by the position of authority entrusted to them.

Rigidity – There are some things to be rigid about, such as values and vision, but for most issues, the leader must be open to change. Good leaders welcome new ideas, realizing that almost everything can be improved.

Laziness – One can't be a good leader and not be willing to work hard. In fact, the leader should be willing to be the hardest worker on the team.

Unresponsiveness – Good leaders don't lead from behind closed doors. They are responsive to the needs and desires of those they attempt to lead. They respond to concerns and questions. They collaborate more than control. Leaders who close themselves off from those they lead will limit the places where others will follow.

Dishonesty – Since character counts highest, a good leader must be above reproach. When a leader fails, he or she must admit their mistake and work towards restoration.

A leader may struggle with one or more of these, but the goal should be to lead "killer-free." Leader, be honest, which of these wrecking balls do you struggle with most?

Give Your Leadership The "Attitude Edge:"
10 Traits to Identify a Promising Person

1. **Leadership in The Past:** The best predictor of the future is the past.
2. **The Capacity to Create or Catch Vision:** When I talk to people about the future, I want their eyes to light up. I want them to ask the right questions.
3. **A Constructive Spirit of Discontent:** Some people could call this criticism, but there is a big difference in being constructively discontent and being critical. The unscratchable itch is always in the leader.
4. **Practical Ideas:** Not everybody with practical ideas is a leader, of course, but leaders seem to be able to identify which are and which aren't.
5. **A Willingness to Take Responsibility:** Leaders will bear work, for the feeling of contributing to other people is what leadership is all about.
6. **A Completion Factor:** In the military, it is called "completed staff work." The half-cooked meal isn't what you want.
7. **Mental Toughness:** No one can lead without being criticized or without facing discouragement. I don't want a mean leader; I don't want a tough leader.
8. **Peer Respect:** Peer respect doesn't reveal ability but can show character and personality.
9. **Family Respect:** The family feelings toward someone reveal much about his or her potential to lead.

10. A Quality That Makes People Listen to Them: Potential leaders have a "holding court" quality about them. <u>**When they speak, people listen**</u>!

Have you noticed that whenever you buy a new car, you suddenly see others of that same model everywhere? I am sure you've figured out that those cars were there all along, you just weren't looking for them before. When we consciously look for the best in people, **their good traits can have a positive impact on our life and leadership**.

<u>**Divorce and Eldership**</u>: "*<u>Thou Shalt Be A Good Minister</u>*"
<u>*1 Corinthians 7:20-24*</u>, <u>*1 Corinthians 7:8-9*</u>, <u>*Matthew 5:32;*</u>
<u>*Matthew 19:9*</u>

> *"Let every man abide in the same calling wherein he was called:*
> *<u>vs.21</u>, Art thou called being a servant? Care not for it: but if thou mayest be made free, use it rather:*
> *<u>vs.22</u>, For he that is called in the Lord, being a servant, is the Lord's freeman: likewise also he that is called, being free, is Christ's servant:*
> *<u>vs.23</u>, Ye are bought with a price; be not ye the servant of men:*
> *<u>vs.24</u>, Brethren, let every man, wherein he is called, therein abide with God." <u>1 Corinthians 7:20-24</u>*

> *"I say therefore to then unmarried and widows, It is good for them if they abide even as I:*
> *<u>vs.9</u>, But if they cannot contain, let them marry: for it is better to marry than to burn:*
> *<u>vs.10</u>, And unto the married I command, yet not I, but the Lord, Let not the wife depart from her husband:*
> *<u>vs.11</u>, But if she depart, let her remain unmarried or be reconciled to her husband: and let not the husband put away his wife." 1 Corinthians 7:8-11:*

Paul again states the remain-as-you-are principle *[I Corinthians 7:17 "But as God has distributed to every man, as the Lord hath called everyone, so let him walk. And so ordained I in all churches]* and illustrates it with a choice faced by slaves: to willingly remain a **servant** or to seek freedom. The apostle did not condemn slaves to a life permanent slavery. By all means use the opportunity to become free if it presents itself, he said. But on the other hand, the fact of being a slave should not be a care. His topic is thus: whether a Christian was free or a slave when he came to Christ, he owes lifetime obligations to the same master, Jesus Christ. In Roman parlance, a ***freeman*** was an emancipated salve, whereas a ***free*** man was one who had never been enslaved.

In the same chapter, **verses 1-11**, **verse 1** represents a Corinthian position, stated in correspondence previously sent to Paul that recommended celibacy in marriage. What a divide in the Corinthian church! Some advocated marital celibacy while others were engaged in gross sexual immorality. **Verses 2-5**, Sexual desires, which can readily lead to sexual immorality, commend frequent sexual union between husband and wife. The phrase **hath not power** in this context refers to sexual relations. Paul issued an apostolic ruling: husbands and wives must not deprive one another sexually in marriage, *except* when mutually agreed upon for the sake of devotion to *prayer*. Like fasting from food and drink, periods of marital celibacy can hone one's focus on the one great desire: God Himself.

Verses 6-11, Paul expressed limited agreement to the celibacy view stated in **verse 1**. He did think it was **good** if the Corinthians stayed single as he was-but only if they had the ***gift*** to do so. Paul gives in verse 9 another apostolic ruling: unmarried persons who lack self-control should get married *[se vs.5]*. Paul reiterates the Lord's ruling to **the married in verse 10**, giving an injunction to wives that they must remain in their marriage *[Matthew 19:1-9; Mark 10:1-12]*. The wife who has separated from her husband has two options: remain apart from him, though celibate, or be ***reconciled to her husband***. Completing his reiteration of the Lord's instructions for marriage. Paul insisted that ***the husband*** is not top leave ***his wife!***

FOOD FOR THOUGHT:

Whenever the subject of divorce and remarriage is discussed, the inevitable question of whether a divorced and/or remarried man can ever serve as an elder follows closely behind. This discussion has led to much confusion as well as a great deal of heartache for many individuals and churches. Multitudes of men who have desired the work and service of an elder have also encountered great opposition to that desire simply because of a previous divorce.

The opposition often comes from those who believe that regardless of any past circumstances, no one who has had a previous divorce is biblically qualified to serve as an elder. Yet on the other side of the spectrum, many today are advocating that we abandon all efforts to examine the nature of anyone's past marital status. They say we should appoint men to the eldership based on present-tense circumstances alone. Their argument follows that because divorce is so rampant in our society, affirming non-divorced men is becoming an even greater challenge.

In addition, increasing numbers of pastors are becoming divorced and yet are remaining in positions of elder/pastoral ministry! Alexander Strauch writes that this issue "was dramatically highlighted when a leading evangelical journal in America brought together five divorced pastors and asked them to share their feelings, experiences, and views on divorce and the ministry. The journal's staff published the forum because they believed the growing problem of divorce among ministers needed to be faced openly and honestly." Strauch went on to say that the article "claimed that a recent survey of divorce rates in the United States showed that pastors had the third highest divorce rate—exceeded only by that of medical doctors and policemen!" *("A Biblical Style of Leadership?" Leadership 2,* Fall 1981, 119-29, cited in Alexander Strauch, *Biblical Eldership* [Littleton, Colo.: Lewis & Roth Publishers, 1995], 67).

Who Is A Perfect Man? Who Is A Perfect Woman?

The ultimate answer to this question, of course, must come from the Word of God. But what does Scripture teach on the subject? What insights do we have from God's Word that could help us in this regard? Can a man who is divorced (or who is married to someone who has been divorced) ever serve at the highest level of spiritual leadership? These crucial questions must be answered if we are to maintain the true biblical standards of spiritual leadership.

First of all, those who oppose any divorced man serving as an elder almost universally do so on the basis of the apostle Paul's language in *1 Timothy 3:2*. There Paul says that if a man is to serve as an elder, he must be the *"husband of one wife"* (this English translation comes from the Greek phrase, *mias gunaikos andra*, which when literally translated means, a *"one-woman man,"* or a *"one-wife husband"*). There are generally four different ways this phrase has been understood:

- elders must be married
- elders must not be polygamists
- elders must have married only once in their life
- elders must be sexually pure and therefore totally committed to their wife *(biblical monogamy)*

The following will be an attempt to summarize the various views and a biblical response.

Must Be Married

Those who take the view that an elder is to be qualified only if he is married misunderstand Paul's intent in this passage. If this were Paul's meaning here, he would obviously be contradicting himself in what he wrote to the Corinthians (cf. *1 Corinthians 7:7-9, 32-35*; see also *Matthew 19:12*). There, he states that it would be better if believers were to remain single *"even as I myself am"* (v. 7). He reiterates this in verse 8 when he says, *"But I say to the unmarried and to widows that it is good for them if they remain even as I."*

Paul was not only an apostle, but also a pastor (he served for three years as the pastor at Ephesus, for instance), so he certainly could not be commanding Timothy to examine potential elders on the basis of what he himself was not qualified to undertake. Likewise, he also says to the Corinthians that as apostles, they had *"the right"* to *"take along"* (marry), a believing wife, **"even as the rest of the apostles and the brothers of the Lord and Cephas [Peter]" (1 Corinthians 9:5).** Even though he did not personally choose the option of marriage (or that he had in fact been married before but at the time of his statement, was speaking as a widower (as many would contend from *1 Corinthians 7:40)*, Paul could have served as an elder and yet have remained single.

To put it another way, if one of an elder's requisite qualifications is his marrying, then every single man would be automatically disqualified, including, of course, Jesus Himself! It is obvious that this view is not a serious consideration of what the phrase, *"one-woman man"* really means.

No Polygamy

The second possibility is that Paul intends to convey that no elder candidate is qualified if he has more than one wife at the same time *(polygamy)*. This was certainly an issue on Paul's day, but it is unlikely that this is what he had in mind. The main reason is again the use of the specific phrase, *"one-woman man."*

Paul could have used a couple of different phrases to speak against polygamy if he had truly wanted to. For instance, he simply could have said, *"An overseer, then, must be above reproach, having no more than one wife,"* or *"having no more than one wife at a time."* This would have most assuredly dealt with any polygamy sins that were occurring at this time. Another reason Paul must have meant something else is that the phrase, *"one-woman man"* occurs three other times in the New Testament *(1 Timothy 3:12; 1 Timothy 5:9; Titus 1:6)*, which by their usage help us conclude that polygamy was probably not in view.

In the *1 Timothy 5:9* passage, the phrase is used to speak of a widow and whether or not she is to receive some financial assistance from the church. Even though Paul uses the corresponding phrase, *"one-man woman,"* or *"one-husband wife,"* he is essentially speaking of the same kind of qualification and speaks to whether a female widow had demonstrated a faithfulness to her one husband (who is obviously now deceased).

We can conclude that because *polyandry* (a woman who would be having at least two husbands at the same time) was repugnant both to the Jews and Romans, Paul would have no real need to address this issue in the church. Therefore, if Paul used the corresponding phrase to refer to these polygamist men in 1 Timothy 3, he would be very confusing to his readers, and certainly should have been far more specific.

Only One Marriage

A third group of interpreter's view on this *"one-woman man"* phrase as meaning that a man could marry only once in his lifetime. This view also will often reflect the belief that once divorced, a man could never remarry, with some even going so far as to say that a widower could not remarry! As in the first view however, this plainly contradicts other passages of Scripture. ***I Corinthians 7:39*** distinctly says, "A wife is bound as long as her husband lives; but if her husband is dead, she is free to be married to whom she wishes, only in the Lord." Likewise, Romans 7:2 says, "The married woman is bound by law to her husband while he is living; but if her husband dies, she is released from the law concerning her husband."

Nowhere in God's Word does it state that remarriage after the death of a spouse automatically renders a man no longer "above reproach." Indeed, Paul himself urges *young* widows (meaning those who were still in their prime childbearing years) to "get married, bear children, keep house, and give the enemy no occasion for reproach" ***(1 Timothy 5:14)***. Immorality being rampant in that pagan society, and with Christianity being so new, Paul was saying the best way to avoid a lasting reproach was to become married.

Finally, Paul even warns Timothy a chapter earlier that some false teachers were actually forbidding marriage ***(1 Timothy 4:3)***, and those men should be exposed. Surely, this *no-marriage view* in *1 Timothy 3:2* would need to be clarified since he condemns those false teachers only a chapter later! Lastly, it would also set up a very difficult double standard. Those outside the spiritual leadership of the church could marry or remarry, while those within leadership could not.

Marital Faithfulness

The fourth view says that Paul is simply emphasizing in this phrase, *"one-woman man,"* the concept of marital faithfulness to one's present spouse. This seems to be the most natural way to interpret the phrase. Strauch concludes, the phrase 'the husband of one wife' is meant to be a positive statement that expresses faithful, monogamous marriage. In English we would say, 'faithful and true to one woman' or 'a one-woman man.'...Negatively, the phrase prohibits all deviation from faithful, monogamous marriage. Thus, it would prohibit an elder from polygamy, concubinage, homosexuality, and/or any questionable sexual relationship. Positively, Scripture says the candidate for eldership should be a 'one-woman man,' meaning he has an exclusive relationship with one woman. Such a man is above reproach in his sexual and marital life (Alexander Strauch, *Biblical Eldership*, 192).

In other words, are you completely committed to the wife you now have? Is your love for her ever growing and do you serve and love her as Christ loves the church *(Ephesians 5:25)*? It is possible that if our English Bible translators had simply translated the phrase literally, much confusion could have been avoided. But since the phrase has been translated as *"the husband of one wife,"* it has evoked much needless debate and anguish.

Elder Qualification

The only remaining question regards the general question of whether a divorced man should *ever* serve as an elder, *even if he has proven to be a present and faithful husband to his wife.* This matter is covered in Paul's first qualification of **_1 Timothy 3:2_**, "An overseer, then, must be *above reproach.*" Being above reproach means that there is nothing for which one can be accused or blamed; those things which could render a man as being validly accused of sinful behavior. He must not have a chargeable character; that is, he has an impeccable reputation. He lives his life in such a way that no one can accuse him of scandalizing the body of Christ in any way. This is the kind of man that, even with his critics, can find no fault in his character.

Another very important reminder is this: we must remember that the qualifications listed in 1 Timothy 3 and Titus 1 are *present-tense* qualifications. The main evaluation of a man's life must take place in the present, not in the past. Does this automatically mean that a man's past actions have utterly no bearing on his present life? No. A man's past could, in fact, render him reproachable in some way. What ways could this be true? A man could be disqualified if his past divorce has continuing implications. For instance, a man who has had a divorce in his past (whether it is his pre-Christian past or his Christian past), might be rendered reproachable in the eyes of the congregation *if the man's former spouse is in the same community as his local church, or in the same local church itself.* In some cases, this may mean he is not qualified to serve as an elder there. Another example is if his children from a previous marriage(s) are not believers or are a reproach to him in some way. This may also become a disqualifier.

It is most unlikely that any man who has had a divorce in his past, whether pre-Christian or post-Christian, will *not* be able to serve as an elder. Usually, there are circumstances which render him as not above reproach in the eyes of the church's leadership and/or the congregation. This does not mean that he cannot serve the Lord in the local church. It simply means that his service will by necessity be in a non-elder capacity. Indeed, he can serve in a variety of ways by God's design. ***It would seem to be an extremely rare occurrence for a man who has had a divorce, whether biblically allowed or not, to fulfill the role of elder in the local church.*** This is never intended to make anyone think that he, because of the fact of his divorce, is a second-class Christian, and that his divorce is a stigma which follows him forever. But at the same time, however, it is true that divorce oftentimes is a stigma, and it has tragically become a stigmatic reproach for many. God's grace can cover the sin, but the consequences sometimes do have lasting effects.

Finally, regardless of the specifics of any one situation, the general principle is this: Does he enjoy the complete and full affirmation of the leaders and people of his own congregation, and is he presently living out the qualifications listed in 1 Timothy 3 and Titus 1? If a particular local church scrutinizes his life and ministry and sees nothing in his present character or past conduct that brings a reproach, he may, in God's good providence, serve as an elder in that place. Strauch gives wise words on this account:

What does 1 Timothy say about sexual and marital sins committed before a person's conversion to Christ? What about people who have legally divorced and remarried (assuming the local church allows for such)? What about the forgiveness and restoration of a fallen spiritual leader? These and many other painful and controversial questions are not answered directly here. They must be answered from the whole of Scripture's teaching on divorce and remarriage, forgiveness, grace, and restoration, as well as its teaching on leadership example and the full spectrum of elder qualifications.

All deviations from God's standard of marital behavior confuse and perplex us. Sin always confuses, distorts, and divides, so there will always be diverse opinions on questions such as these. This in no way, however, diminishes the local church's obligation to face these issues and make wise, scripturally sound decisions. In all these heartbreaking situations, the honor of Jesus' name, faithfulness to His Word, and prayer are the supreme guides (Alexander Strauch, *Biblical Eldership*, 192-93).

WISDOM FOR LEADERS:

Whatever might be going on or that you might be going through remember, God did not use anyone in the Bible until He put them in the University of adversity!

1. You want to think about Abraham? After the age of 90 he had no child of his own; he later had Isaac who begat Jacob who became Israel and great nation!
2. You want to talk about Joseph? He spent 15 years in prison for sin he did not commit, he
3. You want to think about Moses? He escaped from the wrath of Pharaoh to tend his father-in-law's sheep for forty years, he spent another forty years in the wilderness, the people forsook him; he became the author of the first five books of the Bible!
4. What about Isaiah and Jeremiah? Think about their lives and what they went through before they became some of the major prophets of the Bible!
5. God will take you through some adversities before He now perfect you for His own use, our success as leaders hinges on how we scale though the temptations that come our way in the process of making.
6. No one can make you inferior without your consent, if you think you can't, you can't; if you think you can, you can if you believe in yourself!
7. Do not risk the loss of divine favour over a knicle of tithe you ought to pay, the tithe is not yours it belongs to God.
8. We are supposed to walk and live in divine dominion, stop discussing what you want to forget, stop discussing what you don't want!
9. Anything you do not recognize you cannot celebrate, anything you cannot celebrate will exit your life! Whatever you honour will increase in your life!
10. Our future is decided by the voice we honour; honour the voice of the Lord!
11. Until you decide to walk away from your Egypt, you cannot taste manna, when you ask God for a harvest; He will ask you for a seed!

12. If you insist on taking what God did not give you, He will take what He gave you!

LEADERSHIP AND THEOLOGY:

It's possible to love what we're learning about God more than we love God himself.

What's more dangerous to the human soul—money or theology?

Money is the easy answer. Paul warns us, "The love of money is the root of all kinds of evil. It is through this craving that some have wandered away from the faith and pierced themselves with many pangs" *[I Timothy 6:10]* Treasure money, and what it can buy, more than God, and it will rob you of him and buy you terrifying, unending pain, apart from him.

Jesus himself says, "No one can serve two masters, for either he will hate the one and love the other, or he will be devoted to the one and despise the other. You cannot serve God and money" *[Matthew 6:24]*, see also *[Hebrews 13:5]*. The God of Christianity and the god of money are irreconcilably opposed. They cannot room together in the human heart. If you find yourself serving money—consuming yourself with earning, gathering and spending—by definition you are not serving God.

But is money more spiritually dangerous than theology? The answer may be trickier than we think, especially within the numbing comfort of a proudly affluent and educated American Church. Money is a tangible, countable, often visible god. Theology, on the other hand—if it is cut off from truly knowing and enjoying God himself—can be a soothing, subtle, superficially spiritual god. Both are deadly, but one lulls us into a proud, intellectual, and purely cosmetic confidence and rest before God.

Theology will kill you if it does not kindle a deep and abiding love for the God of the Bible and if it does not inspire a desire for his glory, and not ultimately our own.

Good Theology Is the Only Path to God

We all love theology: Paul's one aim in life and ministry was to know Christ and him crucified (i.e., to know Christian theology), and he wanted to know God in Christ as truly and thoroughly as possible, with all of its implications for everything he thinks and says and does *[I Corinthians 2:2]*. You cannot read this man's letters and not come to the conclusion that theology was his heartbeat. He lived to know as much about this unsearchable God as possible, and he was ready to die for those truths.

Psalm 119 is a passionate love letter written to the revelation of God in his word. What we know about God from the Bible is unbelievably, inexhaustibly profitable for teaching, reproof, correction, training in righteousness and *life [II Timothy 3:16; John 6:68]*.

Without theology, you will not know God—literally and spiritually. So, this article is not meant to be a prohibition against theology— God forbid—but a caution and a warning about theology. Knowledge about God can replace an authentic knowing of him to our destruction, especially for the theologically refined and convinced. We all should want our theology to be not only true, but Spirit-filled and fruitful.

It's possible to love what we're learning about God more than we love God himself.

The Best Readers Can Be the Worst Listeners

The Pharisees fought Jesus at every turn. They doubted and even hated much of what he said and did and tried again and again to trap him in a lie or inconsistency. They had read God's word over and over again. They knew this book really well—or so it seemed— and yet they did not know the Word living, breathing and speaking in front of them—the Word through whom all things were made and without whom nothing was made that was made *John 1:3]*, the Word who became flesh and walked the earth *John 1:14]*, the Word who is the perfect picture of God and who upholds the universe with the words of his mouth *[Hebrews 1:3]*.

Mark recounts one of these confrontations between Jesus and the so-called spiritual experts of his day. "The Pharisees and the scribes asked [Jesus], 'Why do *Your* disciples not walk according to the tradition of the elders, but eat with defiled hands?'" *[Mark 7:5]*. We know this was not Pharisaical humility and genuine curiosity

Mathew 12:14; 22:15]. This was defiance—an attempt to undermine and shame the Son of God.

They were so confident in their theology that they confronted the Christ himself. They tried to pin him down under the featherweight and wading-pool-depth of their theology—the One who was the fulfillment and pinnacle of all the pages they had read. They challenged God's own understanding of God. Their education and pride—their knowledge and confidence in their own system—had blinded them to the very image and voice of God. They knew so much about God, and yet knew him so little.

Even the Literate Need to Learn to Read

Jesus responds to their ignorant and murderous criticism with the very Scriptures they seem to know so well. "Well did Isaiah prophesy of you hypocrites, as it is written, 'This people honor me with their lips, but their heart is far from me'" *[Mark 7:6-7].* Hypocrisy, according to Jesus, disconnects knowledge of God from true love for God. Hypocrisy is not just about disobedience to the Bible—the Pharisees would have been thought of as clearly "obedient"—but about disillusionment with the God of the Bible. You can know him and not *know* him. And that might be the most dangerous place in all the world—however comfortable, safe and informed it may feel. Jesus goes on to say, "You leave the commandment of God"—an awful, terrifying condemnation—"and hold to the tradition of men" *[Mark 7:8].* You have traded the truth about God for images of the truth, manufactured by your own mind. You've loved what you've learned about God more than God himself. You've trusted your knowledge and obedience more than the mouth of God. "For the sake of your tradition, you have made void the word of God" *[Mathew 15:6].*

You Can Tithe Theology, Too

So, we *should* fear money when it leads our hearts and allegiances away from God. And we should fear our system of theology when it more subtly does the same. In our good disciplines of learning about God—reading, asking, listening, writing—we must take care to develop habits of treasuring and worshiping Him, too. Be committed to having a right theology but be as committed to having a relational theology—a growing, humble and heartfelt intimacy with God. Do not simply search the Scriptures for soteriology, but search for salvation—the eternal life—that is only found in the flesh, blood and person of Jesus Christ *[John 5:39]*.

Tithe your theology. Just like all money is God's, all good theology is God's, too—it's all about Him, all from Him and all for Him. Still, we give 10 percent or more of our money to declare week after week our gratitude, faith and joy in God, even to say that it is *all* His. Likewise, we need rhythms of responding to God in worship when we learn more about Him. Look for every opportunity to offer what you've seen about God back to Him in prayer and worship.

Stop, and pray God's words about God back to Him. Journal as a way of stimulating your heart over the things your mind is beginning to understand. Put the truths you're learning on your lips for others to hear and love—share them with someone. The psalmist responded this way to knowing God and His love more deeply in **Psalm 63:** "Because your steadfast love is better than life, my lips will praise you. ... My soul will be satisfied as with fat and rich food, and my mouth will praise you with joyful lips" ***Psalms 63:3&5]***.

We will never be truly satisfied by knowing about God. We need to know *Him*. If that dichotomy doesn't make sense to you, beware. Facts about God without feelings for Him and fellowship with Him—without a sense that you are God's chosen, redeemed and known son or daughter—will give you a false sense of God's love and security. But facts about God can also draw you closer to Him.

You cannot serve both God and theology, but you can serve and love and treasure God *with* good theology.

"We need our theology to be not only true, but Spirit-filled and fruitful."

DRESSING FOR OCCASSIONS:

"And a voice came out of the Throne, saying, Praise our God, all ye His servants, and ye that fear Him, both small and great:
<u>vs.6</u>, And I heard as it were the voice of a great multitude, and as the voice of many waters, and as the voice of mighty thundering, saying, Al-le-lu-ia: for the Lord God omnipotent reigneth:
<u>vs.7</u>, Let us be glad and rejoice, and give honour to Him: for the marriage of the Lamb is come, and His wife hath made herself ready:
<u>vs.8</u>, And to her was granted that she should be arrayed in fine linen, clean and white for the fine linen is the righteousness of saints." <u>Revelation 19:5-8</u>

"And I saw heaven opened, and behold a White Horse; and He that sat upon him was called Faithful and True, and in righteousness He doth judge and make war:
<u>vs.12</u>, His eyes were as a flame of fire, and on His head were many crowns; and He had a name written, that no man knew, but He himself:
<u>vs.13</u>, And He was clothed with a vesture dipped in blood: and His name is called The Word Of God:
<u>vs.14</u>, And the armies which were in heaven followed Him upon white horses, clothed in fine linen, white and clean."
<u>Revelation 19:11-14</u>

Like I said, you are addressed by the dressing you put on. If you are dressed up in earthly clothes, you can only influence the earth. It takes putting on Jesus to influence Heaven and earth; what kind of clothes are you putting on? The Book of Revelation tells us the kind of dress the Bridegroom would wear. His dressing reflects His righteousness as well as the battle He is going into. It is important to be well dressed for every occassion. When you are going to dine with the Kings of kings, your dressing should reflect it: you should be in your best. Your dressing will show your attitude to the Lord and that can also affect what you receive from the Lord's Table.

When you are going to evangelize, how do you dress? If you are going for a very important interview, you can be assured that you will be assessed partially by your dressing. When you are going to offer God's greatest gift to man-salvation through our Lord Jesus Christ, you must dress clean, decent and presentable clothes: If your dressing reflects poverty, you are not likely to convert those who seriously mind being poor. They may turn you back for fear of being ***"infested"*** with poverty. You do not need to be extravagant either; let your dressing open door for discussion with unbelievers.

How you are dressed determines how you are received or treated: your dressing is a part of your identity. How you dress equally affects your Kingdom walk: In ***II Kings 1:1-8***, when the king was sick, he sent some people to inquire if he would recover or die. They met Elijah who told them it was a sickness unto death. In order to verify the authenticity of that prophecy, the king asked for the name of the prophet, but they could not tell because he did not disclose his name. But by the time they described the type of clothes he wore; the king immediately knew it was Elijah. Does your dressing portray you as a child of God?

If you as a minister of God were to dress in regular clothes and not priestly robe or cassock, would your dressing showcase you as the servant of the Most High God? If you compare what John the Baptist wore in ***Matthew 3:1-4***, with what Elijah wore, you will find some resemblance. Who do you resemble when you dress? How is your hairdo? What about your beard? How do you adorn yourself with jewelry-moderate or loud? What kind of dresses do you put on?

When Moses fled from Egypt to Midian after killing one of the Egyptians, he met the daughters of the priest of Midian and helped them. When they got home earlier than usual, their father asked why they were back home so soon. They said it was because they received protection and help from an Egyptian ***[Exodus 2:15-20]***.

He was taken for an Egyptian because he dressed like one: If you dress like the world, what follows worldly attires will equally follow you. Worldly fashion is controlled by the lust of the flesh, the lust of the eyes and the pride of life according to *I John 2:16*. Don't be surprised to see pride and worldly lust gaining ground in your life if you are given to worldly fashion. If you are obsessed with the latest fashion and style, rather than running the heavenly race you were called into, you will find yourself running a race that God did not call you to. The unfortunate thing about this is that those who are given to worldly fashion share a common destiny with what they are given to. Are you following fashion or Christ?

7 Basic Things About Marriage:

1. *Marriage Is A Divine Product*:
Mark 10, reading to us from vs.6, *"But from the beginning of the creation God made them male and female:"* when you hear the term, *"God made them male and female,"* then whose product are we? God's product of course, because He made us, He is our Creator, after creating us, He instituted marriage. Marriage belongs to God. It is Holy, it cannot be tampered with, it is fenced around with electric fence, to no extent can anyone, including parents from either side, friends, or relatives interfere in any marriage, that is why it says in *vs.7 & 8*, *"For this cause,"* for this reason, for this cause: same statement in *Mat.19:3-9*.

The reason being stated above in the previous verses; that God created us, God instituted marriage, it is God's ordinance, *"for this cause:"*

> *"Shall a man leave his father and mother, and cleave to his wife: And they twain shall be one flesh: so then they are no more twain, but one flesh."*

Marriage is Divine, it is God's institution, so He only has the solution into any rift in marriage; you can only go to God for counseling by going to your pastor, not just any pastor who doesn't know the divine law and order of marriage, not a pastor who himself is divorced, either taken another wife and married to a divorcee or not, **"as long as either spouses are still alive"** then such a minister is in error. But a pastor, a servant of God who knows the truth, who preach the truth, who does not live in adultery, such a minister is in position to guide you according to God's ordinance of marriage and give you the right counsel.

The Bible says in the first Book of **_Psalms 1:1-2_**

> **_"Blessed is the man that walketh not in the counsel of the ungodly, nor standeth in the way of sinners, nor sitteth in the seat of the scornful: But his delight is in the law of the law Lord; and in his law doth he meditate day and night."_**

A minister who is already divorced whose former wife is still living cannot counsel you rightly; there will be a division of interest: he is too close to the game; he is in error already: A true minister of the gospel of Jesus Christ will not divorce and remarry, if there is a problem in the marriage of a servant of God, they both need to fix it, divorce is not the answer, two wrongs cannot make a right: otherwise what will you preach, what will you teach as a minister what counsel will you give, **_[your own doctrine and your own counsel?]_** and when you pray for people to which God? Is it to the same God of heaven who instituted marriage and said He hates divorce?

This is why a servant of God, a minister of the Gospel must always consult and hear from God before taking any step, because of our position as leaders, elders, pastors, a minister, we must, and must be in line with God's Word so we don't preach and teach error whereby we lead many people to hell!

2. _Marriage Is Accountable_:
It is Trust, and we will give account as husbands, we will give account as wives, all of us both will give account of how we manage that institution; if we are such that orders our husbands around, that

the man has no say in the house, we are not doing His will, you are walking against His will.

If you're like the people of Ephraim in <u>Judges 8</u> you always turn everything into a brawl, arguments, always looking for a fight, so disrespectful, or that you call your husband by name when God says to call him 'lord!' you can't cook for him nor prepare meals in the house for the children if there are, you are the boss in the house as a woman which the Bible forbids, in fact Bibles commands for you to be *"submissive to your own husbands:"* if you're not being submissive, you will give account; you cannot *"Dwell"* neither can you *"Abide"* with the Father!

If you are such a husband that always boss your wife when the Bible says she is your helpmate; someone by your side not behind you; the Bible says, *"Husbands, love your wives:"* you cannot provide for the home; the home is always in lack because you are lazy to *"go out and gather"* mind you, you made your wife to be your boss and the spiritual leader in the home because you are lazy even to serve the Lord, the wife has to push you to go to church, she has to push you to do everything listen to who the Bible says you are:

> *"But if any provide not for his own, and especially for those of his own house, he hath denied the faith, and is worse than an infidel." <u>I Timothy 5:8</u>*

The strong language in this verse indicates that provision for one's own house is a spiritual responsibility; let the husband fulfill his own responsibility in their home likewise the wife to the husband. The Bible talks about *defrauding one another:* let us read the verse and I will explain what this means:

> *"Let the husband render unto the wife due benevolence: and likewise also the wife unto the husband:*
> *<u>vs.4</u>, The wife hath not power of her own body, but the husband: and likewise also the husband hath not power of his own body, but the wife:*

vs.5, Defraud ye not one the other, except it be with consent for a time, that ye may give yourselves to fasting and prayer; and come together again, that Satan tempt you not for your incontinency." I Corinthians 7:3-5

Let me explain briefly, if we read from **verse 1 of I Corinthians chapter 1** and further; these verses present a Corinthian position, stated in correspondence previously sent to Paul, that recommended celibacy in marriage. What a divide in Corinthian church! Some advocated marital celibacy while others were engaged in gross sexual immorality: in **verses 2-5**, Sexual desires, which can readily lead to sexual immorality, commend frequent sexual union between husband and wife. The phrase **hath not power** in this context refers to sexual relations. Paul issues an apostolic ruling: husbands and wives must not deprive one another sexually in marriage, **except** when mutually agreed upon for the sake of devotion to **prayer**. Like fasting from food and drink, periods of marital celibacy can hone one's focus on the one great desire: God Himself.

So, in submitting, the wife shouldn't be the one to say the last word, the man has to remain quiet, otherwise soon, there will be chaos, there will be tension, there will be calling of names, there will be physical abuse, Satan will take a comfortable seat: then that little argument will lead elsewhere; God did not create marriage to be like that. That is why both of them must be believers; some believers are even worse: A spirit filled wife does not nag. A ***Proverbs 31*** wife cannot be disobedient. A spirit filled wife speaks to the husband with respect, does not shout nor yell on the husband, not even at the children; a spirit filled woman will fill her role as a woman of the house who takes care of her home, makes everywhere look neat and prepare meal in the house.

Likewise, a spirit filled husband provides the need for his home, loves his wife and takes care of her, a spirit filled husband does not bully his wife, spirit filled husbands does not order their wives around, spirit filled husbands don't yell at their wives and children. As a believer, a spirit filled husband don't sit back at home while the wife and children go to church, or just send his family to the church, spirit filled husband brings his family to the church, spirit filled husbands are the spiritual leaders in their homes; remember as a husband/wife, believers or not, marriage is accountable.

3. **_Marriage Is Not Divorceable_**:
What God has joined together, let no man, let no woman, let no child, let no judge downtown, let no relative at home or abroad, let no friend here or there, let no job of **_whatever kind_**, let no amount of money no matter how much, put asunder even if you're making more money than your husband; *[what does that mean?]* God who instituted marriage, God who puts it together says for you, *[to not put marriage asunder;"* do not be a party to any separation or a divider between husband and wife: God says, *"I Hate Divorce!"* Jesus said it, God said it, Paul said it. A broken home will produce dysfunctional children.

You say, "Well Bible says in Mat.19, and in vs.9, *"except it be for fornication,"* there is also the doctrine of *'forgiveness;'* how many times does the Bible say for you to forgive? Some say seven times and then they start to count.

> **_Mat.18:22_**, *"Jesus saith unto him, I say not unto thee until seven times: but Until seventy times seven."*

But you say, *"fornication, that is too much to forgive, I am going to put her/him away,"* perfect, please yourself, you're free to do that, any one can do that but let us see what the Bible says concerning what you just did if you put him/her away, in **_I Cor.7_**, listen very carefully, so you can make up your mind or rescind your decision. **_I Cor.7_**, reading to us in **_vs.11_**, *"But and if she depart,"* and for those women who follow the law of the land and throw their husband out, or men who change wives like changing their underwears, throw one out today, bring another in tomorrow we cannot be getting in and out of marriage: let's see what the Bible says, if you want to remain a good Christian who wants to *"DWELL"* and *"ABIDE"* then you have to remain like Paul who never married!

"But and if he departs, let her or him remain unmarried or be reconciled to her husband: and let not the husband put away his wife."

4. **Celibacy**: **The Condition Of Not Being Married**:
The Bible says, two are better than one: to be alone is unbiblical. But then, there is also the Biblical celibacy, that is abstinence from sexual intercourse, especially by reason of religious vows. After a certain teaching of our Lord Jesus Christ on this issue of marriage in **Mat.19**, His disciples said:

"If the case of the man be so with his wife, it is not good to marry: But He said unto them, All men cannot receive this saying, save they to whom it is given."

Paul did it .... He did not marry, and it is explained in **I Cor.7**, reading to us from **vs.7**, *"For I would that all men were even as I myself:"* meaning to stay 'solo' no marriage at all; but then he goes on to say that, *"every man hath his proper gift of God, one after this manner, and another after that."*

"I say therefore to the unmarried and widows, it is good for them if they abide even as I: But if they cannot contain, let them marry: for it is better to marry than to burn: And unto the married I command, yet not I, but the Lord, Let not the wife depart from her husband."

5. **Re-marriage:**
Re-marriage of divorcee is forbidden by God. **Romans 7:3; Mark 10:11-12**, reading to us from **vs.11**, *"And He said unto them;"* who said something unto who? If we look from **vs.2**, The Bible said that *"The Pharisees came unto Him,"* they came unto Jesus tempting Him if really He knows what He was teaching, if He really knows the Jewish laws and custom regarding marriage, *"Is it lawful for a man to put away his wife?"* They know it is wrong, and they want to see if He will teach or advise otherwise.

What did He do? He threw them back to the law of Moses, but then they told Him that Moses ask whoever want to put his wife away to write give her the bill of divorcement. Now here comes the difference between the Perfect will and the Permissive will.

> *In **vs.5**, "And Jesus answered and said unto them, for the hardness of your heart he wrote you this precept: But from the beginning of creation God made them male and female."* [Read further].

There are many things that constitute 'that hardness of heart' lusting after each other, your own will, will of man, i.e ***[parents, friends, inappropriate affection] etc.*** When you go into a marriage with a man who have had *1, 2, 3*, or more wives, or a woman who have had *1, 2, 3*, or more husbands and you're living together as husband and wife, you're both living in adultery. Listen to what the Bible says, "He made them male and female;" you are with someone else's husband/wife, that home is not the place of your placement, you need to get out of that relationship and look for your own wife/husband. Then in **Romans 7**, reading to us from **vs.1-3**:

> *"Know ye not, brethren, [for I speak to them that know the law], how that the law hath dominion over a man as long as he liveth? **vs.2**, For the woman which hath an husband is bound by the law to her husband so long as he liveth; but if the husband be dead, she is loosed from that law of her husband: **vs.3**, So then if, while her husband liveth, she be married to another man, she shall be called an adulteress: but if her husband be dead, she is free from that law; so that she is no adulteress, though she be married to another man."*

Did we see that? God is a God of order and He has a purpose for all His rules and He expect us to abide by His rules and His commandments but because of our hardened heart, we want to do our own will, we want to force our will on His and live by our own rules, we are rebellious and disobedient, we need to make it right and ask Him for pardon and if we have done otherwise, we need to reconcile with the former wife or husband. It is called restitution! Or stay unmarried and not touching any woman. You say, *"Oh, that is hard, this is one of the reasons I don't like His rules and doctrines,"* well this is His standard for making heaven! Then Jesus asked them, *"will ye also go away?"* And Peter said, *"to whom shall we go? You alone have the Word of Life!"* If you thirst after the *Word of Life*, with Him is where you belong.

6. *<u>Marriage With Unbelievers Is Forbidden</u>*:

Believers are not to marry unbelievers; it does not delight God for His son or His daughter to go outside the Kingdom and marry an unbeliever…

> *"Be ye not unequally yoked together with unbelievers: for what fellowship hatht righteousness with unrighteousness? and what communion hath light with darkness?*
> *<u>vs.15</u>, And what concord hath Christ with Belial? or what part hath he that believeth with an infidel?*
> *<u>vs.16</u>, And what agreement hath the temple of God with idols? for ye are the temple of the Living God; as God hath said, I will dwell in them, and walk in them; and I will be their God, and they shall be my people!*
> *<u>vs.17</u>, Wherefore come out from among them, and be ye separate, saith the Lord, and touch not the unclean thing; and I wil receive you;*
> *<u>vs.18</u>, And will be a father unto you, and ye shall be my sons and daughters, saith the Lord Almighty!"* <u>II Corinthians 6:14</u>

What else is there that the above verses have not explained to us about His feelings? The above verses prove the fact that *"God is a jealous God,"* the verse explained the passion of His love for us, and He cannot dwell in the same temple filled with idols because once you are married to an unbeliever, you have become one body with your spouse *[read I Corinthians 6:12-20];* these verses with explain my narrations. Paul's reply to the slogan in *[verse 12]* is that the Corinthians Christians and all Christians are not their own; they are, and we are *"bodies"* belonging to the Lord *[verse 13, 19-20; 7:22-23;10:26]*. In the Roman world, *"body"* was commonly designated a slave owned by a *"lord"* or master. Making a world play of this, Paul said a person's *body* is not for sexual immorality. It is actually a *"slave body"* for the *Lord*. God will *destroy* many bodily desires at the resurrection, so why be enslaved to them now?

Paul called the believers at Corinth to remember the oneness and sanctity of their union with Christ. The words *"one flesh"* in this context refer to becoming one body through sexual relations with a *harlot*. Because Christians *are joined unto the Lord*, they should never be joined to a prostitute.

7. <u>**Marriage Is Guided By 2 Principles**</u>:
   1. Wives, submit to your own husband.
   2. Husbands, love your wife.

   The Book of Ephesians talks about *'The Domestic Life of Believers;'* and in *Ephesians 5:22-24*, it talks extensively about the: *1ˢᵗ* <u>**Principle**</u>: *'<u>Duties of Wives</u>'*.

- Wives, submit to your own husband. <u>***Eph.5:22***</u>, this same statement is repeated in <u>***Col.3:18***</u>, *"Wives, <u>submit</u> yourselves unto your own husbands, <u>as</u> it is fit in the Lord:"* *"submit to your own husbands,"* what does it means?

It simply means *your own husband*, not to all men on the planet but your own husband <u>*as*</u> it is fit in the Lord; whoever is not your husband cannot just come and order you around, cannot just come with a demand that is ungodly that is why it says, *"your own husband."*

It didn't stop at these two references only, it continues if we will look with me into the Book of <u>***I Pet.3:1***</u>, *"Likewise ye <u>wives</u>, be in subjection to your own husbands."*

Now, in the duties of wives, *I Pet.3*, from *vs.3-6*, continued to advise wives in exhortation to faith and good works, addressing wives, liking wives to Sara as obeyed Abraham, and calling him lord, and you will obey your husbands in the Lord and call him lord. It went further to speak about their ways of appearance when it comes to adorning of hair, the use of gold and putting on of apparel *[while it didn't condemn the use of gold]* but to be modest as a Christian wife or a believer. *I Tim.2:9-15*, went on to letting us, especially women, know that this is a conditional promise to save women from death in childbearing *vs.15*, all God's laws came with conditions and promises when fully obeyed.

- The 2nd Principle *'Husbands, Love your wife.'* Remember, *'The Domestic Life Of Believers:'* we must read all the references above to complete this segment. Anything that violates the principle of submission is a sin: anything that will not pass the test of law, is a sin, God does not change, His law does not change, God's law is universal, it is the same in America, it is the same in Asia, it is the same in Africa, it is the same in Europe, His laws are always the same in all of earth: the Bible is one!

Conclusion:

Sexual immorality is unique among sins insomuch as it is sin against the body, thus assaulting the sanctity of a believer's sacred oneness with Christ [sealed by *the Holy Ghost which is in you]* and the oneness of holy matrimony *[I Corinthians 7:2]*. The point is that the believer's body is a sacred vessel, **bought with a price** by the **Son of God.** Believers thus have no business doing anything with the Lord's body that does not glorify Him.

CHAPTER SEVEN

JEHOVAH RAPHA - THE LORD WHO HEALS:
God has provided the final cure for spiritual, physical, and emotional sickness in Jesus Christ. God can heal us of both spiritual and physical sickness of whatever kind!

THE NEW COVENANT AND THE UNCHANGEABLE PRIESTHOOD:

In *[Hebrews 5:114]*, the Bible talks about **The Priesthood of Jesus Christ** and the priesthood of Aaron; the author established the superiority of Jesus as priest over Aaron. The **Son's** superior work as a High Priest serves as the basis for a call to Christian maturity. *Aaron* was the high priest of Israel who had been *called of God*, thus establishing his authority. His purpose as a priest was to offer to God *sacrifices for sins* on behalf of the people, and to *have compassion on* the ignorance and waywardness of the people on behalf of God.

The problem with Aaron's priesthood was Aaron himself; since he was a sinner, he had to make a sin offering for *himself* as well as for *the people*. Like Aaron, Jesus was called by God, but according to **Psalms 110:4** God gave Him a unique calling as a **High Priest after the order of Melchisedec.** Christ's Priesthood was on an entirely different level than that of Aaron. Like Aaron, He offered *prayers and supplications,* but unlike Aaron, Christ was heard *in that He feared.* Unlike Aaron, Christ learned *obedience* through suffering. Unlike Aaron, the salvation that Christ brought was *eternal.*

In *Hebrews chapter 7:1-19*, These chapters are an extended discourse on the superiority of the priesthood of Christ as demonstrated by the superiority of **His order, His covenant, His ministry** and **His sacrifice.** The Levitical priesthood of the Jews was grounded in the *order of Aaron*, but the priesthood of Jesus Christ is grounded in the *order of Melchisedec*. The mysterious Melchisedec appeared in *Genesis 14:18-20]* and was not mentioned again until the messianic promise was made in *Psalms 110*. The author of Hebrews drew from Old Testament witness to show that the order of Melchisedec was eternal in origin and scope. Melchisedec participated in the divine attributes of eternity, righteousness, peace, and sovereignty. His eternality is evident in that he abides as *priest continually*-without beginning or end. His righteousness is evident in His name since Melchisedec is Hebrew for *"king of righteousness."* His peace is evident in the fact that he was also declared to be the *King of Salem*, which means *"king of peace."*

Finally, Melchisedec's sovereignty was recognized by *Abraham*, who paid this priest-king a *tenth part of all* he had when he returned victoriously from war. if Abraham recognized Melchisedec's superiority by paying him a tithe, then Israel *[the believers of today]* must, too. The author argued that the Levitical priesthood was inferior to that of Melchisedec because the inferior is blessed by the superior. The sovereignty of the *Son of God*, because while the Levitical priesthood was authorized by a *carnal commandment*, the priesthood of Christ was authorized by *the power of endless life*.

The author in *[Hebrews 7 verses 20 - Heb.8:13]*, addressed next the authorizing sources of the two priesthoods. Typically, authority was granted to an agreement or a covenant through the confirmation of an oath. Citing *[Jeremiah 31:31-34]*, the author noted the old covenant between God and Israel was dependent on the oath of man; unfortunately, *they continued not* in this covenant. But the new covenant promised through Jeremiah was different, because the oath here was made entirely by God. Because God swore to the new covenant, it was eternally guaranteed. He said He would be merciful to them and place His laws in their minds and hearts. Because of the divine oath, the new covenant is *a better covenant*. The first covenant is old and *decayeth* and *ready to vanish away*.

The priesthood based on the old covenant was filled with priests who could not remain in office because they died, but the new covenant Priest *ever lived to make intercession.* The old covenant priesthood was filled with priests characterized by *infirmity,* but the new covenant Priest was *consecrated for evermore* through Jesus' obedient suffering. The old covenant priest had to offer sacrifices *daily*, but the new covenant Priest offered a sacrifice *once* for all.

The old covenant priest sacrificed for both himself and his people, but the new covenant Priest, being sinless, *offered up Himself* on behalf of the people.

The author turned his attention to a comparison of the ministries of the old and the new priesthoods. *The ordinances of divine services* given through the old covenant were for a *worldly sanctuary* that represented the transcendence of God insomuch as the people could not enter the sanctuary in the tabernacle. Only the high priest could enter the *holiest* place, and he did so only *once every year.* The sacrificial ministry of the old priesthood was unable to make *perfect* the worshippers' *conscience*. While the old priesthood was incomplete, the sacrificial ministry of the Messiah is able to purge our *conscience*. This perfect cleansing enables the followers of the Messiah to engage in works that *serve the Living God.*

The ministry of the Messiah is that of a new covenant *Mediator*. His ministry is superior because He does not enter an earthly sanctuary, but into *Heaven itself,* and thus into the very *Presence of God.* Unlike the high priest who entered annually into the most holy place, the Messiah entered into the most place *once for all*. Unlike the old covenant that was inaugurated by the death of animals that had no choice in the matter, the new covenant was inaugurated by the Messiah voluntary death. Unlike the old priesthood that offered the blood of animals, the Messiah offered *His own Blood*. Unlike the old priesthood that offered sacrifices continually without effect, the *Blood* of the *Messiah* obtained *Eternal Redemption.*

Bringing his comparison of the new and old priesthood to an end, the author in *Hebrews 10:1-18* focused on the superiority of the sacrifice of Christ. The old sacrifices were only *a shadow* of the *very image* of the blessed realities that come from the personal sacrifice of the Messiah. Citing *[Psalms 40:6-8]*, the author demonstrated that God was no longer interested in the *burnt offerings and sacrifices for sin* of the old covenant. The old sacrifices had to be offered continually, and they did not accomplish anything beyond ritual purification because they could not *take away sins.* This is why it was prophesied that the Messiah would come to *do* God's *will*. Jesus the Messiah offered *one sacrifice for sins forever* by offering Himself. Afterward, He *sat down* at the *Throne of God*. Because of His Blood atonement, the old sacrifices are no longer necessary. He offered the perfect sacrifice that *perfected* believers.

ETERNAL JUDGMENT:
THERE IS NO MIDDLE LINE:
There is Heaven, There Is Hell!

Peter commanded believers, as temporary residents who looked to Christ as their example, to suffer and separate themselves from the practices of those who slandered them. God condemn the slanderers and vindicate the believers in heaven's court while many do not believe that there is Heaven or Hell, their unbelief does not remove the fact of existence. Bible says in *I Peter 4:4-5,*

> *"Wherein they think it strange that ye run not with them to the same excess of riot, speaking evil of you: vs.5, Who shall give account to him that is ready to judge the quick and the dead:" "The quick and the dead," means everyone who has ever lived people of all generations.*

"Them that are dead," refers to deceased believers in Christ. When they were alive, the gospel was preached to them. While on earth they were *judged according to men in the flesh or* condemned and martyred on account of the gospel. But they now live by God in the spiritual realm, heaven.

If we believe in the existence of God; if we believe The Bible is the WORD of God; then we must believe that there is HEAVEN AND THERE IS HELL: and if we are children of God and we know His nature and His standard, then we must also understand and know, that there is no middle line. We are either for Him or for Satan, there is no middle line! The Bible says in **Psalms 94:20,** *"[Shall the throne of iniquity have fellowship with thee ...?]"*

"For the time is come that judgment must begin at the house of God: and if it first begin at us, what shall the end be of them that obey not the gospel of God?" <u>I Peter 4:17</u>

Which means if even believers in Christ will be judged, then what terrible punishment must surely await unbelievers? But if we're not seeing all these warnings as believers and we continue to live as if there is no God and that there are no laws guiding us, it's just too bad what punishment we will face because the Bible does not lie.

"And as it is appointed unto men once to die, but after this the judgment." <u>Hebrews 9:27</u>

"And I saw a great White Throne, and Him that sat on it, from whose face the earth and the heaven fled away; and there was found no place for them:
<u>vs.12</u>, *And I saw the dead, small and great, stand before God, and the books were opened: and another book was opened, which was the book of life: and the dead were judged out of those things which were written in the books, according to their works:*
<u>vs.13</u>, *And the sea gave up the dead which were in it; and death and hell delivered up the dead which were in them: and they were judged every man according to their works:*
<u>vs.14</u>, *And death and hell were cast into the lake of fire. This is the second death:* <u>vs.15</u>, *And whosoever was not found written in the book of life was cast into the lake of fire."* <u>Rev. 20:11-15</u>

Notice in the above reference, *"[... and the books were opened ...]"* be you a father, a wife, a son or daughter, a ruler, kings and queens, a politician or anyone; the Bible says, *"and the Books were opened...."* Everything you ever did while you're here on planet earth is recorded, nothing is added and nothing is removed, **good or bad** and if we ever think that we will escape any un-addressed sin, we lie. Whatever we did here on earth is what determines where we go after our tenor here on earth, remember our text? *"**LORD who shall 'ABIDE' in Thy Tabernacle or who shall 'DWELL' in Thy HOLY Hill?**"* and listen to this .... *"**And the dead were judged out of those things which were written in the books, according to their works:**"* why? so as to determine where they chose to *'abide and dwell'* while on earth as there are only two places, you're either going to the left or going to the right, *"no middle-line."*

The **Great White Throne** emphasizes God's purity and Holiness in judging and His sovereign right both to rule and to judge the earth. Apparently the first earth and the first **heaven fled** giving way at the final judgment to a *"new heaven and a new earth"* *[Revelation 21:1]*. The dead standing before *'The Throne'* come to life in the *"second resurrection"* [implied in vs.5]. There are two sets of books at this judgment. The names of all believers are in the book of life. The names of the *"earth dwellers"* are not in the book of life *[Revelation 13:8; Revelation 17:8]*. Everyone is judged *according to his or her works,* which are recorded in the other books. No one can ever be saved though by works, because that would leave room for human boasting *[Ephesians 2:8-9]*. The eternal dwelling place of all unbelievers is the *lake of fire*. As part of the present creation, *death and hell* [see Revelation 1:18]; Christ's authority over **the keys of hell and of death** was stated in His declaration that He would find the church [Matt.18:18]. This will be exercised when death and hell are emptied and then destroyed at the great white throne judgment [Revelation 20:11-15].

If there is no eternal judgment as many argued, what is the significance of The **Great White Throne?** Why will the *"sea give up the dead which were in it* and why will *"death and hell deliver up the dead* *which are in them"* if not for the reason of accountability? ***All must give account to God!*** The Bible says, listen to this, *"... and they were judged according to their works:"* the false prophets came in to give their own theory that "well, God isn't going to do that, how is God going to destroys millions and millions of people because they refused to believe?"

> *"For this they willingly are ignorant of, that by the word of God the heavens were of old, and the earth standing out of the water and in the water:*
> *vs.6, Whereby the world that then was, being overflowed with water, perished:*
> *vs.7, But the heavens and the earth, which are now, by the same word are kept in store, reserved unto fire against the day of judgment and perdition of ungodly men."* <u>II Peter 3:5-7</u>

Let us not forget that the *false prophets* also rose from among the people, just as the *false teachers*, they were present in Peter's time and were among his readers. The latter spread teachings that are destructive to faith. The effect was so far-reaching that they even denied the Lord *"[The Sovereign Master];"* who paid the price to redeem them *[Matthew 10:33]*. Though many followed the heretics' shameful immorality, and the **way of truth** was blasphemed, little did the *false teachers* realize that denying the Lord would bring **destruction** to themselves. Driven by greed, the *false teachers* invented deceptive stories *[the exact opposite of Peter in I Peter 1:16]* with which they exploited their listeners which we are seeing today by the reason of many fable teachings to lure and deceive many people to hell, it is one of the tricks of Satan to not believe the gospel.

Peter's aim in order to prepare believers for the **Day of Judgment** Peter warns his readers *[all of us believers]* and urge us to action, he recalled in *[II Peter 2:4-10a]*, three examples of God's judgment and deliverance.

[1]. God judged *the angels that sinned Genesis 6:1-4]. Hell,* here translates Tartarus, a subterranean place of punishment lower than hades and reserved for the wicked.

[2]. God also judged the ancient world in the flood *[Genesis 7:17-23]*, but protected Noah and seven others *[Genesis 7:13-16]*.

[3]. He judged the immoral cities of *Sodom and Gomorrah [Genesis 19:23-29]*, yet rescued righteous *Lot*, who was distressed by the immoral behaviour of the ungodly *[Genesis 19:29]*. Peter then pointed out that God was capable of delivering them, *the ungodly,* from the destructive false teachings of heretics in their midst. The unrighteous would not escape God's sovereignty or punishment.

In *[II Peter 2:10b-22]*, Peter further described the *false teachers*. In contrast to the behaviour of the more powerful *angels*, they were slanderously insolent. They were brutish and irrational, blasphemous, and ruled by lust and greed. Peter compared the *false teachers* to *Balaam [Numbers 22-24]* because they had abandoned the straight path, were consumed by greed, and would receive what their sins deserved *[eternal judgment]*. Balaam's donkey showed more moral sense than Balaam did. Like dry *wells* and storm *clouds*, the *false teachers* were unsatisfactory and unstable. With their empty and boastful *words*, and despite their promises of *liberty* to others, these *false teachers and false prophets* led their hearers into the same spiritual slavery and corruption to which they themselves were enslaved.

Although these heretics had once claimed to know Christ and even experienced some freedom from sin, they returned to their old practices and became *entangled* again. They were worse off in the end with their rejection of Christ that they were at the beginning when in a state of ignorance. Just as a *dog* return to its *own vomit* and a *pig* returns *to swallow in mud*, so also these false teachers reverted to the immoral lifestyles they preferred by nature. Their immoral behaviour shows that they had never been genuinely converted, yet they handle the law, yet they teach the people: The Bible says:

"The priests said not, Where is the Lord? And they that handle the law knew me not: the pastors also transgressed against me, and the prophets prophesied by Baal and walked after things that do not profit." <u>**Jeremiah 2:8**</u>
"The prophets prophesy falsely, and the priests bear rule by their means; and my people love to have it so: and what will you do in the end there of?"

<u>**Jeremiah 5:25-31**</u>: *[explains the activity and the corruption of them, false teachers and false prophets that are doomed for hell].*

"The priests said not, Where is the Lord? and they that handle the law knew me not: In order words, they teach the Word of God without having any knowledge of Him, they took no time in searching-out nor study the Word of God which is one of the reasons for their heretics teachings; they teach to deceive the fatherless and the widow, to extort money from the week through which they became filthy rich. Those who have grown rich through dishonest gain and neglect of *the fatherless* were like fowlers lying in *wait*. As fowlers set a net with several tame birds to attract wild, unsuspecting birds, so too *wicked men, false teachers and false prophets* entrapped innocent victims.

The word *"horrible"* in *verse 30*, is derived from a Hebrew stem meaning *"filthiness"* or *"rottenness" [Jeremiah 29:17; Hosea 6:10].* Here it describes the wickedness of the false prophets, priests, and people. The phrase in *[verse 31], "by their means"* implies that the *priests* rule either on their own authority or at the direction of the *false prophets.*

<u>*No Favoritism with God:*</u>
Paul offered an extensive rationale for obedience: [1] servants are ultimately serving the Lord rather than a human master: [2] their service will be gloriously rewarded in eternity: and [3] God does not discriminate when it comes to punishing bad behaviour.

"But he that doeth wrong shall receive for the wrong which he hath done: and there is no respect of persons." Colossians 3:25

"Who shall be punished with everlasting destruction from the Presence of the Lord, and from the glory of His power." Thessalonians 1:9

Which in order words means, we are either ***"Dwelling"*** and ***"Abiding"*** with Him, or we are on the other side, ***there is no middle to it,*** you are either here or there! The penalty of ***everlasting destruction*** is described as being away ***from the Presence of the Lord.*** The word ***"destruction"*** does not imply ceasing to exist or annihilation but separation from God in a miserable state. This is why it is called everlasting. God will throw all His enemies into the lake of fire to be eternally judged ***[Revelation 20:11-15]*** *[please read this on your own].*

[The Two texts below are from two of our associates Pastors who were formerly Muslims and are now serving the Lord with their households and families]!

Sharpening Your Focus: Text: 2 Corinthians 4:

<u>*Introduction*</u>: Some of us have blurred vision and if we don't put on our glasses or contact lenses we cannot see clearly. Our glasses or contact lenses bring the object into sharp focus. We use these lenses to improve our focus. Perfecting our focus has tremendous benefits which are very obvious. So also in our spiritual life, a little improvement could bring a host of answers into sharp focus, very quickly.

In the second letter of Apostle Paul to the church in Corinth, he took a moment to reflect on his own life and ministry. Paul narrated that it had been a difficult journey; he had battled unbelievers who fought the Gospel message, faced great persecution and dealt with his health challenges. All this did not make him lose heart! The only way Paul had managed to keep fighting was to sharpen his focus daily.

What did Apostle Paul mean by "to not lose heart" in the text? It can only be interpreted that he refused to be discouraged or refused to give up despite all those challenges that he faced. The Bible recorded that Saul now Paul encountered the Lord Jesus Christ on his way to Damascus where he was going to persecute the believers. His encounter with the Lord was a turning point in his life. Saul experienced the greatest mercy, love, forgiveness and deliverance from the chain of hell. Therefore, Paul cannot lose heart, his body may be wasted away, and getting to heaven has been his goal for the opportunity to meet the Lord again. Achieving eternal glory far outweighs any other consideration for him. So, he wrote, we fix our eyes not on what is seen, but on what is unseen, for what is seen is temporary, but what is unseen is eternal.

We need a little refining of our own focus, and we can learn from the Apostle's example by reviewing his methods:

1: ***Apostle chooses heaven as his goal:*** Paul's eyes were fixed on "eternal glory," despite his several worthy achievements during his lifetime by starting churches, spreading the gospel to the Gentile world, and planting churches all over those places. But all of it, he said, was based on his goal for eternity. He wrote to the Corinthians, "We fix our eyes not on what is seen, but on what is unseen." Which easily translated; thus, he did not allow his success and challenges affect his focus of eternity. Making heaven to be with the Lord is his goal. Everything he did was kingdom focus.

What is your own focus or where is your own finish line? If making heaven is your finish line, then focus on it and work on it. Do not allow your earthly success to blur your vision. Your accumulated billion dollars on planet earth does not translate or give you visa to heaven. What you stored up in heaven is what you are going to reap. ***(Matt. 6:19-20).***

Unfortunately, nowadays, some of the so-called Pastors are now allowing money to be their focus. What they forgot is that money cannot buy a place in heaven. Jesus Christ admonished the rich man in ***Matthew 19:21*** to go and give all his money to the poor first and come and follow him. If our earthly work cannot translate to heaven's gain, then we are building rubble to be burnt by fire. The Bible says that every Man's work shall be judged.

II. Acknowledge the imperfect nature of this life:

Apostle Paul may have focused on the unseen, which is heavenly, but the things which were seen were challenging enough to take all his attention. According to our text, He was hard pressed on every side, and perplexed. He was shipped wrecked, persecuted, and struck down and was wasting away. These were daily challenges that he encountered but he did not allow those things to shift his focus from his goal.

We have to realize that we are living in an imperfect world. We cannot allow the imperfection to affect our responsibility to God. There is no time to waste because we have a limited time on this planet Earth to carry out our heavenly assignment. If you're waiting for the perfect time, perfect team, perfect church, or even perfect spouse, you're going to wait a long, long time. So many people seem so easily discouraged by the imperfections of their environment that they haven't grasped the fact that life is moving on while they wait.

The person who is able to understand and accept the imperfect nature of this life will be happier, in good health and more fruitful. If your church disappoints you, the Great Commission remains. Don't allow your focus to drop from the great command to the great complaints. ***(Matt. 28:19-20)***

If your friend, your child, or your spouse disappoints you, love will still remain the greatest quality within your control. ***(1 Corinthians 13:1-3)*** The debt we owe any man is to love them. Our Lord Jesus Christ left his glory in heaven to make us sinners His friend so that we can learn of Him and find our ways back to the Father. What a magnificent love of God.

If your plan hits a snag along the way, your mission is to stay the course, especially if you're confident that God has directed your path.

When Paul was in prison, he heard reports that some who enjoyed freedom were preaching against him. What was he going to do, in light of such discouraging news? What kind of positive spin could you put on such a report, something that would justify a little anger? Paul told the Philippians: "In any case the gospel is being preached!" ***(Philippians 1:18)***

To discover that life isn't going to be perfect is to make one of the most important steps toward maturity, and productivity.

III. **Perfecting your focus on Christ daily:**

Paul says this in our text: "... Inwardly we are being renewed day by day." It was important for Paul to know that the perfecting of his faith would be a daily process. It is significantly important to recognize that Paul had no objective of being saved day by day. His salvation was settled outside the Damascus Gate, as soon as he acknowledged Jesus as "Lord." Ever since that day he had been a disciple, growing slowly and steadily studying the scripture and sharing his experiences.

In this chapter alone, Apostle Paul mentioned some of the ways to perfect our daily walk with Christ:
- Renouncing secret and shameful ways *(4:2)* – It is imperative to confess and forsake all those secret sins that easily beset us.
- Fighting deception and distortion *(4:2)* – We must not be partakers of evil discussions or gestures that undermines the

Gospel of our Lord Jesus Christ. Or condone any distortion of the Gospel.
- Preaching for God's glory, and not his own *(4:5)* – We should be the teacher of the gospel is season and out of season without fear or favor, with the assurances that the Lord rewards those that diligently seek him.
- And becoming a light in his culture's darkness *(4:6)* – We should let our light shine in this dark world by upholding the integrity of the Gospel.

If we want to do our best in the race set before us, the best effort is required, and it'll be needed every day.

Conclusion:

Sharpening requires setting time, some space, and a safe place for reflection. We have to reflect whether we are still in the race and on the way. The way to heaven is always narrow, if we find ourselves in a broad way, then we have missed the way to the master. We need some time and solitude to reflect on where we are. Christ always set himself aside from the crowd to commune with the father on a constant basis. We need such setting aside to check if we are still on the way. Though Moses was raised in the palace of Pharaoh, God had to take him to the wilderness to prepare him for his mission. We must continually find the motivation within ourselves to play our heart out before our time is up. May his grace continue to abide with us.

Ganiyu Bisiriyu [associate Pastor]

ETERNAL JUDGEMENT *[please read all references]*.

Hebrews 6: Therefore, leaving the principles of the doctrine of Christ, let us go on unto perfection; not laying again the foundation of repentance from dead works, and of faith toward God, of the doctrine of baptisms, laying on of hands, of resurrection of the dead, and of ***eternal judgment***. (KJV)

Matt. 25:31-34, ³¹"When the Son of Man comes in His glory, and all the angels with Him, He will sit on His throne in heavenly glory. ³²All the nations will be gathered before Him, and He will separate the people one from another as a shepherd separates the sheep from the goats. ³³He will put the sheep on His right and the goats on His left. ³⁴"Then the King will say to those on His right, 'Come, you who are blessed by my Father; take your inheritance, the kingdom prepared for you since the creation of the world.

⁴¹"Then he will say to those on his left, 'Depart from me, you who are cursed, into the eternal fire prepared for the devil and his angels. ⁴²For I was hungry, and you gave me nothing to eat, I was thirsty, and you gave me nothing to drink, ⁴³I was a stranger, and you did not invite me in, I needed clothes and you did not clothe me, I was sick and in prison and you did not look after me.' ⁴⁴"They also will answer, 'Lord, when did we see you hungry or thirsty or a stranger or needing clothes or sick or in prison, and did not help you?' ⁴⁵"He will reply, 'I tell you the truth, whatever you did not do for one of the least of these, you did not do for me.' ⁴⁶"Then they will go away to eternal punishment, but the righteous to eternal life."

There are 2 types of people who faces Judgment.

1. **Judgment of unbelievers/ the goats**

The Great White Throne of God – The Greek word "Thronos"

Rev 20:11-15, And I saw a great white throne, and him that sat on it, from whose face the earth and the heaven fled away; and there was no place for them. (12) And I saw the dead, small and great, stand before God; and the books were opened: and another book was opened, which is *the book* of life: and the dead were judged out of those things which were written in the books, according to their works. (13) And the sea gave up the dead which were in it; and death and hell delivered up the dead which were in them: and they were judged every man according to their works. (14) And death and hell were cast into the lake of fire. This is the second death. (15) And whosoever was not found written in the book of life was cast into the lake of fire.

The judgment here involves those who failed to follow God as revealed to them in their dispensations i.e., from the beginning to the end. Meaning from Adam to the present.

There are 6 dispensations from Adam to the present:
- Dispensation of Innocence — Gen. 2:7-3:24
- Dispensation of Conscience — Gen.3-6
- Dispensation of Man in Authority — Gen.9-11
- Dispensation of Man under Promise — Gen.12- Ex..1
- Dispensation of Man under law — Ex. 19 — Mat.1, Lk.2
- Dispensation of Man under Grace. John.6:47— the second coming.

Please note that in each of the dispensations, salvation messages were presented but man always resisted and consequently failed to live for God. Rom.1:21-29.

2. Judgment of believers/ the sheep

1 Pet. 4:17, For the time is come that judgment must begin at the house of God: and if it first begins at us, what shall the end be of them that obey not the gospel of God?

The Judgment seat of Christ – The Greek word BEMA (pronounced Bay-ma)

2 Cor. 5:10, For we must all appear before the **judgment seat of Christ,** that each one may receive what is due him for the things done while in the body, whether good or bad.

Romans 14:8, If we live, we live to the Lord; and if we die, we die to the Lord. So, whether we live or die, we belong to the Lord.

⁹For this very reason, Christ died and returned to life so that He might be the Lord of both the dead and the living.

¹⁰You, then, why do you judge your brother? Or why do you look down on your brother? **For we will all stand before God's judgment seat.**

¹¹It is written: "'As surely as I live,' says the Lord, 'Every knee will bow before me; every tongue will confess to God.'" ¹²So then, each of us will give an account of himself to God.

We can categorize the Judgment of believers into 3 types:

1. The First Judgment is Past. Our justification or our Judgment as a Sinner:

When we accept the finished work of Christ as an atonement for our sins, we can never again come into judgment as a sinner. However, we must not only believe the righteousness of Christ but practice Christ righteousness in our daily lives.

John 5:24, "I tell you the truth, whoever hears my word and believes Him who sent me has eternal life and will not be condemned [judged]; he has crossed over from death to life.

Romans 8:1, Paul adds, "There is therefore no more condemnation (judgment) to them which are in Christ Jesus."

You see, the purpose of the Judgment Seat is not to determine whether a particular person enters heaven or not, for every man's destiny is determined before he leaves this life.

1 John 1:7-9, ⁷But if we walk in the light, as He is in the light, we have fellowship with one another, and the blood of Jesus, His Son, purifies us from all sin. ⁸If we claim to be without sin, we deceive ourselves and the truth is not in us. ⁹If we confess our sins, He is faithful and just and will forgive us our sins and purify us from all unrighteousness.

When we confess our sins, God cleanses us thoroughly and completely for "the blood of Jesus Christ purifies us from all sin.

Psalm 103:11-12, ¹¹For as high as the heavens are above the earth, so great is his love for those who fear him; ¹²as far as the east is from the west, so far has he removed our transgressions from us.

1 John.2:6, "He that abideth in Him ought himself also so to walk, even as He walked".

1 John.3:6, "Whosoever abideth in Him sinneth not: whosoever sinneth hath not seen Him, neither known Him."

1 John.3:9, "Whosoever is born of God doth not commit sin; for His seed remaineth in Him: and he cannot sin, because he is born of God.

2. The Second Judgment is Present, part of our sanctification, our Judgment as Sons:

Heb. 12:4-11, ⁴In your struggle against sin, you have not yet resisted to the point of shedding your blood. ⁵And you have forgotten that word of encouragement that addresses you as sons: "My son, do not make light of the Lord's discipline, and do not lose heart when he rebukes you, ⁶because the Lord disciplines those he loves, and he punishes everyone he accepts as a son." ⁷Endure hardship as discipline; God is treating you as sons. For what son is not disciplined by his father? ⁸If you are not disciplined (and everyone undergoes discipline), then you are illegitimate children and not true sons. ⁹Moreover, we have all had human fathers who disciplined us, and we respected them for it. How much more should we submit to the Father of our spirits and live! ¹⁰Our fathers disciplined us for a little while as they thought best; but God disciplines us for our good, that we may share in his holiness. ¹¹No discipline seems pleasant at the time, but painful. Later on, however, it produces a harvest of righteousness and peace for those who have been trained by it.

1 Cor. 11:32, When we are judged by the Lord, we are being disciplined so that we will not be condemned with the world.

3. The Third Judgment is Future – our redemption, our Judgment as a Servant.

Now it's this judgment that takes place at the Judgment Seat – the **Béma Seat of Christ**.

Paul says, as we have read in **2 Cor. 5:10** For we must all appear before the **judgment seat of Christ**, that each one may receive what is due him for the things done while in the body, whether good or bad.

Who is Paul talking to? 2 Corinthians is addressed to "the church of God which is at Corinth with all the saints which are in all Achaia."

Now understand, this is not a warning to the unsaved, this is a word addressed to **believers**. The **"we"** in 2 Cor. 5 appears no less than 25 times, and it is clear that it is being addressed to the church, to believers. This judgment is for Christians, but it cannot and doesn't deal with sin or salvation. The Béma is not a judicial bench where someone is condemned, it is a reward seat. It has nothing to do with the Christians Rejection, but everything to do with the believers Reward.

1 Cor. 3:10-15, [10]By the grace God has given me, I laid a foundation as an expert builder, and someone else is building on it. But each one should be careful how he builds. [11]For no one can lay any foundation other than the one already laid, which is Jesus Christ. [12]If any man builds on this foundation using gold, silver, costly stones, wood, hay or straw, [13]his work will be shown for what it is, because the Day will bring it to light. It will be revealed with fire, and the fire will test the quality of each man's work. [14]If what he has built survives, he will receive his reward. ¹⁵If it is burned up, he will suffer loss; he himself will be saved, but only as one escaping through the flames.

Paul teaches here that at the Judgment Seat our Service will be revealed and rewarded. The loss we can suffer is a loss of rewards in heaven, not a loss of Salvation.

Rev. 22:12-13, ¹²And, behold, I come quickly; and my reward is with me, to give every man according as his work shall be. ¹³I am Alpha and Omega, the beginning and the end, the first and the last.

¹The Revelation of Jesus Christ, which God gave unto Him, to show unto His servants things which must shortly come to pass;

Again, He is talking to believers, His servants. Christ comes to fetch us, to separate us from the goats, to take us to His Judgment seat, where we will be rewarded with our inheritance, which is eternal life - in the presence of God!

Isaiah 6: ⁵Then said I, Woe is me! for I *am* ruined; because I am a man of unclean lips, and I dwell in the midst of a people of unclean lips: for mine eyes have seen the King, the LORD of hosts.

The Glory of God is something quite unbelievable…

1 Cor. 3:8-10, ⁸The man who plants and the man who waters have one purpose, and each will be **rewarded according to his own labor.** ⁹For we are God's fellow workers; you are God's field, God's building. ¹⁰By the grace God has given me, I laid a foundation as an expert builder, and someone else is building on it. But each one should be careful how he builds.

Our works CANNOT save us. Only belief and faith can. Does that mean our work is not important? Not at all. Our works on this earth will determine our rewards in the life hereafter.

The principles of Judgment

Gal. 6:7, Be not deceived; God is not mocked: for whatsoever a man sows, that shall he also reap.

Eph. 6:7-8, ⁷Serve wholeheartedly, as if you were serving the Lord, not men, ⁸because you know that the Lord will reward everyone for whatever good he does, whether he is slave or free.

Col. 3:23-25, ²³And **whatsoever** you do, do *it* heartily, **unto the Lord**, and not unto men; ²⁴Knowing that of the Lord you shall receive the reward of the inheritance: for you serve the Lord Christ. ²⁵But he that does wrong shall receive for the wrong which he has done: and there is no respect of persons.

James 2:12-13, ¹²Speak and act as those who are going to be judged by the law that gives freedom, ¹³because judgment without mercy will be shown to anyone who has not been merciful. Mercy triumphs over judgment.

James says that we are going to be judged by the law of liberty. Our lives are going to be examined in the light of God's Word. Those who have shown Mercy, will be shown Mercy.

The Rewards

There are Five main rewards – our inheritance in heaven. The bible speaks of them as crowns. These are the privileges of service for the King of Kings.

1. The Incorruptible crown - for those who strive to serve Christ acceptably.
1 Cor. 9:24-27, ²⁴Do you not know that in a race all the runners run, but only one gets the prize? Run in such a way as to get the prize. ²⁵And every man that strives for it is temperate in all things. Now they do it to obtain a corruptible crown; but we an incorruptible. ²⁶Therefore I do not run aimlessly; I do not fight like a man beating the air. ²⁷But I keep under my body, and bring it into subjection: lest

that by any means, when I have preached to others, I myself should be disqualified. [Practice what we preach!]

2. Crown of Rejoicing - the reward for witnessing for Christ.
1 Thess. 2:19-20, [19]For what is our hope or joy, or crown of rejoicing? Are you not even to be in the presence of our Lord Jesus Christ at His coming? [20]For you are our glory and joy.

Paul was speaking here to the people that he had won over to Christ. It gives one great joy to win another over for Christ, so much so, that those we have won over will actually be our glory when Jesus comes back. We will receive a crown of rejoicing for the souls that we have led to Christ. It is perhaps the greatest reward anyone can receive.

3. The Crown of Glory - the reward for being a good example.
1 Peter 5:2-4, [2]Be shepherds of God's flock that is under your care, serving as overseers—not because you must, but because you are willing, as God wants you to be; not greedy for money, but eager to serve; [3]not lording it over those entrusted to you, but being examples to the flock. [4]And when the Chief Shepherd appears, you will receive the crown of glory that will never fade away.

Being shepherds of the flock of God means we need to be **doers** of the Word, being good examples to others – practicing what we preach! We need to make sure that those we lead to the Lord are discipled properly. We need to take care of those that God has entrusted to your ministry or teaching.

4. The Crown of Life - Reward for suffering for Christ.
James 1:12, Blessed is the man who perseveres under trial, because when he has stood the test, he will receive the **crown of life** that God has promised to those who love him.

5. The Crown of Righteousness - for keeping your faith until the end
2 Tim. 4:6-8, [6]For I am now ready to be offered, and the time of my departure is at hand. [7]I have fought a good fight, I have finished my

course, I have kept the faith: ⁸Henceforth there is laid up for me a crown of righteousness, which the Lord, the righteous judge, shall give me at that day: and not to me only, but unto all them also that love his appearing.

The rewards we will be given will be the responsibility that we are given in God's eternal kingdom, and it will ***never*** be changed, it is forever, eternal. But it is determined here, on earth.

2 Thessalonians 1:6-10, ⁶God is just: He will pay back trouble to those who trouble you ⁷and give relief to you who are troubled, and to us as well. This will happen when the Lord Jesus is revealed from heaven in blazing fire with his powerful angels. ⁸He will punish those who do not know God and do not obey the gospel of our Lord Jesus. ⁹They will be punished with everlasting destruction and shut out from the presence of the Lord and from the majesty of his power ¹⁰on the day he comes to be glorified in his holy people and to be marveled at among all those who have believed. This includes you, because you believed our testimony to you. Possibly the greatest punishment of all! To be shut out from the presence of God!

---

2 Pet. 3:7; Jude 15

Aim: To prepare believers for the Day of Judgment.

Definition: Many scholars have defined it in many ways. We can put all together to say that eternal judgment means the ever-lasting decisive pronouncement or verdict of God concerning everyman according to his works.

Terminology: *1 Cor. 5:5; Acts 17:31; Jude 6*
The great day is the same as the day of the Lord also known as eternal judgment because it is an everlasting judgment that has no appeal. The last judgment is also the same thing as the last day when

all believers will be finally saved and ushered into their mansions. Rejecters will be judged and condemned by the word.

John 12:48

The first judgment: ***1 Pet. 4:17; Deut. 8:5; Ps. 94:12; Prov. 3:11-12; Rev. 3:19***
The first judgment is now in the Church as the beloved of the Lord. God is using evil men as an instrument of judgment to chastise His sons for correction. That is the first judgment. ***Deut. 28:49-50***

Who will Judge? ***Ps. 50:6; Acts 10:42; John 5:22***
The Bible is not contradicting itself. God Himself made an emphatical statement showing that God the Father Himself will sit on the throne of judgment. Because He gave to Human race the most precious gift that will restore them to their lost dignity. Jesus Christ – God the son- An instrument for redemption who had passed through all hardness of life is the voice of judgment to pronounce and reward every man according to his deeds. John 3:18, those who received Him not are condemned already.

Judgment according to works: ***1 Pet. 1:17; Matt. 16:27; Rev. 22:12; Jer. 17:10***
During our lifetime, every work must be accounted for. Both just and unjust people must appear before the judgment seat of God and give account of mysteries of God (Our life, money, salvation, energy, power, Holy Ghost, etc.) in their custody. So we must sojourn with fear and trembling because we are on probation. We should be mindful of every fruit of life we bear because it will be recovered.

Exaltation of the saints: ***Dan. 7:18 & 22; Ps. 91:14; Isa. 58:14***
As we sojourn on earth, we (saints) face humiliation and afflictions. Forsaking every worldly ambition in order to be exalted. The saints will possess the kingdom of God forever. They will judge the world as the redeemed of the Lord and also judge the angels. ***1 Cor. 6:2-3***
Conclusion: ***Rom. 14:10; 2 Cor. 5:10; James 2:13***

The extent of God's love signifies and interprets His fury. The depth of His mercy is equivalent to His anger. So, all will appear before the white throne judgment seat of God that day, to receive according to their works.

Now worship God with fear and trembling.

> *"LORD, <u>who shall</u> abide in THY tabernacle? <u>who shall</u> dwell in THY HOLY Hill?"*

The Bible says in <u>***I Tim.4:6***</u>,

> *"If thou put the brethren in remembrance of <u>these things</u>, thou shalt be a <u>good minister</u> of Jesus Christ, nourished up in the words of faith and of good doctrine, where unto thou hast attained."*

CHAPTER EIGHT

JEHOVAH SHALOM - *THE LORD IS PEACE:*
God defeats our enemies to bring us peace. Jesus is our Prince of Peace. God brings inner peace and harmony!

FOOD FOR THOUGHT:

The Bottom Line: "*Be Humble Therefore and Let God Exalt You*"

IN the Book of Genesis chapter *41 verse 44*, we read, *"And Pharaoh said unto Joseph, I am Pharaoh and without thee shall no man lift up his hand or foot in all the land of Egypt"*.
This is a unique story of how God exalts the humble. Therein we see the transfer of power and authority to His faithful saint. We note that Joseph is a type of Jesus. In Philippians chapter two, from verses five to eleven, we read the story of Jesus' elevation. This compares with the testimony of Joseph.

The Bible says that *'All those who are exalted by God must like Jacob, walk with a limp'.* This is His method of operation. *Isaiah 48:10-11* explains that God chooses His saints in the furnace of affliction. He does this, so that we will not touch His glory. He ensures this so that we will easily give to others the love and comfort He gave in elevating us. *[II Corinthians 1:2-4]. Read and think about this.* God exalts and empowers the humble. Then the faithful ones love others and become light to our dark world.

See Hebrews 5:8. Jesus suffered and humbled Himself. Then He was exalted. Joseph was put in prison and was elevated into the pinnacle of power at Pharaoh's palace. King David is revealed as *"a man after God's own heart"*. He humbled himself and obeyed God totally. He was faithful to write His love songs to God and became the sweet *'Psalmist'* of Israel.

Yes, to this day the Holy Spirit seeks, **"A man after God's own heart."** He seeks everyone who will yield to His Lordship. But even king David lived through God's **'promotion paradox.'** He was moved from the wilderness to the throne. Dedicated Christian disciples must learn this route. This is Christ's **'narrow way'. Read and interact with Matthew 7, 13.**

> <u>**Psalm 22:28**</u> says, **"For the Kingdom is the LORD's and He is the Governor among the nations."**

In ***Psalm 24:1-5***, King David details, ***'the specific realm of almighty power that the King of glory wields,'*** You will notice he alludes to Jesus in verse five – **"He shall receive the blessings from the Lord and righteousness from the God of His salvation."**

Read Matthew 22:37-40-. For us to appreciate the authority we can have in Christ Jesus, I have listed the stories of Joseph and David. Each of these vessels had enviable faith testimonies. Joseph endured ten years of imprisonment for a crime he never committed. He was graceful and never despaired. David suffered multifaceted tribulations, yet he never grew weary in seeking God.

In *II Samuel 24:24*, king David gave us the secret of his **'acceptance in the Beloved.'** He informs that **'we are not to offer unto the Lord what costs us nothing.'** He learns to put God first. He therefore gave God his very best. Self was dethroned. Translated, there is a down-sizing of personal ego demanded of those who seek God's friendship. Why? Because our God does not give His power to arrogant curiosity. He will cast pearls on swine. Jesus confirms this in ***Matthew 13 and Luke chapters 12-14.***

This was Apostle Paul's concern in ***Romans 12:1-3.*** Yes, ***'we are to daily present our bodies a living sacrifice unto the Lord. This is our reasonable service.'*** In fact, most do not know this. The tithe of

Who Is A Perfect Man? Who Is A Perfect Woman?

10% is requested of every **24 hours** of our time. Believe this or not. Take your pick. Those who faithfully wait upon the Lord pay the price and gain His vital friendship. *See Isaiah 66:2*. The majority who refuse this command are Biblical illiterates. They are destroyed by lack of knowledge of what the Spirit is saying. They would not hear God's voice as stated in *John 10:27-30*. Happy are those who read this and upgrade their study of God's book of ancient wisdom. Amen.

Jesus said in *John 3:3, "Verily, verily, I say unto thee, except a man be born again he cannot see the kingdom of God." Then in Matthew 6:33 we read, "But seek ye first the kingdom of God and His righteousness and all these things shall be added unto you."*
I have researched and lived this out. By His grace, I wait upon God to daily hear His voice. *Isaiah 50:4-5, John 8:32-34*. No one can be an authentic Christian except, they have tasted His truth. We are to find out by ourselves, the great faithfulness of Christ's Authority, which He avails us when we fully trust Him. Yes, no one can be a true Christian until they have in their dark moments trusted only in the invisible grace of God. That is why it is written that, *"we learn obedience by what we suffer and triumph". 1 Peter 5:10, Hebrews 5:8.*

Students of the Bible know that our God gives us the end facts from the beginning. *Isaiah 46:10.*
We read in *__Matthew 5:10-12__*:

> *"Blessed are they which are persecuted for righteousness sake for theirs is the Kingdom of heaven."*
> *"Blessed are ye when men shall revile you and persecute you and shall say all manner of evil against you falsely for my sake. Rejoice and be exceeding glad for great is your reward in heaven for so persecuted they the prophets which were before you."*

See *James 1:12-17* which also spells out the above divine paradox.

The key factor points in proving Jesus' authority which He avails His faithful saints in this world is this; *"it is as one rejoices in one's tribulations and trials that the power of Jesus shows up."* This was the faith testimony of Joseph, David and all the prophets. The Book of the Acts of the Apostles powerfully confirms this. Our God delights to turn our *'mess' first into a 'message'* then if we faint not, we obtain His miracles. **Read Luke 18:1-8, Genesis 50:20, Psalm 66:10-12. Job 23:8-10.** Those who know this truth and practice them are blessed indeed. It is also the testimony of countless faithful Christians.

Interact with this faith fact. Yes, in the coming days of global darkness, **"Only those who know their God and have an abiding intimacy with Christ shall be made strong. They shall be quickened to do exploits."** Selfishness will not consume them. They shall win souls. Amen.

The Book of Daniel reveals that, as we obey God the power of the Spirit comes upon us to disarm satanic strongholds. **Daniel 11:32.** God comes in to impose His due order as the king of Glory. He shuts the mouth of lions. He shows up and protects Daniel. He still manifests himself as the Creator, Controller and Commander of the universe. Of course, the Bible stated how Daniel and the three Hebrew children proved their total surrender to God. In obedience to God, they suffered numerous trials, but He delivered them. This was prophesized by king David in **Psalm 34:19**. Give God all the glory.

The New Testament shouts, **"Without faith we cannot please God."** Our faith in God pays off in the fullness of His time. This is a faithful truth. His timing is different from ours. He makes all things that concern His faithful saints beautiful in His own times. We can therefore boast that, **'everything is working out together for our own good. Faith calls the things that be not as though they are. Thus, 'the weak can say I am strong.'**

Our faith testimony shall be miraculous only as we submit to obey God. That is regardless of our personal innate fears. When we do this, we surrender my self-will to honour God's. This is called, *'dying to the self-life.'* This is difficult for the carnal person to consistently obey. I also struggle with this on many fronts. Most people do, but His grace is our sufficiency. He knows our weakness and He is long-suffering to bear with us. He loves us but hates our sins. Amen.

I have observed this truth: 'When I carry my own cross and obey God then as I reach my wits 'end, He comes to my aid'. My extremity becomes the basis through which the hand of God is released to revive and restore me. ***Job 23:10. Read Luke chapter ten***. Therein, we see this principle at work. Jesus commissions His disciples to their first missionary task. He gives them His word of power. ***Luke 10:19-22***. They diligently carry out His instructions. End result is: ***"Their names are written in heaven."*** What a wonderful reward. Conditions precedent when obeyed yields conditions subsequent. Remember, the law of sowing and reaping is very much alive. What you sow, you reap. Praise be to God.

In ***John 16:33***, Jesus gave us this legacy before facing the cross:

> ***"Thosethings I have spoken unto you that in Me ye might have peace, in the world ye shall tribulations but be of good cheer, I have overcome the world."***

<u>***1 John 5:4-5***</u> *concur*:

> ***"For whatsoever is born of God overcometh the world; and this is the victory that overcometh the world even our faith. Who is he that overcometh the world, but he that believeth that Jesus is the Son of God."***

The Bible says that *"The just shall live by faith."* **Romans 14:23** assures that, *"What is not done by faith is sin."* **Of course**, we can attest that *'all things are possible to those who believe that Jesus is Lord and Saviour of their lives.'*

John 3:16-18:

"He that believeth on Him is not condemned, but he that believeth not is condemned already because he had not believed in the Name of the only begotten son of God." Ponder on this.

Those who believe in Jesus prove their trust by their daily devotion to obey His authority. They love and trust Him totally. They labour to work out their salvation. They are lifelong marathon of denying self and carrying their cross. It ends up in glory. ***See Psalm 73:24.***

PRAY THIS PRAYER...*Acts 1:8, John 14:26.*
Ask God that we may obtain daily the freshness, fire power and zeal of the Holy Spirit to revive and quicken us to do good works. ***Acts 10:38, Proverbs 20:24, 4:5-12***

Ask for grace to study God's word. Be sensitive to hear, obey and follow every detailed instruction of the Holy Spirit. Claim ***Isaiah 50:4-5. Psalm 32:8-10, 37:23, 73:24, Hebrews 4;12-16, 11:6, Psalm 119:105,176, Isaiah 66:2, Jeremiah 10:23, John 3:27-30, 10:27-30.***
Ask for increase in your faith to trust and totally believe God's word. ***John 16:7-16, 6:63, Psalm 46:1-10, John 14:26.*** Those who trust God are blessed. ***Psalm 40:4***

Seek to daily bring God pleasure. Get right with Him.

Psalm 37:1-7 says, "Delight yourself in the Lord, He will give you the desires of your heart." Proverbs 3:5-7, Isaiah 50:4-5, Romans 8:14-17, 26-39

When you take the time to ponder on these Bible chapters and verses, you will obtain great mercies. Your joy and peace shall abound in Jesus' name!

The Bible commands this tough task. Make restitution of whatever you may have stolen. *See Numbers 5:6-7, Luke 19:9-10.* **Ask God to deliver you from the love of money.** *1 Timothy 6:10, Luke 6:13-16.* You cannot serve God and money. *[Mammon Luke 16:13,15]*

Practice every Christian disciplines you learn. Share what you have with others. God delights in those who give cheerfully. *Matthew 6:1-5.* Make your daily needs minimal. Follow peace with all people. *Hebrews 12:14-15, Psalm 119:165, Matthew 5:3-8,40-48*

We are to *"Forgive 70 x 7 times."* Therefore, leave your battles at the Lord's feet. Trust Him with your perplexities.

Read Romans 12:19-21, 2 Thessalonians 1:6. It is as we seek to live the spirit filled life and abide in His presence, that we obtain great peace.

Daily ask God to give you victory to surrender yourself life to become His bride. Then your flesh will be crucified, sanctified and all selfishness cum self-seeking will be put to death. ***2 Timothy 2:2-4, Mark 8:32-38,1 Timothy 1:5-9, 2 Timothy 1:7.*** No one said this will be easy, but we can do it if we try. May the Good Lord be our strength in Jesus' name!

It is when we choose the way of the cross that we manifest His power in our life. ***II Corinthians 6:2-10, 12:7-10, John 15:10-16, 13:30-34, 14:21-23, Romans 8:12-17, 26-39.***
Jesus has given us the Holy Spirit. When we daily call upon His assistance, He comes to abide and actively quicken us. His presence gives us vital freshness, liberty and boldness. He gives us the unique power gifts to function as Christ's temple. These gifts are listed in ***II Corinthians 12, 14:3, II Timothy 1:7, II Chronicles 16:9 John 7:38***.

Knowing the above, let us ask God to daily fill us up with His Holy Spirit. He fills us up inch by inch. First as a cup, next as a well, then as a river. That is 30%, 60% & 100%. He gives according to our

faith. Let us covet the gifts and the Presence of the Holy Spirit. He will keep us strong in faith and we will finish well. We will inherit eternal and glorious heritage.
Revelation 19:1-9.

Let us ask God to give us His specific assignment and ministry. God seeks those who will worship Him in spirit and in truth. Wait upon Him to make you, His Bride. That you may function in life as His prophetic and apostolic vessel. Ask by faith and pay the price to obtain His attestation. In ***II Samuel 24:24***, we note King David's word that *"we are not to offer unto the Lord what costs us nothing."* Therefore, daily give your utmost for His highest. Pursue God "bumper to bumper." ***Jeremiah 29:11-14***

This is because in ***John 3:27*** – **we find that, *"A man receives nothing except Heaven gives it"***. ***James 1:17*** **concurs**,

> *"Every good gift and every perfect gift is from above and cometh down from the Father of light with whom is no variableness neither shadow of turning."*
> *See also, 1 Chronicles 29:10-13*

The key factor and Biblical strategy to growing deeper into Christ have been listed above. It is as we seek Him that He wakes us morning by morning to give us His wisdom. **Read Proverbs 23:23, 4:5-12.** Know that Jesus is the wisdom of God and is the principal Amour.

Through our pragmatic use of our time and resources, we put on the Lord Jesus. ***Romans 13:14***. We are to also put on the whole amour of God. ***Ephesians 6:10-18. John 15*** lists how we shall be in-dwelt by the Holy Spirit. When abides, He will make us sanctified and holy to reign as His kings on earth. ***Revelation 1:5-6***. Therefore, prayerfully interact with this. Be bold to claim the anointing released as you meditate on these prophetic power words. Keep increasing in your faith and trust God to obey and obtain all He has promised to make you finish strong. Watch out for His Soon Coming and be

Rapture Compliant. Praise God, give Him all the glory and rejoice that He has written your name in the Lamb's Book of Life. This is a faithful saying. Believe this. Why? Because *"All things are possible to those who believe.'* **Assignment for everyone:** *[please read I, II & III John]* **He Will Speak to You!**

<u>*FINALLY WAIT A MINUTE!*</u>

In the early sixties in my teen ages, I've always thought that America is a Christian nation just like Saudi Arabia and most middle east nations are Islamic nations. I also thought and believe that, that was what made this great nation of America great but I soon realized as the years go-by probably for whatever reasons, we deviated from the service of the Lord by not countenancing Him and we're putting Him last in all we do, we left the worship of the Lord to worship money *[the god of mammon].* Permit me to please take us back to a statement that once brought tears to my eyes and still do, the 1863 President Abraham Lincoln's Thanksgiving Proclamation as we see below: maybe this will change our mind towards God, and we will remember all His mercies and compassion then we will turn from our ways worldwide and begin to seek Him from now on!

<u>***Lincoln's 1863 Thanksgiving Proclamation***</u>: "It is the duty of nations as well as of men to own their dependence upon the overruling power of God; to confess their sins and transgressions ***<u>in humble sorrow</u>***, yet with assured hope that ***<u>genuine repentance</u>*** will lead to mercy and pardon; and to recognize the sublime truth, announced in the Holy Scriptures and proven by all history, that <u>those nations are blessed whose God is the Lord</u>.

We know that ***<u>by His divine law, nations, like individuals, are subjected to punishments and chastisements in this world,</u>*** May we not justly fear that the awful calamity of civil war which now desolates the land may be a punishment inflicted upon us for our ***<u>presumptuous sins</u>***, to the needful end of our national reformation as a whole people?

We have been the recipients of the choicest bounties of heaven; we have been preserved these many years in peace and prosperity; we have grown in numbers, wealth and power as no other nation has ever grown.

But we have forgotten God. We have forgotten the gracious hand which preserved us in peace and multiplied and enriched and strengthened us, and we have vainly imagined, in the deceitfulness of our hearts, that all these blessings were produced by some superior wisdom and virtue of our own. Intoxicated with unbroken success, we have become too self-sufficient to feel the necessity of redeeming and preserving grace, ***too proud to pray to the God that made us***.

It has seemed to me fit and proper that God should be solemnly, reverently and gratefully acknowledged, as with one heart and one voice, by the whole American people. I do therefore invite my fellow citizens in every part of the United States, and also those who are at sea and those who are sojourning in foreign lands, to set apart and observe the last Thursday of November as a day of Thanksgiving and praise to our beneficent Father who dwelleth in the heavens." – ***A. Lincoln, October 3, 1863***

If we read the above statement closely and understand what he was saying especially this: *[We know that by His divine law, nations, like individuals, are subjected to punishments and chastisements in this world. May we not justly fear that the awful calamity of civil war which now desolates the land may be a punishment inflicted upon us for our presumptuous sins, to the needful end of our national reformation as a whole people?]*

So, judging by the devastating state of affairs and evil occurrences like rape, abortions, shedding of blood, random killings, drug trafficking, drug use and abuse both in schools and at other places, fire incidences are happening, airplanes with innocent lives men women and children are dropping out of the skies; all kinds of accidents that are taking lives in the thousands daily in this nation and the world at large, we will realize if we haven't, that we are at war with the **Higher Powers** the Bible says:

> *"The people of the land have used oppression, and exercised robbery, and have vexed the poor and needy: yea, they have oppressed the stranger wrongly." Ezekiel 22:29: we must also read, Ezekiel 21:24-27:* The Lord then said this:
> *"Thus said the Lord GOD; Remove the diadem, and take off the crown: this shall not be the same: exalt him that is low, and abase him that is high.*
> *vs.27, I will overturn, overturn, overturn, it; and it shall be no more, until he come whose right it is; and I will give it him."*

The *diadem* or mitre was worn by priests, but it also served as setting for the *crown [Exodus 28:36-37; 29:6; 39:31; Leviticus 8:9]*. The *removal* of these signs of dignity implies degradation, as in *[Job 19:9]* and the Book of *[Lamentation 5: 16]*. The *removal* of the priesthood and the kingship from Judah is symbolized by the removal of the h*igh priest's diadem* and the *king's crown.* Let me explain briefly what all of these can mean, we can as well look at it as in the area of God's verdict for disobedience, *[Psalms 9:17]* says, *"The wicked shall be turned into hell, and all the nations that forget God];* reading and understanding the meanings all of the above references. May the Lord not remove the crown of this nation of America, may the Lord not degrade this nation and may the dignity of this nation as one of the world's power remain!

But it lies with leaders and the law makers of this Great Nation; question is, are we sincerely following God, and the Constitution with respect and integrity in enacting the rule of law, are we not greedy for money and power and neglecting the masses, are we not forgetting God? The Bile says you are wicked! *[Psalms 9:17]* says, *"The wicked shall be turned into hell and all the nations that forget God]!*

SOLUTION:

Focus is on the ministers of God worldwide, teachers of the gospel, churches and members of the congregations to *daily evaluation of self, check and balance, renounce secret sins and dishonesty, deception and filthy lucre; to know and understand that narrow road is to be walked by self!* To seriously engage in spiritual warfare, constantly praying for our nations, praying for our leaders on national and state levels that the Lord will give them wisdom with which to rule and to govern, to desist from oppressing the poor, to take care of the strangers in our midst. We must also remember that it took Moses forty years to prepare as a servant of God!

With the church praying and leading, we can go back to being and remaining the greatest nation on earth that no nation will be able to withstand, we can be a blessed people of God, our economy can be great again by going back to our roots and following the plan of our founding fathers seeking and serving the only God of the Bible, we can repent of our sins and turn away from our iniquities, *we can re-introduce Bible readings in schools and let God begin to work in us and in the hearts of our youths through that. We can be great and remain great!*

> *"If my people which are called by my name, shall humble themselves, and pray, and seek my face, and turn from their wicked ways; <u>then</u> will I hear from heaven, and will forgive their sins, and will heal their land!" <u>II Chronicles 7:14</u>*

If we truly believe there is a GOD in Heaven, and we are believers, let us follow Him, let us seek Him, let us serve Him in truth and in spirit and *He will Perfect us!*

> *JEHOVA MEKADDISHKEM - THE LORD WHO SANCTIFIES:*
> *God sets us apart as a chosen people, a royal priesthood, holy unto God, a people of his own; He cleanses our sin and helps us mature in Him!*

Let Us Pray!
Our God in heaven we thank you for the privilege of calling You Father; and this is what Jesus Christ has thought us; that we become children in the family of God brothers and sisters, brethren; Lord we pray, that we take our place as children of God; children of the heavenly Father, around the table of the Lord even today in
Jesus' name; that childlike faith, that childlike affection; and a childlike supplication; that we will be able to call upon You and look at You and say, Abba! Father.

Your word says: *"If my people which are called by my name, shall humble themselves, and pray, and seek my face, and turn from their wicked ways; <u>then</u> will I hear from heaven, and will forgive their sins, and will heal their land!"*

Truly we are your people. And on behalf of myself, ourselves, our brothers and sisters, the ministers, teachers, the people in authority, the inhabitants of the lands worldwide, Presidents and rulers, Kings and Queens because that's who You called us; we sincerely humble ourselves before You; we pray while seeking Your face to hear from Heaven and forgive our sins, and heal our lands worldwide that these calamities, wars, shedding of blood, violence in all of the nations of planet earth be over dear Heavenly Father!

And then we can have great expectations of new beginnings, confidence trust and faith, that You will do what You have said You will do; that childlike attitude, and affection and faith and love, give to every one of us today in Jesus' name! And so we pray that these simple Words of Scripture, in this Study Book that we have studied and learnt, You will take them to reform and transform our lives in Jesus' name; we pray O Lord, that every prayer that is prayed in this Book and in all the places we gather together to hear the Word of God You will answer those prayers in Jesus' name!

Give us the key; the key of answered prayer; let it be in our hearts; that anytime, and every time we call upon You, there will be the great expectation of the answers to our prayers and well-being in Jesus' name; do marvelous and wonderful things in the lives of Your children all over the world. Thank You Father because we know you have answered. In Jesus' name we pray. Amen!

Amen. Shalom. Maranatha.

Psalm 15

> *<u>Vs.1</u>, "LORD, <u>who shall</u> abide in THY tabernacle? <u>who shall</u> dwell in THY HOLY Hill?"*
> *<u>Vs.2</u>, "<u>He that</u> walketh uprightly, and worketh righteousness, and speaketh the truth in his heart."*
> *<u>Vs.3</u>, "<u>He that</u> backbiteth not with his tongue, nor doeth evil to his neighbour,*
> *nor taketh up a reproach against his neighbour."*
> *<u>Vs.4</u>, "In whose eyes a vile person is contemned; but he honoureth them that fear the LORD. <u>He that</u> sweareth to his own hurt, and changeth not."*
> *<u>Vs.5</u>, "<u>He that</u> putteth not out his money to usury, nor taketh reward against the innocent. <u>He that</u> doeth these things shall never be moved."*

> *"Every WORD of GOD is pure, He is a shield unto them that put their trust in Him; therefore, I receive the WORD of GOD, not as the word of men, but as it is in truth the WORD of GOD, which effectually worketh also in me that believe. And so I am holding forth the WORD of Life, that I may rejoice in the Day of Christ, that I have not run in vain neither laboured in vain."*
> ***Amen!***

www.ingramcontent.com/pod-product-compliance
Lightning Source LLC
Chambersburg PA
CBHW042028050526
44107CB00103B/735